# PREEMPTS

## FROM

## A TO Z

### *Ron Andersen*
### *and*
### *Sabine Zenkel*

*Magnus Books*

*Magnus Books*
41 Ursula Place #3
Stamford, Connecticut

First Edition published 1993.
Printed in the United States of America.
10 9 8 7 6 5 4 3 2 1


Library of Congress Catalog Card Number
  93-079256


ISBN 0-9637533-0-4

# DEDICATION

*<u>Preempts From A to Z</u> is appropriately dedicated
to the most important A Z in our lives.*

**ALBRECHT ZENKEL**

# TABLE OF CONTENTS

## PART TWO
## NON-TRADITIONAL
## PREEMPTIVE OPENINGS ..... 165

# ACKNOWLEDGEMENTS

Like most authors who are deeply indebted to several individuals who have made substantial contributions, we would be remiss if we did not acknowledge our principal accomplices so that they can share the blame (or credit) for Preempts From A to Z.

First, (or more accurately last), there were Donna Gradt, Lew Finkel, Donna Hay, Janice Seamon, Gene Saxe, Tom Smith and Andrew Tarkington. They spent hours reviewing the publisher's final proofs. Your authors are happy to report that their endeavors were not followed by a single optometrist's bill.

Several leading bridge authorities made major contributions to the content of this book. Eric Rodwell clearly deserves to be recognized first. His contributions to bidding theory — as well as his stature as a player — are legendary, despite his youth. Eric and his regular partner, Jeff Meckstroth (who collaborated on the introduction) have been friends, teammates and occasional partners of your authors for more years than they would (probably) like to remember.

Another partnership that deserves special recognition for their contributions to this book includes the most knowledgeable authority on Bergen preempts, Marty Bergen. Chapter 8 would not have been possible without his assistance, support, and excellent illustrations and examples. Marty's frequent partner and friend, Larry Cohen, was also a major contributor. His help with the sections about the LAW was as valuable as his insights about "Two Under" preempts. We highly recommend that you read Larry's book, To Bid or Not to Bid — The Law of Total Tricks.

Whenever your authors did not see eye-to-eye on a subject, example or illustration, their final arbiter was their long-time friend, Paul Soloway. Several ideas presented in this book are essential features of the methods used by the Goldman-Soloway partnership.

On the other side of the Atlantic, George Nippgen, Daniela von Arnim (Sabine's favorite partner from Germany) and Tony Forrester (Great Britain's leading authority) made substantial contributions to the material in this book.

The late Barry Crane and C.C. Wei also deserve to be acknowledged. Wei co-authored <u>Profits From Preempts</u> with one of your authors. This was a book in the Precision Series on preemptive openings. A few of its traditional ideas and methods that have stood the test of time have been repeated herein.

No list of credits for this book would be complete without noting the contributions of Mexico's leading player, Dr. George Rozenkranz, and his wife Edith, the bridge world's perfect lady and expert in her own right. A number of George's ideas on preemptive bidding are reported in this book.

David Berkowitz, Bob Hamman, Edwin Kantar, Zia Mahmood, Kathie Wei-Sender and Kit Woolsey all deserve our thanks. Each made contributions for which your authors are grateful.

Our penultimate "Thank you" goes to a red pen and the man who wields it. That red pen is the best friend any bridge author ever had. It is held by the best bridge editor in the world. He edits the Daily Bulletins at North American Championships and WBF Championships. He is known for his many contributions to <u>The Bulletin</u> in his role as Executive Editor. Thank you Henry Francis. This is the only paragraph that will appear in this book over Henry's objections.

You may find it a bit monotonous to come across so many hands with exactly the same number of cards — always thirteen — no two alike, never more, never less. This repetitive pattern is no coincidence. The guilty party is Patricia Magnus. Her role in producing and publishing <u>Preempts From A to Z</u> was limited to handling all the material for this book after it left your authors' hands (or typewriter or computer or chicken scratch on the back of envelopes or airline tickets), until it reached its final destination under the printer's camera. Patricia is a master of detail and other matters which authors, preoccupied with supposedly higher matters, are apt to overlook. Should you find a hand with twelve cards (or two deuces of spades), a misspelled word or other technical error, please let your authors know. We'd love to keep it on file for the next time Patricia sadly shakes her head after receiving a less than perfect paragraph or two.

So to Patricia (Magnus), Henry (Francis), and those who contributed to the content of <u>Preempts From A to Z</u> goes the lion's share of the credit (or blame). In addition, we would like to thank McNaughton & Gunn, our printer, for making this book possible, and our creditors for making it necessary. We hope you will find it a worthwhile addition to your bridge library. That will constitute your authors' reward — the Internal Revenue Service will get the rest.

Ron Andersen                    Sabine Zenkel

# INTRODUCTION

When Sabine and Ron asked us to write the introduction for Preempts From A to Z, we happily agreed. We did so for several reasons.

First, we were consulted during the research phase of writing this book. Most of our favorite preemptive tactics — openings, responses and rebids — are presented, in addition to the defensive measures we use to combat our opponent's preempts.

Second, this is the first **comprehensive** book on preempts that includes both traditional, standard preempts and the highly sophisticated modern preemptive weapons. Defensive measures are presented for every preemptive bid discussed. The subject matter is very important; it fills a long-standing "void" (or at best, "short suit") in bridge literature.

Third, there is no pair better qualified to write a comprehensive book on this subject. Sabine was born, raised and educated in the European tradition of preempts. Ron has a similar background on the other side of the Atlantic in North America. Their partnership is one of the best travelled in the entire bridge world. Sabine and Ron are uniquely suited to this task.

Preempts From A to Z has a number of qualities that are noteworthy at the outset. Perhaps the most important theme is the objective (at all levels of competition, from local duplicates to World Championships) of making life difficult for your opponents and preventing them from reaching their optimum contract. We heartily endorse this objective. The success our partnership has enjoyed is due as much to accomplishing this goal as it is to the results we have achieved with our constructive bidding methods.

The examples and illustrations in this book have been selected carefully. We know, having been asked to review most of them. The amusing stories, anecdotes and wit in this book are typical of the humor that has made Ron one of the best and most entertaining speakers, Vugraph commentators, and writers in the world. Even if you gain nothing substantive from the following ten chapters (impossible), you will add considerable depth to your repertoire of bridge humor.

Finally, perhaps the greatest quality of <u>Preempts From A to Z</u> is that it is designed for all bridge players — from novice to expert, from casual social player to serious students of the game. Whatever your level of play, if you don't make life more difficult for your opponents, and handle their preempts more successfully after you have finished this book, do not blame the authors. Instead, try reading it again.


Jeff Meckstroth
Eric Rodwell

# PART ONE

# TRADITIONAL
# PREEMPTIVE OPENINGS

Although we use the word traditional to describe the bids discussed in the first six chapters, this is not completely accurate. Several of these bids are more preemptive in nature as they are played today than when they were when originally designed. For example, Howard Schenken — the designer of the modern weak two-bid — would not have envisioned:

$$\spadesuit \ KQ983 \quad \heartsuit \ 7 \quad \diamondsuit \ J1076 \quad \clubsuit \ 1093$$

as a 2♠ opening, even at favorable vulnerability. Today, such weak two-bids are not uncommon. Similar evolutionary changes have taken place in preemptive openings beyond the two-level.

Many significant improvements have also been made to the responding tools available over preemptive openings. These responses not only raise the accuracy of the bidding for the side that preempts, they also make life difficult for the side that is defending against them. All of these methods and treatments are reviewed in Chapters 1 through 6.

As preemptive openings and responses have become more effective, so have countermeasures against them. You will not find a preemptive opening presented in Part One without a suggested defense.

The general principles that apply to all preempts are explained in Chapter 1. Chapters 2 through 5 explore traditional preemptive openings from 2♦ through 5♦. Chapter 6 is different. It deals with preemptive overcalls, responses and rebids when the bidding starts at the one-level.

Three themes reviewed and developed in Chapter 1 are an important part of all the subjects discussed. In fact, these three themes are an integral part of the entire book. They are: **be aggressive, be disciplined, stay on the right side of the LAW.**

Consider these themes throughout your study of the pages that follow. They are critical elements in the prime objective of all preempts — making life difficult for your opponents. In short, they are the key to winning preempts.

# CHAPTER 1

## WINNING PREEMPTS —

## MAKING LIFE DIFFICULT FOR YOUR OPPONENTS

> "Twice armed is he who knows
> his cause is just;
> But thrice armed is he who
> gets his blow in fust!"
>
> *Anonymous*

Bridge is similar to warfare in many ways. Ely Culbertson was wont to compare bridge with the maneuvering of an army. In fact, the first sentence of his famous Gold Book began: "The road to the best final bid is strewn with the bones and boners of millions of pasteboard soldiers." The paragraph continues: "It [bridge] has this in common with the strategy of actual warfare (which it so strikingly resembles in many other particulars): the side that makes the fewest blunders is victorious."

If bridge in the Culbertson era could be compared with the maneuvering of an army, today's modern bidding arsenals could accurately be likened to "Star Wars" technology. Despite all the advances that have been made in bridge and warfare technique, one successful tactical strategy has stood the test of time for both — the advantage of the preemptive strike. If well-designed and well-directed, preemptive strikes can prove decisive on both the battle-field and at the bridge table; if ill-conceived, preemptive attacks can destroy the side that uses them.

For decades, winners at the bridge table have realized that preemptive openings are among the most important weapons in their bidding arsenal. The reason is simple. In addition to describing a specific type of hand, **preempts make life difficult for opponents**. The purpose of preemptive bids is not to pave the way to the best contract, but to prevent your opponents from reaching theirs. In that sense, preempts are purely destructive; they are a piece of calculated sabotage. Even the best partnerships in the world cannot bid as accurately when they have been denied two, three or four levels of bidding space. Players who maintain that preempts do not affect their bidding accuracy are either kidding themselves, you, or both.

The importance of making life difficult for your opponents at the bridge table has never been greater. To be a consistent winner requires more than simply avoiding blunders; which was all it may have taken in the Culbertson era. The standards of bidding (and even play) have improved dramatically over the years. Left to their own devices, most partnerships today will reach reasonable final contracts in non-competitive auctions. (And having your opponents play reasonable contracts most of the time is not good for your side irrespective of the form of scoring; it makes winning very difficult at rubber bridge or IMPs [International Match Points] and practically impossible in matchpoint events.)

When the hand belongs to the enemy, a good preemptive opening is one of the most effective ways of putting your opponents to the test. For example, you pass and LHO (left hand opponent) is in second seat looking at:

♠ 7  ♥ AKQ105  ♦ K3  ♣ AQJ94

Using standard bidding methods, LHO will happily describe this "battleship" by opening 1♥, intending to jump-shift in clubs to reveal his powerful two-suiter. No problem. Suppose, however, you open 3♠ in front of LHO. Now your opponent's task of describing his hand is far more difficult: the three levels of bidding space you have consumed will prove extremely costly.

When you open the bidding with a preempt, there are really only three auctions you usually do not want to hear:

4

| 1. | | North | East | South | West |
|----|-----|-------|------|-------|------|
| | (a) | 2♠ | Dbl. | P | P |
| | (b) | 3♠ | Dbl. | P | P |

These auctions are dangerous but may not prove disastrous for your side. On a good day your opponents will be able to score more by playing the hand. On a great day, partner will lay down a useful dummy and you will make your doubled contract. At least if trumps are stacked, they are in front of you.

| 2. | | North | East | South | West |
|----|-----|-------|------|-------|------|
| | (c) | 2♥ | P | P | P |
| | (d) | 3♥ | P | P | P |

It is hard to believe, but these auctions are often far worse for your side than the ones where LHO doubles your opening preempt. Optimistically, you may have "stolen" the hand, but far more often your opponents remained silent because the hand did not belong to them. If that is the case, your only hope is that 2♥ (c) or 3♥ (d) is your best contract. To make matters worse, it is usually bad to be the declaring side when the hand is a misfit (as it so often is when three passes follow an opening two- or three-level bid).

| 3. | | North | East | South | West |
|----|-----|-------|------|-------|------|
| | (e) | 2♠ | P | P | Dbl. |
| | | P | P | P | |
| | (f) | 3♠ | P | P | Dbl. |
| | | P | P | P | |

This is the worst! The spades are no doubt stacked behind you, and West's strength in the other suits is well-placed behind any high cards in dummy. Unless your opponents have totally misjudged their side's offensive and defensive potential, your side is headed for a poor result.

That is the extent of the "bad news;" all other auctions rate to be "good news" when you make an opening preempt. You are well placed for a favorable result. If partner bids, he does so knowing a great deal about your hand and is in an excellent position to judge your side's defensive and offensive prospects. If the opponents bid, you have consumed bidding space that they may have needed to reach their side's optimum contract.  When the opponents do compete, partner will often know when to double, bid or pass.

An excellent gauge to determine whether or not to preempt on a given hand is to decide how well prepared you are for one of the three auctions you do not want to hear.  As we will discuss in our review of specific preemptive openings, several factors help determine the likely outcome of a preempt.  All should be considered prior to opening at the two-, three- or four-level.

This is what a model preempt looks like NV (non-vulnerable):

(a)     ♠ KQJ987   ♥ 7   ♦ J109   ♣ 984

(b)     ♠ KQJ10954   ♥ 54   ♦ 7   ♣ J106

Hand (a) is a classic weak 2♠ bid, hand (b) is a perfect 3♠ opening.  Both hands contain excellent trump suits, adequate playing strength, (with your trump suit as the source of tricks, as it should be), little defense, and a less-than-useful dummy if your suit is not trump.  When you hold either of these hands and the opponents either pass or double (those "dreaded" auctions we examined earlier), you rate to get a decent result.

You cannot wait until you pick up a hand like the two above to open a weak two- or three- bid.  If you do, you are not preempting enough and you are failing to put pressure on your opponents as often as you should.  Nevertheless, all your weak two-bids should have some of the features of (a), and your three-level openings should approximate (b) as closely as possible.

Since you cannot always hold a model hand when you preempt, there are several factors to take into account when you are considering preempting with less than an ideal hand.  These factors will determine whether the odds favor, or are against, a preemptive opening:

(1)     **Internal trump strength** — NOT just HCP (high card points).  QJ109873 is a far better suit for a three-level preempt than AQ85432 because of its internal strength.  If the suit breaks terribly, you will lose only two tricks with the first holding; with the second, you might lose three or four.

(2)　**Length of your trump suit**. Although weak two-bids with five-card suits (and three-bids with six-card suits) used to be as rare as the Edsel, they are commonplace today. We support the modern trend, provided a reasonable amount of discipline is used. If your suit is shorter than the time-honored standard for a preemptive opening, its internal trump strength becomes more important.

(3)　**High cards outside your suit**. These are definite liabilities when you preempt beyond the two-level. Outside Kings and "Quacks" (Queens and Jacks) are often of little value on offense, but may provide the setting trick against enemy contracts. Partner may underestimate your side's defensive potential when he is not sure about your outside strength and may therefore take an expensive (sometimes phantom) sacrifice.

(4)　**Possession of the Ace of trump**. Like high cards outside your suit, the Ace of trump is often a liability because it may become a major factor in defending against an enemy contract. The defense can start with the Ace and a ruff against a suit contract, or provide an entry to your long suit against a notrump contract. We would rather hold KQ109652 than AQ107643 when we preempt.

(5)　**Voids**. Preempting with voids makes it difficult for partner to judge your side's offensive and defensive potential. When you have a void you often have a second suit — something to guard against when preempting. The opponents will often favor a notrump contract after your two- or three-level preempt. When you have a void, you would prefer they play in a suit contract.

(6) **Support for alternative contracts**. It is best if your hand is relatively worthless unless your long suit is trump. Beware of preempting when your hand would provide excellent support for another suit, particularly when opening a minor-suit preempt holding good support for a major. Although we would open 3♣ in first seat NV with:

    (a)  ♠ 7  ♥ 5  ♦ 7643  ♣ KQ108752

it would more dangerous to open 3♣ with:

    (b)  ♠ 10975  ♥ 5  ♦ 2  ♣ KQ109653

because of the great likelihood that your side might belong in spades. Partner would pass 3♣ holding:

    ♠ AJ432  ♥ A984  ♦ A95  ♣ J

when 4♠ would be a make opposite (b).

Other factors which have nothing to do with your hand or the trump suit also influence the advisability of preempting.

(7) **Vulnerability**. The greatest danger of any preempt is that it will suffer a larger set than the score the enemy could record by playing the hand. If the opponents double when you are at unfavorable vulnerability, they need only a two-trick set to more than compensate for the value of a game. The odds are far better for the preempter when he is at favorable vulnerability, since a four-trick set is required to show a profit when the enemy has a game (and even if a four-trick set is available, the opponents may fail to realize their side's defense against the preempt). Obviously, you can afford to be a more enterprising with your preempts when you are non-vulnerable than when you are vulnerable. If a partscore is the limit of the hand for both sides, you must avoid -200 (a two- trick set undoubled), particularly when

playing matchpoint duplicate. Your preferred order of vulnerability is:

a. Not vulnerable vs. vulnerable

b. Neither side vulnerable

c. Both sides vulnerable

d. Vulnerable vs. not vulnerable

(8) **Position at the table**. This factor is often overlooked, even by experienced players. If you hold a good, long suit and a weak hand in first chair, you are in an excellent position to preempt. You have two opponents and only one partner who may hold a strong hand: good odds. Second seat is not as good a proposition for a preemptive opening. The reasons are simple. If RHO (right hand opponent) passed, there is a greater chance that the hand belongs to your side because your partner and LHO are equally likely to hold a strong hand. Furthermore, your opponents are in a better position to judge their side's best course of action since they have already exchanged some information: RHO does not have an opening bid and his partner knows it. Third seat is without question the safest position for a preemptive opening. Partner is a passed hand and LHO is marked with a good hand. You know the hand belongs to the enemy.

(9) **Your opponents and partner**. Preempts work best against opponents who are either overly aggressive or too conservative in their bidding. Your preempt may "steal" the contract from conservative opponents and produce a huge plus score against the aggressive types (who have to make sure you do not steal from them). Against sensible

opponents with well-established partnerships, marginal preemptive openings will rarely show a profit unless most other conditions are favorable.

Do not violate your partnership understandings and agreements regarding preempts. Even if a "violation" of your agreements works out well, you are likely to pay for it later in lost partnership confidence.

(10) **The state of your game.** Preemptive openings are often an effective weapon when you are in need of a good result at the bridge table. Avoid the marginal preempts when things are going well for your side.

Despite the length of the list of factors to consider before preempting, most successful bridge players look for reasons to make a preemptive opening before they look for reasons to pass. The explanation for this is simple; winners on the battlefield and at the bridge table attack their opponents. Aggressive preempts at the bridge table are one of the most useful tools available to achieve this goal and make life difficult for the enemy.

Keeping our list of factors in mind, consider a few examples and determine whether or not the odds favor a preempt. Suppose with neither side vulnerable, you pick up:

♠ AJ107653 ♥ QJ10 ♦ 10 ♣ J4

RHO passes. Should you open 3♠? The internal strength of the spade suit and playing strength are adequate for a preemptive opening: two pluses. The QJ10 of hearts, J4 of clubs and Ace of spades are liabilities: three minuses. The vulnerability is good, but being in second chair after LHO's initial pass is bad. In addition, you have reasonably good support for a heart contract and would not be ashamed to put this hand down as dummy for a notrump contract: two more minuses. All things considered, there are simply too many minuses for a 3♠ opening. You should pass and hope to introduce spades later in the auction. Remove one of the minus factors (for example, put yourself in first seat) and you have a marginal preempt. Eliminate a second minus (such as the QJ10 of hearts) and the preempt is clear-cut.

With favorable vulnerability, you pick up:

♠ KQ985　♥ 5　♦ QJ94　♣ 983

Partner and RHO pass. Your hand is a considerable distance from a classic weak two-bid. Nevertheless, it is clear to bid 2♠. The vulnerability and your position at the table are perfect. Your 9-8 of spades are decent intermediates. In addition, you are taking away two levels of bidding space from your opponents. On a good day partner will have a fit for spades and be able to deprive the enemy of even more bidding space. Admittedly, the bid could work out poorly, but the odds are in your favor.

You are the dealer at favorable vulnerability and pick up:

♠ 7　♥ KJ10　♦ A976432　♣ Q5

Despite the ideal vulnerability and good position, you should not even consider opening 3♦ with this hand. Your suit contains the Ace and has no internal strength. You have far too many HCP outside diamonds and good support for a heart contract: two more minuses. There are far too many experienced bridge players who would open 3♦ and feel they were most unlucky when the opening bid led their side to a poor result (most of the time). Do not be one of them.

With both sides vulnerable, you pick up the following in first seat:

♠ 7　♥ 54　♦ 9874　♣ AQJ1074

Open 3♣. Yes, we know that you have the club Ace and only a six-card suit. We know the vulnerability is not ideal. However, you have more to gain than lose by opening hands like this at the three-level. If you are uncomfortable opening 3♣ on this hand, pretend your diamond and heart suits are reversed: then we would not open it 3♣ either.

Finally, suppose you are in second chair, unfavorable, holding:

♠ 98　♥ 7　♦ KQ109852　♣ J109

Despite the vulnerability and position — as well as our respect for time-honored institutions such as the "Rule of Two and Three" (being within two tricks of your contract vulnerable and within three tricks when you are not) — we would venture a 3♦ opening. Except for the vulnerability and position, the hand is perfect for a preemptive opening. Although a 3♦ opening could go for a four-digit number, you may escape when your opponents overcall — rather than double — your aggressive preempt.

Once you have decided to make a preemptive opening, the only remaining question is: how high are you going to bid? Rigid guidelines such as the "Rule of Two and Three", or the more sophisticated "Rule of One, Two and Three" (going down one, [or making], at unfavorable vulnerability; two at equal; and three at favorable) have been discarded by winning bridge players as far too conservative.

For decades, most experts have known that you have to take some chances if you want to make life difficult for your opponents. Your objective is to put pressure on the enemy as often as possible. In terms of the playing strength required for preempts, many of today's leading players have replaced the "Rule of Two and Three" (or the "Rule of One, Two and Three") with the "Rule of 8, 11 and 14." Simply stated, this rule says that if dummy is suitable, the loss will be only 800 if the preempt gets doubled; if the dummy is average the penalty will be 1100; and if the dummy is unsuitable, the cost will be 1400!

Although we do not subscribe to the "Rule of 8, 11 and 14," we do advocate that you preempt as high as you reasonably can given the conditions: vulnerability, playing strength, suit quality, position, etc. Following this philosophy, an opponent will occasionally ask you for your area code and you will go for a telephone number. If you do not, you are not preempting often enough or high enough. In return, the damage you do to your opponents will more than compensate for the occasional number your opponents collect from your preemptive attacks.

We advocate preempting as high as you reasonably can because an extra level of preemption often makes a great deal of difference. To appreciate the validity of this approach, consider it from your opponents' perspective. Suppose, vulnerable versus not, your LHO picks up:

♠ AQ ♥ 74 ♦ AKJ954 ♣ K32

and hears you open 2♥. No problem. LHO has a clear-cut 3♦ overcall with a confident expectation of reaching his side's optimum contract. His partner might bid notrump, or bid spades at the three-level if that is his suit and the proper strain for the partnership. Should RHO have a worthless hand, 3♦ will end the auction.

Now let us change your opening bid — to 3♥. LHO is not so happy anymore. He is too strong to pass and cannot bid 3NT with the 7-4 of hearts (even though 3NT might be the best spot). A takeout double with only two spades is out of the question. So LHO will have to choose 4♦ as the least of evils. 3NT is gone forever, and 4♦ might not even make if RHO has a worthless hand. Over the 4♦ overcall, holding spades, RHO might not be able to bid. After all, his partner did not double and therefore would be unlikely to have a fit.

As this simple example illustrates, and as American expert Kit Woolsey noted in his excellent book, Matchpoints, "In keeping with Newton's law of gravitation, it is not unreasonable to say that the accuracy of the opponents' bidding varies inversely with the square of the level of the preempt."

Although there are clearly numerous reasons to preempt as high as is prudently possible, there is a danger that must be considered. You do not want to hear one of those "dreaded" auctions where you end up playing in your preempt, either doubled or not. The higher you preempt, the more likely it is that you will buy the contract, whether you want to or not. A weak two-bid may not give your opponents a serious problem, but it is unlikely to end the auction. A 4♥ or 4♠ opening bid, on the other hand, is quite likely to produce the final contract. Consequently, when you open 4♥ or 4♠ you had better be prepared to play there.

The rank of opener's suit is also a factor in preempting. A 3♠ opening, for example, is a much "higher" preempt than a 3♣ bid, even though both are on the same level. Keep in mind that a 3♠ opening bid wipes out the entire three-level while 3♣ leaves room for the opponents to play 3♦, 3♥ or 3♠. Therefore, your opponents are more likely to remain silent over 3♠ than they are over 3♣. You must be better prepared to play the hand as the level of your preempt rises.

# DISCIPLINED PREEMPTS

We like discipline, as did General George Patton: "Give me one disciplined battalion for every three undisciplined ones my enemy has, and I will win any battle. They may win a few skirmishes, but I will win the war." That does not mean we are not aggressive; it simply means that we urge you to make sure your preemptive openings are disciplined. On the surface this may seem contradictory, but it is not. By disciplined, we do not mean conservative; we mean in accordance with partnership agreement. For example, you may agree with your partners that at favorable vulnerability, a 3♣ or 3♦ opener might look like:

(a)     ♠ 7   ♥ 95   ♦ 9843   ♣ QJ10974
(b)     ♠ 52   ♥ 9   ♦ J1098542   ♣ J107

No problem: your partnership obviously enjoys preempting and putting considerable pressure on your opponents; you probably would not be our favorite opponents. However, if (a) and (b) constitute a three-level minor suit opening for your partnership at favorable vulnerability, you cannot open 3♣ under the same conditions with:

(c)     ♠ 7   ♥ 98   ♦ K107   ♣ AQJ10652

Some partnerships envision (c), not (a) when the opening bid is 3♣, even at favorable vulnerability in first seat. Perfectly legal, but such partnerships cannot open 3♣ with (a) or (b).

Effective preempts require that you be on the same wavelength as your partner concerning what constitutes a preemptive opening given the conditions. Once you have reached an agreement, it is vital that you stay consistent with it.

Disciplined preempts clearly limit and define the following, which we advocate:

(1)     Opener's suit: in terms of both length and strength.

(2)     Opener's distribution.

(3)     The strength in high cards opener may hold outside his suit.

(4)       Opener's approximate playing strength assuming normal breaks.

When your hand does not meet with your partnership agreements for all these conditions, particularly in first and second positions, you CANNOT open with a preempt.

For years, Marty Bergen has been in the vanguard of experts crusading for the reduction of traditional requirements — and creating more frequent opportunities — for preemptive openings. His sub-standard suits and strength for preemptive openings are legendary in North America, but his preempts are disciplined. He always has a bad suit and a poor hand when he preempts non-vulnerable, particularly at favorable vulnerability. His partner can count on it. We feel it is his discipline, not necessarily his methods, that accounts for the success his preempts generate. (We will discuss Bergen preempts at greater length and examine his specific preemptive weapons in Chapter 8.)

One of the reasons we favor aggressive preemptive openings is that we enjoy seeing our opponents (even world champions) guess the best course of action for their side when denied considerable bidding space for exploration. However, we do not want to force our partners to guess at high levels with (usually) hundreds of points hanging in the balance. Lack of discipline takes away most of the advantage an opening preempt should give and often creates a "third opponent" — the person sitting across the table from you. Preemptive openings should be designed to put pressure on the enemy, not your partner. To accomplish that objective, your preempts must be disciplined in accordance with your partnership agreements.

The task of responding to partner's preemptive openings is greatly simplified when the opening bid is both limited and disciplined. Responder usually knows immediately whether the hand belongs to his side, and can use the "Law of Total Tricks" to determine how high to compete. When the hand rates to belong to his side, responder generally knows whether the combined partnership assets are in the partscore, game or slam zone. Your side's defensive prospects will also be clear to responder since opener's outside high card strength and distribution are clearly defined.

One area of bidding that has been neglected by most partnerships (except for experts) and writers is responding to opening preempts.  The reason is simple.  Most partnerships play "catch-as-catch-can" wide-range preemptive openings.  These do not lend themselves to careful probing and exploration — when responder's interest is beyond the game level — or to determining which game the partnership should play.  Responder is often forced to simply take a shot in the dark at what he hopes will be the right contract.

We hope this book will enable you to bid as accurately after a preemptive opening as you do when the opening bid is at the one-level.  In order to do so, it will be necessary to modify some conventions and add a few new weapons to your responding arsenal when the opening bid is a preempt.

The preemptive openings we are about to describe can be used when playing just about any system.  They are designed to complement both limited (as in Precision or other "forcing club" systems) and unlimited (as in Standard American) opening one-bids.

The responses we recommend permit maximum exploration when responder has a good hand, and maximum preemption when he has a poor hand with a good fit for opener's suit.  To be effective, however, these responses require opener to have the agreed values and playing strength for his opening bid.  Without disciplined openings, this responding arsenal is as ineffective as loading a BB gun with M1 ammunition.

## THE LAW

When we make periodic mention of the LAW in our discussions of various preempts, we are referring to the "Law of Total Tricks." The idea of the LAW came to North America in 1969 in an article by Jean Vernes titled "The Law of Total Tricks" that appeared in the Bridge World magazine.  It received little fanfare at the time, perhaps because the author was relatively unknown.  Today, more than 20 years later, the LAW is a force to be reckoned with, particularly in reference to preemptive tactics and competitive bidding.  The concept of the LAW is endorsed by many bridge authorities on both sides of the Atlantic and is the sole subject of an excellent book by American expert Larry Cohen titled To Bid or Not to Bid — The Law of Total Tricks.

Application of the LAW to various preempts is worth noting at the outset. Simply stated, according to Cohen's book, the "Law of Total Tricks" asserts:

> The Total number of tricks available on any deal is approximately equal to the total number of trumps.

Of more specific importance to preemptive bidding is the most important adjunct of the LAW. It states:

> You should always bid to the level equal to the combined number of trumps held by your side.

Like most other laws, the "Law of Total Tricks" must on occasion be modified slightly and tempered with reason and judgment. This, however, does not negate its overall effectiveness and usefulness when applied to preemptive bidding.

It does not take a mathematical genius to figure out that if you have a long suit, partner's expected length is one-third of the remaining cards in that suit. Let us see how we can apply that simple maxim to opening bids at the two- and three-level.

Traditional wisdom dictates that when you open the bidding at the three-level (in a suit), you will have a seven-card suit. The LAW concurs. If opener has a seven-bagger in his suit, there are six remaining. Assume that each of the other three players at the table has two cards in that suit. Hence, the opening bidder's side is favored, on balance, to have nine trumps; opener's seven plus partner's expected doubleton. Nine trumps should mean we can bid successfully to the three-level. So far so good.

Now let us see if traditional weak two-bids have the LAW on their side. The most widely accepted, and played, suit length requirement for a weak two-bid is six. That leaves seven cards outstanding to be divided among the remaining players. Responder's expected length in opener's suit is two and a third; for a total of eight and one-third; more than the amount required by the LAW for success at the two-level.

Today we see an increasing number of two-level preempts based on five-card suits by such experts as Marty Bergen, Larry Cohen and Meck-Well. What does the LAW say about this violation of the traditional wisdom? When you open a weak two-bid with a five-card suit, there are eight outstanding cards in the suit. Partner's expectancy is two and two-thirds, giving the partnership approximately eight cards in the suit (seven and two-thirds to be exact, but no one is going to put you in jail for missing a third of a card). Once again, the LAW is on the side of those who open weak two-bids with five-card suits.

ALL PREEMPTS ARE A GAMBLE (except perhaps at one of your author's Mother's bridge clubs — where a 3♠ opening bid might look like ♠ AKQJ9865 ♥ 4 ♦ QJ10 ♣ 7). Therefore, when your side preempts the bidding, you are betting that if your opponents defend, they will score less than if they had elected to bid on to their optimum contract (left to their own devices). The gamble is the preemptive opening, not partner's decision to sometimes make it with a trump less than you were expecting. Therefore, as long as partner has done his job, you do yours. Once a fit has been established, responder should raise the preempt to the proper LAW level with impunity (according to the LAW adjunct).

Many of us have followed the dictates of the LAW without knowing it for many years. For example, we were all taught to raise a traditional two-bid to the three-level (preemptively) holding three-card support. According to the LAW, that is the right thing to do. When you have nine trumps, you bid to the three-level.

Similarly, if partner shows a seven-card suit by opening 3♥, the LAW urges us to raise to 4♥ with three-card trump support (and lacking a good reason for disobeying, we do). The LAW does not make it easy for the player in fourth seat, who is holding a "battleship" and hears the bidding around the table go 3♥-P-4♥ (by a "LAW-abiding" citizen) to him.

The LAW should also be followed when the enemy opens the bidding and partner makes a preemptive jump overcall. With neither side vulnerable the bidding proceeds 1♣-2♠ (preemptive)-double (negative) and it is your turn holding:

♠ K1074  ♥ A52  ♦ QJ107  ♣ 94

If you are "LAW-abiding," you have nothing to think about. Bid 4♠. You obviously do not expect partner to make it, but that does not matter; you have ten trumps and the LAW is on your side.

Cohen did a remarkable amount of research prior to writing To Bid or Not to Bid — The Law of Total Tricks. His regular bridge partner for years, Marty Bergen, has also done a fantastic amount of research regarding how the LAW is applied to preempts. Collectively, they discovered two noteworthy trends concerning preempts. In researching bridge deals from important bridge tournaments and events from the 1970s and 1980s, they discovered that there was an increasing frequency (as the years went by) in the number of preempts made. The other noticeable trend they reported was that aggressive preempting proved to be the winning action 60-70% of the time — even against outstanding opponents — when compared with the conservative action taken at the other table(s).

Our own research prior to writing Preempts From A to Z supports this conclusion. Aggressive, disciplined preempts are winning preempts. If you do not accept this premise, perhaps the rest of this book — and an understanding of the LAW — will convince you.

# CHAPTER 2

# WEAK TWO-BIDS
## 2♦, 2♥ and 2♠

According to <u>The Official Encyclopedia of Bridge</u>, a weak two-bid is the use of suit openings of two, other than clubs, as preemptive bids. Its prototype was used in auction bridge, and adopted in the Vanderbilt Club System in the early 1930s. The modern weak two-bid was developed by Howard Schenken and was later incorporated into most American systems. It is part of almost all bidding systems throughout the world in one form or another.

As a result of this popularity, the most frequently used (and **misused**) preemptive opening is the weak two-bid. Despite almost universal agreement regarding the requirements to open a weak two-bid, fewer than half of most partnership's two-bids meet the partnership's agreements and understandings. Unfortunately, this lack of discipline considerably reduces the effectiveness of preempting and often creates insoluble problems for the responder to a weak two-bid. In addition, even many experienced partnerships lack sufficient methods to accurately reach the best final contract after a 2♦, 2♥ or 2♠ opening.

We hope this chapter will solve most — if not all — of your partnership's problems in opening, responding to and defending against weak two-bids.

Let us start with 2♥ and 2♠ openings since there are a few special considerations in dealing with the weak 2♦ opening.

## 2♥ AND 2♠ OPENINGS

The following box outlines our recommended requirements for opening major suit weak two-bids:

---

### REQUIREMENTS FOR OPENING 2♥ AND 2♠

(1) A good six-card suit with at least two of the top four honors.

(2) 5-11 HCP, with a majority of the points in the suit opened.

(3) A one-suited hand. You may occasionally have a four-card minor, but **never** four cards in the other major.

(4) Preferably, no more than one Ace or King outside your suit.

(5) Preferably, no void(s).

---

If you follow these recommendations strictly, particularly in first and second positions (3rd and 4th seat two-bids are special cases which we will discuss separately), your opening 2♥ and 2♠ bids will promise a very specific type of hand that contains very definite assets. These preempts are constructive as well as preemptive. They are not preemptive openings in the sense that they are primarily designed to interfere with the opponents' communications. They may, however, serve that purpose when partner has a poor hand with a good fit and is able to make a preemptive raise.

Effective weak two-bids always contain a good suit. These suits all qualify for a 2♥ or 2♠ opening:

| (1) | AQ10864 |
|-----|---------|
| (2) | KQJ762 |
| (3) | KQ10752 |
| (4) | AKQ865 |
| (5) | AJ10984 |
| (6) | KJ10872 |
| (7) | QJ10732 or QJ9873 (weakest) |

These suits do NOT qualify because they do not contain two of the top four honors:

| (1) | A97643 |
|-----|---------|
| (2) | K98432 |
| (3) | Q107542 |
| (4) | K106532 |
| (5) | Q98543 |
| (6) | J109743 |

You will note that all the suits we would open with at the two-level preempt are six-cards in length. Does this mean that your authors never open a weak two-bid with an exceptional five-card suit? Does this mean we never open with a seven-card suit at the two-level? If so, what should you do if you pick up the following hand at favorable vulnerability in first seat?

♠ AKJ109   ♥ 2   ♦ J1094   ♣ 976

Following our guidelines, you cannot open 2♠. But, you can do what your authors would do: move the ♣ 6 next to the ♠ 9 and then open 2♠. If it works out poorly, apologize for missorting your hand and ask partner to remind you to make an appointment with your optometrist in the not too distant future. Most partners can charitably forgive failing eyesight, but few have the same charity for violations of partnership agreements or bad bids.

Although your authors may violate their agreements with a relatively rare five-card 2♥ or 2♠ opening, we practically never open a weak two-bid with a seven-card suit. If we hold seven hearts or spades and the suit or hand fails to qualify for a three-level opening, we simply pass and hope we get to introduce our suit later.

One simple rule of thumb regarding suit quality often proves helpful from both sides of the table when the opening bid is 2♦, 2♥ or 2♠. If responder holds a high doubleton honor in opener's suit (Ax, Kx or Qx), there should not be more than one loser in that suit, assuming normal breaks.

Regarding high card strength for a weak two-bid, we find nothing wrong with the most commonly played range of 5–11 HCP. As in all matters related to point count, a bit of reason and judgment is required. For example, open 1♠ holding:

(a)      ♠ AK10984   ♥ 7   ♦ KJ105   ♣ 98

because you do not have a 2♠ bid, under any circumstances. This hand has two suits with good intermediates and an easy rebid. We hope your partnership agrees.

(b)      ♠ KQ10643   ♥ QJ   ♦ QJ   ♣ J62

Open 2♠ with (b). Even though this hand contains 12 HCP according to the 4-3-2-1 point scale, it is full of "Quacks" and is NOT an opening one-bid.

The ideal distribution for an opening weak two-bid is 6-3-2-2 or 6-3-3-1. Occasionally, you might open 2♥ or 2♠ when your distribution is 6-2-4-1 (with a singleton in either minor) when you have a relatively poor four-card minor. Avoid opening weak two-bids with 6-4-3-0 or 6-3-4-0 distribution. It is simply too difficult for responder to judge the best course of action for your side when you have both a four-card side suit and a void.

We categorically refuse to open 2♥ or 2♠ with four cards in the other major. The reason is simple. Suppose you open 2♥ holding:

(a)      ♠ K1087   ♥ AQ7654   ♦ 95   ♣ 7

Armed with the knowledge that you have less than an opening bid and a one-suited hand, partner should pass 2♥ with:

(b)      ♠ AQ965   ♥ 10   ♦ K62   ♣ A854

"Wunderbar!" as one of your authors would sarcastically say in her native tongue. You may be struggling to make a low-level partscore in hearts while game in spades is almost ironclad.

Problems frequently occur when you open a weak two-bid with a void. In the 1989 European Ladies' Team Championships a player opened 2♠ holding:

♠ AJ10652   ♥ —   ♦ Q1095   ♣ J54

Unlucky for opener, partner passed holding:

♠ 7   ♥ 9872   ♦ AKJ762   ♣ A6

Spades split 3-3 and after a club lead, declarer won nine tricks for +140. The German team holding these cards bid to a small slam in diamonds and took all 13 tricks for a considerable gain. Once again, the fault was with the opening bid, not responder's pass. You cannot make a weak two-bid with a void: your hand simply has too much support for two of the other three suits.

Some players may object to our requirements for 2♥ and 2♠ openings because these guidelines limit your opportunities to open 2♥ and 2♠. That is true. Your purpose is not to see how often you can preempt, but to get maximum value when you do. The goal is to win points, IMPs and matchpoints, not to bid just to listen to the sound of your own voice.


## RESPONSES TO 2♥ AND 2♠

Many gadgets, conventions and special treatments have been devised for responding to weak two-bids. The most common forcing response is 2NT. Most partnerships use 2NT to ask opener to bid a high card feature (Ace or King) outside of his trump suit. The mechanics are simple: with a high card feature, opener bids the suit which contains the Ace or King; lacking a high card feature, opener simply rebids his suit at the three-level[1]. Most partnerships require that the majority of HCP be in the suit opened, so when opener does show a feature (or rebids 3NT), we know that he holds a maximum. When opener does not show a feature, (or rebid 3NT), we may assume that he holds a minimum 2♥ or 2♠ opener.

---

[1]   With a solid suit (AKQxxx or better), opener should rebid 3NT over responder's 2NT inquiry.

For regular partnerships we recommend a conventional set of responses to 2NT (called "Ogust") which give responder considerably more information about opener's hand than simply whether or not he holds an Ace or King outside of his suit. Designed by New York expert Harold Ogust, the conventional responses to the 2NT inquiry are:

---

## OGUST RESPONSES TO 2NT

3♣ = Minimum strength; poor suit.

3♦ = Maximum strength; poor suit.

3♥ = Minimum strength; good suit.

3♠ = Maximum strength; good suit.

3NT = Solid suit.

(Note: some partnerships prefer to reverse the meaning of opener's 3♦ and 3♥ rebids.)

---

Playing Ogust responses to 2NT, what rebid would you make after partner responds 2NT to your 2♠ opening holding:

(a)  ♠ AQJ1065  ♥ 7  ♦ 874  ♣ 632
REBID 3♥. This shows your good suit with minimum strength.

(b)  ♠ KJ8754  ♥ 74  ♦ AJ10  ♣ J10
REBID 3♦. You have a good hand in terms of strength, but a relatively poor suit for a weak two-bid.

(c)  ♠ KQ10985  ♥ A5  ♦ J107  ♣ 74
REBID 3♠. Your 10 HCP and good spade intermediates (10, 9, 8) qualify this hand as a maximum weak two-bid. If your hand were any stronger, it would qualify for an opening one-bid.

(d)     ♠ AKQ985  ♥ 65  ♦ 874  ♣ 93
REBID 3NT. This tells partner that your suit
is solid. It is headed by at least the AKQ.

In addition to 2NT, your partnership needs a firm understanding about whether new suits are forcing, non-forcing, or invitational. Some pairs play that over any opening weak two-bid, major suit responses are forcing while minor suit responses are not. There are various treatments of jumps in new suits. Do you play splinter bids over weak two-bids? How about control asking bids?

There are numerous conventions which individually (and in combination) may be playable. Most of them are designed to complement the undisciplined weak two-bid. The following are recommended to complement **disciplined** weak two-bids.

---

## RESPONSES TO 2♥ AND 2♠

(1)  A single raise is defensive — not invitational. Jump raises are sign-offs; they are made with preemptive hands or with game-going values.

(2)  2NT asks opener to describe the precise nature of his weak two-bid via Ogust responses. If opener later bids 3NT, opener can correct to four of his major. (Alternatively, you may agree to show high card features or shortness in response to 2NT).

(3)  Simple changes of suit (except 3♣) are natural and forcing for one round. Opener then:
  • Raises responder's suit with three-card support (xxx) or high honor doubleton.
  • Rebids his suit, suggesting a minimum.
  • Bids a new suit, showing a high-card feature in the suit bid (not a second suit).
  • Jumps in a new suit to show support for partner's suit with shortness in the suit bid (splinter).

(continued)

---

(4) 3♣ asks opener to bid a distributional feature — singleton or void (rare). Opener then:
- Rebids his suit with no outside shortness.
- Bids a new suit, showing a singleton or void in that suit (**3NT is club shortness**).
- Jumps to game in his opening suit if it is solid (AKQxxx or better).

(5) Jumps in new suits are CABs (control asking bids) for the suit bid. Opener responds:

> 1st step = **no** 1st or 2nd round control.
> 2nd step = 2nd-round control (King or singleton).
> 3rd step = 1st-round control (Ace or void).

**After** opener has shown first- or second-round control, responder bids the same suit again, asking whether the control is distributional or based on high cards. Opener responds:

> 1st step = distributional (singleton or void).
> 2nd step = high card (King or Ace).

Subsequent bids by responder are CABs. Responder may also make a CAB after a conventional 2NT or 3♣ inquiry and response by simply bidding a new suit.

(6) 3NT and all other game bids are to play (except 4♥ over 2♠ [CAB]. In order for responder to set the contract in 4♥ over a 2♠ opener, he must bid 3♥ and rebid 4♥.)

(7) 4NT is Blackwood — simple Blackwood unless responder has shown a fit via a 2NT or 3♣ inquiry (when a fit has been established or implied, Keycard Blackwood is best).

(8) 5NT is the Grand Slam Force.

Since opener's suit, distribution and possible outside strength can be clearly defined using the methods outlined above, responder should rarely have any problem setting the final contract after a 2♥ or 2♠ opening. See how this works by choosing your response to partner's 2♥ opening with each of the following hands:

(a) ♠ K85  ♥ K94  ♦ KJ1095  ♣ 98
RAISE TO 3♥. Game is out of the question. You have a good fit for hearts and your opponents are likely to have a good fit elsewhere. Raise the bidding to the three-level, adhering to the LAW, and make it hard for the opponents to compete. You want partner to know you would like a heart lead if the opponents end up playing the hand.

(b) ♠ QJ10  ♥ 7  ♦ AKQJ107  ♣ AJ10
JUMP TO 3NT. This is not correctable.

(c) ♠ AKQ10964  ♥ 8  ♦ 7  ♣ A1073
JUMP TO 4♠. Again, bid what you think you can make.

(d) ♠ AJ64  ♥ 2  ♦ 7  ♣ KQ107632
PASS. Although 3♣ might be a better spot, it is forcing and conventional, asking partner to bid his shortness. 4♣ would be a CAB.

(e) ♠ 8742  ♥ KJ5  ♦ A  ♣ AKQ104
JUMP TO 3♠ (CAB). Partner's spade holding will determine whether you should play 4♥, 6♥ or even 7♥. Find out with the conventional inquiry.

(f) ♠ AKQ1065  ♥ AJ109  ♦ —  ♣ 965
JUMP TO 4♣ (CAB). Partner's club holding will determine your contract level.

Partner opens 2♠. What action would you take holding:

(a) ♠ 5  ♥ AKJ107  ♦ KQ10  ♣ A1043
RESPOND 3♥, forcing. If partner bids 4♥, pass. If partner rebids spades, bid 3NT.

(b)    ♠ J104 ♥ AK109 ♦ 7632 ♣ A7

RESPOND 3♣. If partner is short in diamonds, 4♠ should be an excellent proposition. You may be forced to game if opener holds either solid spades or club shortness (requiring a 3NT rebid), but 4♠ will probably make under those circumstances.

(c)    ♠ AQ52 ♥ A ♦ 753 ♣ AKQJ10

JUMP TO 4♦ (CAB). If your side can avoid two fast diamond losers, slam in spades should be cold. The ♦ A coupled with the ♠ K will make 7NT a claimer.

(d)    ♠ 10842 ♥ 63 ♦ 873 ♣ AJ76

JUMP TO 4♠. That is what Betty Ann Kennedy bid on this hand, at favorable vulnerability, when Carol Sanders opened 2♠ in Seattle at the 1984 Olympiad. Amazingly, 4♠ undoubled became the final contract. The many-time world champions conceded 150 (down three) to their embarrassed opponents who had 12 tricks on top in either hearts or notrump.

(e)    ♠ 7 ♥ AQJ10973 ♦ KQ10 ♣ K4

RESPOND 3♥. Remember, a direct jump to 4♥ would be a CAB. To sign off in 4♥ you must first make a forcing 3♥ call, intending to rebid 4♥ if opener does not raise your suit. This is a small price to pay for all the good results generated by CABs.

Control asking bids have not been given the recognition and popularity they deserve as a responding tool to weak two-bids and other preempts. This is unfortunate, since they often play a crucial role in improving the accuracy of your slam bidding when your side opens at the two-, three- or four-level.

A good example of the effective use of a CAB over a weak two-bid can be seen in the following deal played by one of your authors with world champion Kathie Wei-Sender.

## North
- ♠ KQ73
- ♥ 32
- ♦ Q752
- ♣ 953

## West
- ♠ 1042
- ♥ AQJ1084
- ♦ 96
- ♣ K6

```
Board 3
Dlr. - South
Vul. - E/W
```

## East
- ♠ A5
- ♥ K95
- ♦ A3
- ♣ AQJ1072

## South
- ♠ J986
- ♥ 76
- ♦ KJ1084
- ♣ 84

---

OUR TABLE

Opening Lead ♥ 7

E/W + 2220 (25 matchpoints/25 top)

| *Wei-Sender* | | *Andersen* | |
| West | North | East | South |
| — | — | — | P |
| 2♥ | P | 4♣ (a) | P |
| 4♥ (b) | P | 5♣ (c) | P |
| 5♥ (d) | P | 5NT (e) | P |
| 7♥ (f) | P | 7NT (g) | |

| (a) | Control Asking Bid (CAB) in clubs. |
| (b) | Second round control (King or singleton) |
| (c) | "King or singleton?" |
| (d) | "Club King." |
| (e) | Grand Slam Force. |
| (f) | "I have two out of the top three heart honors." |
| (g) | Barring unforeseen bad breaks, I can count 14 tricks: 1 spade, 1 diamond, 6 hearts and 6 clubs. |

# 2♦ OPENINGS

Most partnerships play 2♦ as preemptive for the same reason they use a particular toothpaste! They have tried most of the other brands and eventually end up back where they started. The weak 2♦ bid has the advantage of being consistent with weak 2♥ and 2♠ openings. Since your authors have tried other toothpastes and come back to the preemptive 2♦ bid, we suggest that you do likewise.

As you might expect, most of our requirements for a weak 2♦ are similar to those we recommended for 2♥ and 2♠.

---

## REQUIREMENTS FOR OPENING 2♦

(1)  A good six-card suit, with at least two of the top four honors.

(2)  5-11 HCP, with a majority of the points in diamonds.

(3)  No four-card major; a four-card club suit is acceptable.

(4)  Preferably, no more than one Ace or King outside the diamond suit.

(5)  Preferably, no void(s).

---

Since a weak two-bid in diamonds is of dubious preemptive value, there is never any reason to stretch to open 2♦. Tactically, it is far better to confine your 2♦ openers to hands with sound values. This will assist responder in locating your side's optimum contract when the hand belongs to your side. It will also prove helpful in finding profitable sacrifices when partner has a fit and the hand belongs to your opponents.

The following hands technically meet our requirements for a 2♦ opening, but we would decline. We would PASS with hands (a) and (b) in first and second positions. Simply stated, 2♦ openings should be made of sterner stuff!

(a)     ♠ Q5   ♥ J4   ♦ QJ8742   ♣ J32

(b)     ♠ J43   ♥ 7   ♦ KJ7642   ♣ 1074

On the other side of the spectrum (c), (d) and (e) are too strong for a weak 2♦ opening. Open 1♦ with these hands:

(c)     ♠ 7   ♥ 109   ♦ AKJ1086   ♣ K1098

(d)     ♠ A109   ♥ 5   ♦ AK10874   ♣ 985

(e)     ♠ 7   ♥ A107   ♦ KQJ1053   ♣ J109

Finally, we **would** make a weak 2♦ bid with any of the following three hands:

(f)     ♠ K5   ♥ 74   ♦ KQ10974   ♣ 1093

(g)     ♠ 6   ♥ 1094   ♦ AQJ1073   ♣ J105

(h)     ♠ 7   ♥ 643   ♦ KQJ108   ♣ QJ109

Hand (f) is a classic 2♦ opening. Both your suit and outside strength are ideal. You will be delighted if partner drives the bidding to 3NT or preemptively bids more diamonds. Hand (g) is another classic 2♦ opening. Although (h) is not a classic since your suit is a card short, most experts we respect would open 2♦, even vulnerable. The determining factor for (h) is the strong intermediates in your trump suit.

## RESPONSES TO 2♦

The responding structure to 2♦ is consistent with the methods we recommended over major suit weak two-bids. For partnerships who elect not to use CABs over preemptive 2♦ openings, it may be best to play 2♥ and 2♠ as constructive, invitational, but **not** forcing; jumps to 3♥ and 3♠ will then be game-forcing. These agreements should make it easier to play in a major suit or locate major suit fits after a weak 2♦ opening.

# RESPONSES TO 2♦

(1) 3♦ and 4♦ are defensive — not invitational.

(2) 2♥ and 2♠ are natural and a one-round force. Opener then:
  - Raises with Qx, Kx, Ax or xxx in the major.
  - Rebids diamonds with a minimum.
  - Shows a feature:
    2♠ over 2♥ = ♠ feature.
    2NT over 2♠ = ♥ feature.
    3♣ shows a club feature.
  - Bids three of the other major with a solid diamond suit (AKQxxx or better), enabling responder to play 3NT from the "right" side of the table
    3♥ over 2♠ = solid ♦s.
    3♠ over 2♥ = solid ♦s.

(3) 2NT asks opener to clarify his weak two-bid via Ogust responses. (Alternatively, you may agree to respond high card features).

(4) 3♣ asks for a distributional feature (shortness). Opener rebids:
  - 3♦ without shortness.
  - 3♥ or 3♠ with shortness in the opened major.
  - 3NT with club shortness.

(5) 3NT, 4♥, 4♠, 5♣ and 5♦ are to play.

(6) 3♥, 3♠ and 4♣ are CABs.

(7) 4NT is Blackwood.

(8) 5NT is the Grand Slam Force.

Here is an example of our methods in practice:

## North
- ♠ J105
- ♥ A32
- ♦ KQ8764
- ♣ 7

## West
- ♠ 93
- ♥ KQ85
- ♦ 105
- ♣ KJ1054

Board 21
Dlr. - North
Vul. - N/S

## East
- ♠ 762
- ♥ J1094
- ♦ J32
- ♣ AQ3

## South
- ♠ AKQ84
- ♥ 76
- ♦ A9
- ♣ 9862

Opening Lead ♥ K
N/S +1430 (12 matchpoints/12 top)

| West | *Zenkel*<br>North | East | *Andersen*<br>South |
|------|------|------|------|
| — | 2♦ (a) | P | 2♠ (b) |
| P | 4♣ (c) | P | 4♦ (d) |
| P | 4♥ (e) | P | 4NT (f) |
| P | 5♦ (g) | P | 6♠ (h) |
| P | P | P | |

- (a) Typical sound weak two-bid.
- (b) One-round force.
- (c) Splinter in support of spades.
- (d) This is getting good. "I have the Ace of diamonds."
- (e) "And I have the Ace of hearts."
- (f) Keycard Blackwood.
- (g) One keycard.
- (h) 12 tricks should be available after we lose a club trick.

Most pairs played this hand in 4♠, some landed in 3NT which went down on a club lead, and a few did not even reach game. We were the only pair to reach this excellent slam via North's most informative 4♣ bid. The key bid was the rare (and highly unusual) splinter bid by opener after the 2♦ opening.

As a result of this deal played in a Madison, Wisconsin (silver-point) Sectional, one of your co-authors, namely Sabine, broke Jeremy Flint's record for length of time spent in becoming a Life Master of the ACBL[1].

## LESS DISCIPLINED WEAK TWO-BIDS

Despite the advantages presented for playing sound disciplined weak two-bids (particularly in first or second seat), some partnerships will prefer to place considerably fewer restrictions on their 2♦, 2♥ and 2♠ openings. In such partnerships, requirements for both the quality and (even) the length of the suit are reduced from those we have outlined and discussed. The same is true for playing and high-card strength.

In the world of tournament bridge, the most successful advocates of opening weak two-bids with a broad range of suits and hands are Jeff Meckstroth and Eric Rodwell — considered by many to be the finest pair in the world[2]. A reasonable five-card suit is more than adequate for a Meck-Well weak two-bid; and under ideal conditions, a less than "reasonable" five-card suit will suffice.

Your authors have played numerous sessions over the years with Jeff and Eric as partners, and have had the good fortune of having

---

[1]   Jeremy Flint (of London, England), held the record for becoming an ACBL Life Master in less than 11 full weeks. This record stood for a quarter of a century until Sabine Zenkel became an ACBL Life Master in less than **eight** weeks in 1988.

[2]   When referring to, or making references about, the Jeff Meckstroth-Eric Rodwell partnership, it is common practice throughout the bridge world to call them simply "Meck-Well."

them as teammates, playing their "undisciplined" preemptive style. We have also played with other experts who utilize a similar approach to two-level openings. Frankly, we find it remarkable that so many excellent results are generated by such openings and that so few poor results are produced.

A few words of caution seem appropriate before we go any further. Wide-range bids — whether weak two-bids or others — require firm partnership understandings and sufficient tools for responder to inquire about the exact nature of opener's hand. In addition, wide-range bids should be played only by regular experienced partnerships.

Having issued the "warning," if you want to open a weak two-bid on all of the following hands

| | | | | | |
|---|---|---|---|---|---|
| (a) | ♠ AQ1073 | ♥ 7 | ♦ 9842 | ♣ 1093 | NV only |
| (b) | ♠ AQ10976 | ♥ A74 | ♦ 3 | ♣ 982 | |
| (c) | ♠ 43 | ♥ KQ10763 | ♦ 432 | ♣ 43 | |
| (d) | ♠ KJ3 | ♥ KQ10952 | ♦ J106 | ♣ 7 | |
| (e) | ♠ QJ1097 | ♥ 7 | ♦ Q1054 | ♣ 983 | NV only |
| (f) | ♠ 7 | ♥ K105 | ♦ KQ1094 | ♣ 10953 | |
| (g) | ♠ 54 | ♥ AJ1097 | ♦ 9854 | ♣ 85 | NV only |
| (h) | ♠ KJ1095 | ♥ 7 | ♦ QJ95 | ♣ 874 | |
| (i) | ♠ 832 | ♥ 4 | ♦ AQ1098 | ♣ J1094 | NV only |

…we suggest a few changes in your responding arsenal from those recommended over more disciplined openings. For example, playing "wide-range" preempts it is desirable to have methods that enable you to show **three** ranges of strength in addition to the length of your suit. Unfortunately, even the Ogust responses to 2NT outlined earlier in this chapter can show only two ranges of strength and have no way to distinguish between five- and six-card suits.

If you decide to venture out with "wide-range" weak two-bids, we recommend the following responses to the conventional 2NT inquiry. They enable opener to reveal his strength and suit length quickly and precisely.

# CONVENTIONAL RESPONSES TO 2NT OVER "UNDISCIPLINED" WEAK TWO-BIDS

(1)  3♣ shows a 5-card suit.
  Then, 3♦ by responder asks about opener's
  hand strength. Opener rebids:
    3♥ = minimum.
    3♠ = medium.
    3NT = maximum.

(2)  3♦ shows a 6-card suit with minimum strength.

(3)  3♥ shows a 6-card suit with medium strength.

(4)  3♠ shows a 6-card suit with maximum strength.

(5)  3NT shows AKQxxx or better.

Using these responses, consider the following hands. You open 2♠ and partner bids 2NT. What is your response holding:

(a)  ♠ AQ1094  ♥ 7  ♦ 9843  ♣ 873
  REBID 3♣. You have a 5-card 2♠ opener.
  If partner then bids 3♦ you will bid 3♥ to
  show your minimum.

(b)  ♠ AK10975  ♥ 7  ♦ QJ75  ♣ 98
  REBID 3♠. You have a maximum weak
  two-bid with a 6-card suit.

(c)  ♠ AJ10965  ♥ 3  ♦ 984  ♣ Q109
  REBID 3♥. You have a 6-card suit with
  medium strength.

(d)  ♠ AKJ109  ♥ 7  ♦ 875  ♣ 10983
  REBID 3♣. This is a medium strength
  weak two-bid with a 5-card suit. If partner
  inquires with 3♦ you will bid 3♠ to show
  medium values.

After opener's response to 2NT, responder rarely has any difficulty setting the final contract. Should his interest be beyond game, it is reasonable to play that a new suit after opener's response to 2NT is a CAB.

Although we recommend playing new suits as forcing over disciplined weak two-bids, it may be best to adopt Meck-Well's approach over the undisciplined variety since you may have only a five-card suit. They play new suits as non-forcing over their weak two-bids. Personally, we feel it is best to play new suits as forcing over all types of weak two-bids even though the advantages of this approach are diminished considerably when playing wide-range weak two-bids.

With the exception of your responses to the conventional 2NT, (and possibly playing new suits as non-forcing), we see no reason to change the meaning of other responses we recommended over disciplined weak two-bids when playing wide-range preempts. Even over undisciplined 2♦, 2♥ and 2♠, you need tools for exploration when responder has a good hand.

## THIRD AND FOURTH SEAT WEAK TWO-BIDS

Most partnerships relax their requirements for weak two-bids in third seat, since partner is a passed hand. This is perfectly reasonable and meets with our approval, provided a modicum of discretion is used. In other words — as our teenage nephews and nieces would say — "Let's not go nuts!"

Speaking of "going nuts," and much as we hesitate to criticize other authors, one book on weak two-bids advocates opening 2♦ in third chair holding:

♠ 96432   ♥ 5   ♦ AKJ42   ♣ 53

The reason given for this "unusual" opening is its lead-directing value. This text goes on to suggest that:

♠ AKQJ   ♥ 9432   ♦ 65   ♣ 852

"will probably work out as a third-seat weak two-bid in spades more often than not...," adding this brief note of caution: "Like fine wine, this sort of weak two-bid should be used sparingly." Distasteful as the thought of finding fine wine in any way culpable may be, it is only possible to justify making an opening preempt with these hands after imbibing the wine.

What does constitute a third seat preempt? Although the following would not qualify in first or second chair, we would open 2♦ in third seat with:

♠ 986   ♥ 73   ♦ AK1095   ♣ J104

In third seat, 2♠ (at any vulnerability other than unfavorable) is a reasonable call holding:

♠ KJ1097   ♥ 7   ♦ QJ105   ♣ 1093

The following is NEVER a 2♥ bid, in any position, at any vulnerability, at any form of scoring:

♠ AJ104   ♥ J87432   ♦ —   ♣ KJ10

You might, however, open 2♠ at unfavorable vulnerability in third chair holding:

♠ AK97542   ♥ 85   ♦ 109   ♣ 43

As we shall discuss in Chapter 3, it is too dangerous to open this hand 3♠ at this vulnerability. Consequently, **with partner a passed hand**, 2♠ is not unreasonable. Opening 2♠ denies your opponents most of two levels of bidding space and should get partner — if he is on lead — off to the optimum beginning for the defense. Even if vulnerable versus non-vulnerable, the quality and extra length of your suit offers considerable safety at the two-level.

We recommend a few adjustments to your responding structure after a third seat preempt. There is no longer any reason to play simple changes of suit forcing. It is best to play new suits as non-forcing since responder — a passed hand — may have a reasonable six- seven- or even eight-card suit of his own (with a hand that did not qualify for a disciplined preemptive opening).

Two notrump and 3♣ should remain unchanged by responder. They should be used as game tries by a maximum passed hand and they should promise a good fit. They are both excellent tools which can be used to reach good game contracts when the partnership is short on high-card strength, but has an exceptional fit and sufficient controls.

Control Asking Bids (CABs) are no longer needed because passed hands cannot be interested in exploring for slam facing a third chair weak two-bid. Your authors play that jumps in new suits are "fit-showing" with good support for opener's suit and a good side suit (the suit bid). This treatment is designed to handle competitive auctions where your side may have a good sacrifice and be forced to decide whether to defend or bid on at a high level. If you do not like the idea of playing "fit-showing" jumps, it is perfectly reasonable to play jumps in new suits as splinter bids.

Partner opens 2♥ in third chair. Plan your response holding:

(a)    ♠ QJ95  ♥ —  ♦ KJ109543  ♣ 94
RESPOND 3♦. This is not forcing. Correct 2♥ to your exceptional diamond suit. You did not make a diamond preempt initially because of your four-card spade suit.

(b)    ♠ A1096  ♥ —  ♦ J1087  ♣ Q10943
PASS. You have nowhere to go. You may redouble — S.O.S. — later in the auction.

(c)    ♠ A10953  ♥ J1075  ♦ A1053  ♣ —
JUMP TO 4♥. This is the same bid you would have made if partner had opened 2♥ in any other seat.

After three passes, the only tactical consideration in opening the bidding is your side's chances of **going plus on the scoresheet**. With a passed partner and a typical sound preemptive opening (6 to 9 HCP), you should pass the deal out for no score. Therefore, you have more high cards, defense, and playing strength for a fourth chair weak two-bid than you have in the other three positions. We suggest the following requirements:

# REQUIREMENTS FOR FOURTH SEAT WEAK TWO-BIDS

(1)   10+ to 13 HCP.

(2)   Two defensive tricks.

(3)   A **good** suit (usually a six-card suit, but could be an exceptional five-card or a reasonable seven-card suit).

In fourth seat, you will often have full values for an opening one-bid and elect to open a weak two-bid as a better description of your one-suited hand. When you open in fourth chair at the two-level, you make it difficult for the opponents to compete while suggesting the level and strain of your side's final contract (partner may only try for game with an excellent fit).

Consider what you would do holding these hands in fourth seat:

(a)   ♠ AQJ983  ♥ 6  ♦ A104  ♣ J107
OPEN 2♠. Although you would have opened 1♠ in any other position, 2♠ is a good tactical opening in fourth seat. Partner knows you have more than a typical weak two-bid, and you may prevent your two (passing) opponents from competing as they might have done over 1♠. You would have rebid 2♠ had you opened 1♠, so you might as well get your hand off your chest now. Opening 2♠ will not stop your side from reaching game if partner holds a useful hand and spade fit; in fact, it may help.

(b)   ♠ 7  ♥ AKJ1052  ♦ 9732  ♣ J5
PASS. In first, second or third positions, we would open 2♥. However, in fourth seat we pass. We hold only 9 HCP. Our suit is hearts, and the opponents might easily outbid

us in spades (if you do not expect to go plus it is best to pass). Partner may expect us to hold more strength for our bid and get us too high. If we ever opened this hand with 2♥ in fourth chair (perhaps against timid opponents, or looking for a swing), we would have to be prepared to defend ourselves.

(c)    ♠ AK10974  ♥ A1097  ♦ J109  ♣ —

OPEN 1♠. It is very possible that your side should play hearts, or even diamonds, depending on partner's hand. Opening 2♠ might very well prevent you from reaching your optimum contract. Remember, even fourth-seat weak two-bids should suggest a one-suited hand. With six-four in the majors and three quick tricks, the danger of effective competition is relatively remote.

(d)    ♠ 10  ♥ AJ10985  ♦ A95  ♣ K108

OPEN 2♥. Although you would have opened 1♥ in first, second or third chair, 2♥ is a better choice in fourth seat. Your additional strength will not be misleading to partner, and opening 2♥ will make it more difficult for the enemy to compete.

(e)    ♠ 7  ♥ 97  ♦ AKJ1075  ♣ K1085

OPEN 2♦. There is obviously some danger that your opponents can successfully outbid you in one of the majors. Nevertheless, your side rates to make at least a partscore and even a game is not out of the question. Opening 2♦, instead of 1♦, should make it a bit more difficult for the enemy to compete.

Responses to fourth seat weak two-bids are simple. However, responder must keep in mind that opener has a stronger hand than he would have in any other seat — often with an extra King or Ace — when he makes a weak two-bid in fourth chair.

# RESPONSES TO FOURTH SEAT
# WEAK TWO-BIDS

(1) 3♣ asks for shortness.
Opener bids 3NT with club shortness; bids the suit in which he is short; or rebids his trump suit (showing no shortness).

(2) New suits are **invitational**, not forcing, and deny a fit for opener's suit.

(3) 2NT asks for a high card feature.

(4) Simple raises are invitational, not preemptive (responder's failure to bid 2NT or 3♣ suggests interest in opener's **general** overall strength and controls).

(5) 3NT and all other game bids are to play.

Using these methods, consider a few illustrations. Partner opens 2♥ in fourth seat. Choose your action holding:

(a) ♠ 74 ♥ 2 ♦ AJ109743 ♣ A107
RESPOND 3♦. This is **not forcing** by a passed hand. Your hand did not meet the requirements for a 3♦ opening. Since 3♦ rates to be a better contract than 2♥, bid it now, denying a heart fit and suggesting a contract where you can go plus.

(b) ♠ A10 ♥ 984 ♦ K102 ♣ KJ1096
RAISE TO 3♥. Invite partner to bid on to game with a maximum fourth chair weak two-bid. You are not interested in a specific high card or distributional feature, so the simple raise is your most effective game try.

What action would you take with the following hands over partner's fourth seat 2♠ opener?

(c)      ♠ 10   ♥ KJ974   ♦ QJ106   ♣ K85
PASS. Game is out of the question; you have no reasonable alternative. Hope that your scattered Kings, Queen and Jacks will permit partner to make 2♠.

(d)      ♠ J105   ♥ AKQ   ♦ 87643   ♣ 94
RESPOND 3♣. If opener is short in a minor, you should have an excellent play for 4♠. On the other hand, if partner is short in hearts, 3♠ may well be too high. Nevertheless, your hand is definitely worth a game try over a fourth chair weak two-bid.

(e)      ♠ 1093   ♥ 7   ♦ AQ94   ♣ A10732
JUMP TO 4♠. Facing a fourth chair weak two-bid, game should be an excellent proposition. Bid what you think you can make!

(f)      ♠ —   ♥ QJ107   ♦ KQJ1093   ♣ 1093
RESPOND 3♦. A diamond contract rates to play better than spades. Remember, 3♦ is **not** forcing when you are a passed hand.

The key to responding to fourth seat weak two-bid openings is **going plus**. Remember, partner could have passed the deal out for no score. Any minus score you get probably will be a disaster. Beware of game tries when the three-level may be too high if your attempt to reach game is rejected.

## WHEN THE OPPONENTS COMPETE

When the opponents double your weak two-bid, they have not deprived you of any bidding space. Therefore, responder's bids are the same as they would be had the opponents remained silent, with one notable addition; the redouble. Our guidelines for **redoubling** 2♦, 2♥ and 2♠ are:

# REDOUBLES OF WEAK TWO-BIDS

(1) Sound values for an opening bid or better (13+ HCP).

(2) A hand that "belongs" to your side, thus creating a forcing auction. For example:
2♥-Dbl.-Redbl.-P
P- 3♣-P is 100% forcing.

(3) Considerable interest in penalizing the opponents with a double. You invite partner to double an enemy "escape" despite his preemptive opening.

(4) Sufficient strength to be willing to play in opener's suit redoubled at the two-level, just in case both opponents elect to pass.

(5) A hand that is better suited for defense than offense in light of partner's opening weak two-bid.

We would recommend redoubling 2♠ holding:

(a)     ♠ 10  ♥ AQ109  ♦ KJ95  ♣ A1097

(b)     ♠ J10  ♥ KQ108  ♦ AQ1043  ♣ A9

With (a) you intend to double anything your opponents bid, irrespective of the vulnerability. Game is no certainty for your side and a double of any "escape" rates to yield a substantial plus score.

With (b), you have a problem, depending on the suit your opponents bid and the vulnerability. Game, particularly with your opponents' strength well placed, is virtually certain. Therefore, a double must produce more than the value of a game in order for you to net a profit. If your side is vulnerable against non-vulnerable opponents, we would plan to double either red suit but simply bid a spade game over 3♣ (+800 is not likely against this contract).

You must consider the consequences before redoubling a weak two-bid. Do not redouble just because you have a good hand. If you are not interested in doubling at least one or two of the other suits, make a constructive response over a takeout double just as you would have if the opponents had remained silent.

On the following hands, partner opens 2♥ in first seat, and RHO doubles for takeout. Plan your bid holding:

(a)     ♠ A   ♥ KJ32   ♦ AKQ104   ♣ 762
JUMP TO 4♣ (CAB). Despite your opponent's takeout double, your side has a good chance for 6♥ if partner has a first- or second-round club control. If you redouble, the opponents may find their save, particularly if they are at favorable vulnerability. Since the answer to a simple question will determine the optimum contract for your side, ask it (taking up enemy bidding space) and set the contract. Do not redouble.

(b)     ♠ A1094   ♥ KJ3   ♦ 7   ♣ KQ874
JUMP TO 4♥. Bid what you think you can make. Should the enemy compete further, you will determine the best course of action.

After a takeout double of a weak two-bid, some partnerships prefer to play new suits as corrective or rescue. This is certainly playable and is particularly useful when playing less disciplined weak two-bids which are frequently based on a five-card suit.

Several expert partnerships play that a new suit by responder after an opponent's takeout double of 2♥ or 2♠ is lead directing — if their side defends — and shows support for opener's suit (where they intend to play). Then, 2NT is used as the vehicle for responder to sign-off in his own suit; it forces opener to bid 3♣. Responder then passes if he holds clubs, or corrects to his own suit. This treatment is commonly called the McCabe adjunct and was described by J.I. McCabe in the 1955 January issue of the <u>Bridge World</u>. The following box outlines the McCabe adjunct:

## MCCABE ADJUNCT
## OVER TAKEOUT DOUBLES OF 2♥ AND 2♠

(1)   2NT forces opener to bid 3♣. Responder then:
- Passes to play in 3♣.
- Bids a new suit as a sign-off.

(2)   Simple changes of suit are lead directing and show a fit for opener's suit (forcing to three of opener's suit).

Using these methods, what would you bid after partner opens 2♥ and RHO doubles?

(a)      ♠ 82   ♥ 764   ♦ AKJ10   ♣ 9832
RESPOND 3♦   This is lead directing and shows support for partner's hearts.

(b)      ♠ 943   ♥ —   ♦ KQ109543   ♣ 983
RESPOND 2NT.   This forces partner to bid 3♣.  You will sign off in 3♦.

Such methods are fine for regular partnerships with good memories.  They are not, however, recommended for casual partnerships or partnerships with less than perfect memories.

The bidding space consumed by an overcall may deny you the opportunity to make the response you would have made in a non-competitive auction.  You cannot use the conventional 2NT or 3♣ inquiry after a 3♦ overcall; and some bids which would be CABs in a non-competitive auction become simple changes of suit after an overcall.  For example, your 4♦ response to partner's 2♠ opening is a CAB in a non-competitive auction; your 3♦ response would be natural and forcing.  However, after a 3♥ overcall of 2♠, 4♦ is no longer a jump and therefore cannot be a CAB.

We advise the following adjustments in your responding structure after an overcall of partner's weak two-bid:

# RESPONSES WHEN THE OPPONENTS BID A SUIT OVER OUR WEAK TWO-BID

(1)   Double is penalty.

(2)   All raises carry their non-competitive meaning. Jumps to the five-level in opener's suit are preemptive.

(3)   Simple changes of suit below game are natural and forcing. Simple changes of suit at the level of game are natural sign-offs.

(4)   2NT and 3♣, if available, retain their conventional meaning in spite of the interference.

(5)   **Jumps** in new suits (even to game) are CABs.

(6)   3NT is a natural sign-off (to play).

Review these principles in the following auctions:

(a)   2♥-3♦-<u>3♠</u>  =   Natural and forcing.

(b)   2♥-4♦-<u>4♠</u>  =   Natural sign-off.

(c)   2♠-3♥-<u>4♣</u>  =   Natural and forcing.

(d)   2♠-4♥-<u>5♠</u>  =   Preemptive.

(e)   2♥-3♣-<u>4♠</u>  =   CAB.   Start with 3♠ to sign off in 4♠.

(f)   2♠-3♥-<u>5♣</u>  =   CAB.

(g)   2♥-3♠-<u>4♦</u>  =   Natural and forcing.

(h)   2♥-3♠-<u>5♦</u>  =   CAB.

(i)     2♦-2♥-<u>2NT</u> =   Conventional inquiry.

(j)     2♥-2♠-<u>3♣</u> =   Conventional, asking for
                              shortness.

(k)     2♥-2♠-<u>3NT</u> =  To play.

Just as the redouble was available over a takeout double of partner's preemptive opening, the penalty double is a weapon you can use when your opponents have made an error in contesting the auction with an overcall. Doubling an enemy overcall is similar to a real estate investment: "How much do you stand to gain" vs. "how much do you stand to lose," coupled with "what is the likely result of alternative courses of action?" In short, when you double, you believe your side can score more points on defense than on offense; the penalty double must provide a profitable tradeoff.

Consider a few examples. Suppose partner opens 2♠ and the opponents overcall 3♣. Choose your action, holding:

(a)     ♠ 7  ♥ AKQ10972  ♦ K105  ♣ K4     V vs. V
        RESPOND 3♥.  Although you intend to
        play 4♥, you must first bid 3♥ because the
        immediate jump to 4♥ would be a CAB.

(b)     ♠ Q106  ♥ 8  ♦ AJ10754  ♣ 863    NV vs. NV
        JUMP TO 4♠.  You may be able to prevent
        your opponents from finding their excellent
        heart fit.  Such jumps to game are either
        preemptive or made with game-going values
        (as in a non-competitive auction).

(c)     ♠ 3  ♥ K10752  ♦ AJ10  ♣ K1092    V vs. NV
        DOUBLE.  Despite the vulnerability, 3♣
        doubled should yield an excellent score for
        your side on a deal where you were not
        destined to bid or make a game.

(d)     ♠ J104  ♥ A1093  ♦ J965  ♣ 85    NV vs. NV
        RESPOND 3♠.  Stay on the right side of
        the LAW.

After a 3♦ overcall of partner's 2♥ opening, what action would you take holding:

(a)    ♠ K5 ♥ 5 ♦ KJ2 ♣ AKQ10943    V vs. V
RESPOND 3NT. You have a better hand for offense than defense. Although we would anticipate beating 3♦ doubled a trick or two, our virtually laydown notrump game rates to produce a greater plus score. Since your opponents are known to have at least an eight-card spade fit and may well have a fit in diamonds as well, you should bid the notrump game you would have reached in a non-competitive auction.

(b)    ♠ 63 ♥ KJ52 ♦ A ♣ AKQJ95    V vs. NV
JUMP TO 4♠ (CAB). Opener's spade holding will determine the number of hearts you should bid. A jump in a new suit (even to game) is a CAB, not a sign-off.

There are two overcalls that do not consume any valuable bidding space — 2♥ over 2♦ and 2♠ over 2♥. If responder has a natural, forcing response in the enemy suit, he will be delighted to double. All other non-competitive responses are available. Therefore, we recommend using our non-competitive structure of responses in these auctions.

When an opponent overcalls 2♦, 2♥ or 2♠ with a natural 2NT (showing the values for a strong 1NT opening with opener's suit well stopped), our approach is similar to the methods we use to handle a 1NT overcall of a one-level opening. Double is the only strong action. Raises and new suits are non-forcing and simply competitive. 3NT after a natural 2NT overcall would be unusual, describing a two-suiter.

After a jump overcall of a weak two-bid, there is no substitute for reason and judgment. Usually, very little room will be available for exploration.

The guidelines that follow will help you avoid any possible partnership misunderstandings when the opponents bid 2NT or make a jump overcall over your weak 2♦, 2♥ and 2♠ openings:

## RESPONSES WHEN THE OPPONENTS BID 2NT OVER YOUR WEAK TWO-BID

(1)  Double is the only strong response.

(2)  Simple raises are competitive.

(3)  Jump raises to game are either preemptive or made with highly distributional hands.

(4)  New suits are natural and non-forcing. With forcing values, you begin with a double.

(5)  3NT is unusual showing a two-suiter.

## RESPONSES WHEN THE OPPONENTS MAKE A JUMP OVERCALL OVER 2♦, 2♥ AND 2♠

(1)  New suits below game are natural and forcing.

(2)  Simple (non-jump) new suits bid at the game level (and 3NT) are all natural sign-offs.

(3)  Jumps in new suits are CABs.

(4)  Simple raises are either defensive or made with game-going values. Jump raises (to the five-level) are preemptive.

(5)  Double is for penalty.

Sometimes the bidding space consumed by an enemy overcall or jump overcall will prove costly to your side. To compensate, there will also be times when this intervention presents you with a lucrative penalty double on a partscore deal. No partnership goes "right" in every competitive auction. Using our guidelines, and a little common sense, you should reach reasonable contracts in most contested auctions after your side has opened with a weak two-bid.

# DOUBLES OF WEAK
# TWO-BIDS

Your defense against weak two-bids should be quite similar to the methods you use against enemy one-bids. True, you are a level higher, but their bid is weaker in strength — so it comes out about even. Additionally, you will have the advantage of knowing more about your opponents' strength and distribution when your side plays the hand. Nevertheless, we feel you should add a few conventional agreements and methods to your defensive strategies when the opponents preempt at the two-level.

---

## REQUIREMENTS FOR
## DOUBLING WEAK TWO-BIDS

(1)  Takeout-oriented hand with at least three-card support for the unbid suits.

(2)  Values for a sound opening bid.

(3)  The more HCP, the less perfect the support for all the unbid suits need be, but support for any unbid major(s) is essential.

### OR

(4)  A hand that is too strong for a simple overcall. You will bid your suit at your next turn.

---

We would double a 2♥ opening with both these hands:

(a)   ♠ KJ105  ♥ 4  ♦ KJ103  ♣ K1063

(b)   ♠ AK10  ♥ 52  ♦ AKQ105  ♣ J103

Hand (a) is a good illustration of perfect distribution with adequate strength for a takeout double of 2♥. The high card strength of (b) compensates for the less than ideal support for the black suits.

(c)    ♠ K7  ♥ 743  ♦ AQ105  ♣ KQ76

Although the strength is more than adequate, do not double 2♥ with hand (c). You are short in spades. Pass and hope partner can get your side into the auction.

## RESPONDING TO THE DOUBLE

(1)  New suits at the two-level are non-forcing.

(2)  Jumps in new suits below game are invitational.

(3)  3NT, 4♥, 4♠, 5♣ and 5♦ are to play.

(4)  Cuebids are game forcing. Use them to either locate your best strain or suggest slam interest.

(4)  2NT over 2♦ (doubled by partner) is invitational and denies a four-card major.

## LEBENSOHL

(5)  2NT over 2♥ and 2♠ (doubled by partner) forces doubler to bid 3♣ with any normal takeout double. Responder then:
   • Passes 3♣ with a sign-off in clubs.
   • Signs off in a suit, showing weakness.
   • Bids 3♠ (over 2♥ doubled) with four spades and invitational values (an immediate jump to 3♠ therefore shows an invitational hand with a five-card suit).
   • Cuebids opener's suit, asking partner to bid 3NT with a stopper (a direct cuebid is game-forcing and asks partner to confirm his four-card major).

(6)  Simple three-level responses are constructive and invitational, suggesting at least 7+ HCP (with less, responder signs off via Lebensohl).

The reason for the Lebensohl application is easily demonstrated by the following hands. Suppose partner doubles a 2♥ or 2♠ opening. What bid do you make with the following hand?

(a)   ♠ 742   ♥ 97   ♦ KQ1094   ♣ A109

You would most likely respond 3♦, hoping that if partner has anything extra he will bid again so you can reveal your **good** 3♦ response. Admittedly, 3♦ does not do this hand justice, but you do not have a viable alternative.

Remember, you would also have been forced to bid 3♦ holding:

(b)   ♠ 32   ♥ 43   ♦ 65432   ♣ 5432

There is quite a difference between hands (a) and (b); yet in both cases 3♦ would be your only reasonable response if you were not playing Lebensohl. You certainly would not want to jump to 4♦ with hand (a) because that would take you past 3NT which might be your only makeable game.

Using Lebensohl you can bid 3♦ directly in response to partner's takeout double on hand (a). With hand (b), bid 2NT and then sign off in 3♦.

To make this even clearer, look at the hand from the other side of the table. RHO opens 2♥ and you double holding:

♠ QJ109   ♥ A5   ♦ AJ8   ♣ AQ76

Partner responds 3♦. If responder holds (a) or slightly better (which is possible), you had better bid 3NT since you have an excellent play for game. However, if partner has the misfortune of having been dealt (b), you had better pass fast before the lights go out. Any move beyond 3♦ is likely to be greeted with a very profitable penalty double when your opponents did not have game possibilities.

Clearly, in such situations, both responder and the player doubling a weak two-bid are on the horns of a dilemma if they lack methods to distinguish immediately between hands like (a) and (b). Our Lebensohl solution is simple and effective; it requires only that you give up the natural meaning of a relatively infrequent response to the double of a preemptive two-bid; i.e., 2NT.

Applying the Lebensohl convention, consider a few examples:

(a) &spades; 52 &hearts; KJ73 &diams; 1094 &clubs; K1095
**The auction is 2&spades;-double-pass to you.**
BID 3&hearts;, constructive.

(b) &spades; 763 &hearts; J1095 &diams; Q1062 &clubs; 85
**The auction is 2&spades;-double-pass to you.**
BID 2NT, Lebensohl. Partner is forced to bid 3&clubs; and you correct to 3&hearts;, non-forcing.

(c) &spades; KQ1092 &hearts; 4 &diams; 1083 &clubs; 9872
**The auction is 2&spades;-double-pass to you.**
PASS. Defending 2&spades; doubled rates to produce your side's best result. Remember, you can still convert a takeout double.

(d) &spades; AKQ10 &hearts; A5 &diams; AKQ107 &clubs; J10
**RHO opens 2&hearts;. What do you do?**
DOUBLE. Should partner now bid 2NT, suggesting a weak hand, bid 3NT.

(e) &spades; J109 &hearts; 94 &diams; AKQ106 &clubs; K73
**The auction is 2&hearts;-double-pass to you.**
CUEBID 3&hearts;, forcing to game. Although 3&diams; would be a constructive response, it is **not** forcing.

(f) &spades; AKJ6 &hearts; 9 &diams; KQ104 &clubs; KJ42
**2&hearts;-double-pass-2NT-pass.**
BID 3&clubs;. You have a good hand — 17 HCP — but not nearly enough to do anything other than make the forced 3&clubs; response. Your 4-1-4-4 pattern gives you no convenient alternative.

(g) &spades; 7 &hearts; AKJ10 &diams; AQJ1095 &clubs; A5
**2&spades;-double-pass-2NT-pass.**
BID 3&diams;. Your side could still have a game if partner was intending to pass 3&clubs;; besides, 3&diams; rates to be a far better contract than 3&clubs; if responder is completely broke. Breaking the relay **promises** extra values.

As hands (d) and (f) above illustrate, when the doubler holds a "battleship" for his initial action, he must not make the simple 3♣ relay over the conventional 2NT response. A few extra points, however, do not constitute a "battleship." You must hold a sufficiently good hand to produce a game when partner may have wanted to sign off in 3♣.

As an aside, if a passed hand makes a takeout double of a weak two-level bid, Lebensohl no longer applies. You may play that 2NT by a passed hand is natural; OR your partnership agreement may be that 2NT suggests that your side has more than one place to play, requesting that the doubler bid four- or five-card suits up the line.

## OVERCALLS OF WEAK TWO-BIDS

Overcalls are by far the most frequently used weapon in your competitive bidding arsenal against weak two-bids. They are also the most dangerous. The effectiveness of an overcall will depend on various factors.

The quality of your trump suit and the playing strength of your hand — with your suit as trump — is most important in terms of safety. A suit which is good enough for an overcall at the one-level may not be sufficient for a two-level bid. For instance, AK765 or AQ1043 are perfectly reasonable suits for a one-level overcall. They are at best marginal suits for a two-level overcall of a weak two-bid, and at the three-level they would be totally unacceptable without considerable compensating values and conditions.

You should also evaluate the risk versus possible gain of making a bid. Factors that make a difference here are the vulnerability, the level of your overcall, the form of scoring (or type of game you are playing, including the state of your game or match), and your position at the table. Also consider partner's judgment and bidding style as well as your partnership understandings regarding overcalls.

We recommend using the following guidelines for overcalls of weak two-bids:

# REQUIREMENTS FOR OVERCALLING WEAK TWO-BIDS

(1) Overcalls promise a **good** suit and approximately opening one bid strength. Then:
  - New suits are a one-round force.
  - Jumps in new suits are splinters (support, game-going+ values).
  - Cuebids are game forcing.
  - 2NT is invitational, showing a stopper in opener's suit.
  - 3NT is natural, promising a sure stopper in opener's suit.

(2) 2NT shows a strong (15-18 HCP) balanced hand, with the enemy suit well stopped. Responses:
  - 3♣ is Stayman.
  - 3♦, 3♥, 4♦ and 4♥ are transfers.
  - 4♣ is Gerber.
  - 4NT is a quantitative notrump raise.

(3) 3NT shows a stopper in the enemy suit and a source of tricks via a long, good suit (with 18+ HCP, balanced, you double initially).

(4) 3♦ over a weak 2♦ is takeout for the majors.

(5) Cuebids over 2♥ and 2♠ are conventional, asking partner to bid 3NT with a stopper in the enemy suit. They promise a source of tricks via a long running suit.

(6) Jump overcalls to 3♥ or 3♠ show strong one-suited hands and are highly invitational.

(7) 4♣ or 4♦ over 2♥ or 2♠ show a strong two-suiter (5/5 or better) with the minor plus the other major. 4♥ over 2♥ and 4♠ over 2♠ show a strong minor two-suiter.

Using these guidelines, let us consider a few examples. Suppose RHO opens 2♥ and you hold:

(a)　♠ K10　♥ AJ9　♦ KJ107　♣ AJ103
OVERCALL 2NT. This is a perfect overcall of a 2♥ opening.

(b)　♠ A9843　♥ Q42　♦ KJ　♣ KJ3
PASS. 2♠ would qualify as a "Marie Antoinette" overcall (a description coined by the late Victor Mollo and one of your authors). It is not surprising how often a guillotine awaits a direct 2♠ overcall with this garbage. Yes, you have 14 HCP, but neither your suit nor your playing strength are even close to a two-level overcall. Your Queen-third of hearts is a danger sign.

(c)　♠ KQJ108　♥ 873　♦ 74　♣ A109
OVERCALL 2♠. You have the exact same distribution as (b) with four fewer HCP; yet this is a reasonable two-level overcall. Your suit quality is good and you therefore have good playing strength.

(d)　♠ A5　♥ 94　♦ AKJ1085　♣ K93
OVERCALL 3♦. You have a good suit and sound values for a three-level overcall.

Failure to show at least some restraint when overcalling weak two-bids can have disastrous consequences. One of your authors fondly recalls an opponent's "explanation" for a minus 1400 on the third deal of her first North American Championship event[1]. Playing with Rhoda Walsh, Sabine heard her partner open 2♠ in first seat and was delighted when RHO overcalled 3♥ on AQ854. Here is the complete deal:

---

[1]　Sabine won this National Championship in Lancaster, Pennsylvania, in 1989 — even though she was not yet a Life Master and had to receive special permission to enter.

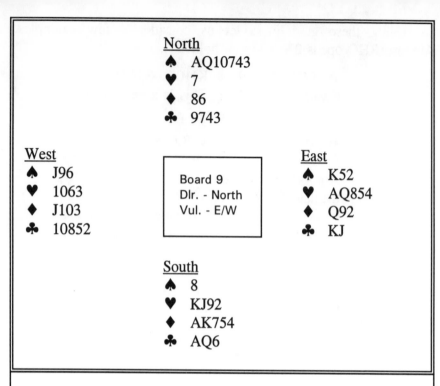

**North**
- ♠ AQ10743
- ♥ 7
- ♦ 86
- ♣ 9743

**West**
- ♠ J96
- ♥ 1063
- ♦ J103
- ♣ 10852

Board 9
Dlr. - North
Vul. - E/W

**East**
- ♠ K52
- ♥ AQ854
- ♦ Q92
- ♣ KJ

**South**
- ♠ 8
- ♥ KJ92
- ♦ AK754
- ♣ AQ6

Opening Lead ♠ 8
N/S +1400

| West | *Walsh* North | East | *Zenkel* South |
|------|-------|------|-------|
| — | 2♠ | 3♥ (!!) | DBL. |
| P | P | P | |

After winning her fourth — and final — trick, East "explained," "But I had to bid...I had 15 high card **points** and a good suit!" When East departed, West (unimpressed), removed East's hand from the board, shook her head and cooed, "Points...schmointz ... I wonder whether the **15** included the one on top of her head?"

The object lesson of this deal is simple. Points are not the key ingredient to sound overcalls of weak two-bids. Good suits and playing strength are.

Cuebids of enemy weak two-bids can be used to describe a variety of different hand types.  They can:

(1)     Ask partner to bid 3NT with a stopper in the enemy suit;

(2)     Describe a game-forcing hand; or,

(3)     Show a good two-suiter.

We recommend that cuebids over 2♥ and 2♠ (1) ask partner to bid 3NT with the enemy suit stopped.  If you use cuebids over 2♥ and 2♠ to describe hands types (2) and (3), you may create confusion.  A 3♦ cuebid over 2♦, however, should show the majors.

We strongly urge your regular partnerships to adopt our suggested approach — which has become standard practice among most expert pairs — to describe strong two-suiters.  This method uses a jump to four of a minor over a major suit weak two-bid to show the suit bid plus the other major.  This treatment is advantageous because it allows you to show two specific long suits (at least 5/5) in a hand with excellent playing strength.  The key to jumps to 4♣ and 4♦ over 2♥ and 2♠ is the quality of your suits.  We would jump to 4♦ over 2♥ with:

(a)     ♠ AKJ74  ♥ 7  ♦ KQJ1075  ♣ 7

(b)     ♠ AKQ109  ♥ 32  ♦ AQJ104  ♣ 3

We would **not**, however, bid 4♣ over 2♠ holding:

(c)     ♠ A  ♥ Q10652  ♦ AQ  ♣ KQ732

(d)     ♠ K4  ♥ AKQ108  ♦ A  ♣ K7632

The distribution in hand (c) is acceptable, as is your high card strength, but the quality of your suits is simply not good enough.  The poor texture of your suits, and the fact that many of your HCP are outside of them, give you a hand with insufficient playing strength.  Hand (d) is closer to a jump to 4♣.  The heart suit is more than adequate but the club suit is far too weak.  Your playing strength falls short in hand (d) as it did in (c).  Remember, these jumps are practically forcing to game; partner must not pass.  Similarly, we recommend using a jump to four of the two-bidder's suit as "unusual," showing both minors.

We would jump to 4♠ over a 2♠ opening holding:

(e)  ♠ —  ♥ A4  ♦ KQJ109  ♣ KQ10963

## BALANCING OVER WEAK TWO-BIDS

Our discussion so far has been confined to actions by the defender sitting directly over the weak two-bid. If LHO's weak two-bid is passed around to you in balancing seat, your problems (and risk) are considerably reduced with marginal values. It is reasonable to play partner for some strength in light of RHO's pass. You still must exercise discretion since RHO's pass may be based on what he knows to be a misfit. He may still have considerable strength. Nevertheless, it is reasonable to lower your requirements for doubles and overcalls in the balancing chair, particularly playing matchpoint duplicate. We would, for example, make a balancing double of a preemptive 2♥ opening in the pass-out seat with:

(a)  ♠ QJ93  ♥ 65  ♦ AJ7  ♣ K985

(b)  ♠ KQ10  ♥ 3  ♦ Q10943  ♣ K1062

(c)  ♠ Q1097  ♥ 4  ♦ KJ98  ♣ KJ87

None of these hands, however, would meet our requirements for a direct double. Similarly, we would balance with 2♠ over 2♦ or 2♥ with the following hands, even though we would pass in direct seat.

(d)  ♠ AJ1075  ♥ 54  ♦ 53  ♣ AJ94

(e)  ♠ K9753  ♥ A4  ♦ 85  ♣ KJ98

(f)  ♠ AJ753  ♥ K7  ♦ Q2  ♣ Q985

Although we lower the requirements for balancing doubles and overcalls, we see no reason to change the meaning and requirements of other competitive weapons and responses. All bids — including 2NT, jump overcalls, cuebids — and responses (e.g., Lebensohl) should remain the same.

# IF YOU ARE FIXED,
# STAY FIXED

Unfortunately, the partner of the two-bidder does not always remain silent. He can raise or jump-raise the weak two-bid, make a conventional inquiry asking for additional information from the opening bidder, or make a forcing, non-forcing or sign-off bid in another suit or notrump. Any of these actions may make the life of the defending side more difficult. For example, suppose you pick up:

♠ AJ75　♥ 72　♦ KQ10　♣ KQ62

and the bidding goes 2♥-P-4♥ to you. You are vulnerable, they are not. You double, right? WRONG. Partner has a completely worthless hand and the 4♥ bidder, armed with a great hand, is going to send your side to the "promised land." So you pass, right? WRONG. This time it is partner who has a useful hand and your side has a laydown game; the 4♥ bid was an advance "save." You passed and they stole the hand for a tremendous profit. So, what is the solution to such problems? The answer is that there is no answer. You just cannot get these hands right all the time.

There is also the possibility that the partner of the preempter is psyching. He is in an excellent position to make such a bid with impunity because you are the one in the dark, not he. Therefore, beware of auctions that begin 2♦-P-2♥ and 2♥-P-2♠. To guard against psyches by responder here, your authors play that a bid of 3♥ after 2♦-P-2♥ and 3♠ after 2♥-P-2♠ are natural. We also recommend playing doubles of the forcing responses as penalty-oriented.

More dangerous than the above auctions are those where the partner of the weak two-bidder passes — particularly at favorable vulnerability. With a weak hand, they will almost always bid when partner opens with a weak two-bid (at favorable). So if they do not bid against you, be forewarned — something may be "rotten in Denmark."

Rely on your judgment when one opponent opens a weak two-bid and the other elevates the bidding. Occasionally you will not be able to reach your side's optimum contract. Accept that and try for the best result possible (as opposed to the best possible result).

This concludes our discussion of defenses against enemy weak two-bids, except for one common situation. Often a weak two-bid will be preemptively raised by the partner of the opening bidder. In such instances, all competitive bids carry their usual meaning over the "sum" of the opponents' action. For example, suppose your LHO opens 2♥, partner passes, RHO bids 3♥ and it is your turn. Your bids mean the following:

Double shows values to double a 3♥ opening.
3♠ shows the values for a three-level overcall of a 3♥ opening.
3NT shows the values necessary to bid 3NT over a 3♥ opening.

You must be aware of potential bluffs by the partner of the preempter. While jumps and raises to game in opener's suit may show values, they may just as easily be advance saves, or strictly preemptive, (an attempt to keep you from reaching your optimum contract). Keep in mind, we discussed such tactics in regard to our own weak two-bids. To combat such tactics, simply use the "sum of the enemy action" approach.

# CHAPTER 3

# THREE-LEVEL OPENINGS

When you open the bidding at the three-level you may be wielding a two-edged sword. Carefully utilized you will make life difficult for your opponents and profit when they misjudge; misused, you will create disasters — often of considerable magnitude. Your goal is to preempt the opponents out of the bidding space they need to conduct an auction to their optimum contract.

Exercise discipline and discretion when opening at the three-level so that partner will know what to expect. This will put partner — who will usually know more about whose hand it is than the opponents — in an excellent position to bid accurately to a game (or slam), sacrifice, or double the opponents.

Several important factors must be considered when you contemplate opening the bidding at the three-level. These include:

(1) **The length and strength of your suit**. This is by far the most important consideration in determining whether to open 3♣, 3♦, 3♥ or 3♠. Most guidelines call for a seven-card suit. Six- or eight-card suits may be acceptable under certain conditions. As with weak two-bids, it is best to have your honor

strength concentrated in the suit bid. This automatically increases your trump strength, decreases the danger of suffering a substantial penalty, and limits your defensive prospects against an opposing contract.

(2) **Vulnerability.** At the three-level, vulnerability is an extremely important factor. The traditional rule was to take the playing strength of the hand and add three tricks when not vulnerable or two tricks when vulnerable (the time-honored "Rule of Two and Three"). Some partnerships have found this rule too restrictive and have liberalized it to the "Rule of Two, Three and Four" — to open a three-bid you must be within two tricks of your contract at unfavorable vulnerability, three tricks with equal vulnerability, and four tricks at favorable vulnerability.

Obviously, rules like the "Rule of Two and Three" are oversimplifications. Experts have always made preemptive openings more freely than such rules would permit. In the most favorable circumstances, not vulnerable versus vulnerable in third seat, most successful tournament players would venture 3♥ with as little as:

(a) ♠ 32   ♥ J1097643   ♦ 5   ♣ QJ10

(b) ♠ 7   ♥ KJ10963   ♦ J1095   ♣ 32

Although (a) may get partner off to an unfortunate lead, one of the prime objectives of three-level openings is to make trouble for your opponents. Although (b) qualifies perfectly for a 2♥ bid, most experts would make the more aggressive three-level preempt at the table.

(3) **Position at the table**. The best position for a preemptive opening is third seat. Third hand cannot "preempt" partner, who is a passed hand with limited strength. Fourth hand, almost certain to have the best hand at the table, may be devastated when third hand deprives him of three levels of bidding.

Three-level openings by the dealer are also attractive. Admittedly, they run the risk of finding partner with a strong hand, thus giving him a problem. However, there are two opponents and only one partner, so chances are the hand belongs to the enemy.

Preemptive bids in second chair are less attractive, so they should always be based on sound values. Three-level openings in fourth seat are extremely rare and — unlike those made in the other three positions — must suggest that the hand belongs to opener's side.

(4) **Partnership methods, agreements and understandings**. It is critical that you abide by your partnership agreements and understandings regarding three-level openings. It is equally critical that you have definite understandings regarding suit length and quality, playing strength, distribution and values outside the suit when you preempt at the three-level.

For example, your authors recommend that you DO NOT OPEN 3♠ with the following (neither side vulnerable)

(a) ♠ KQJ10965　♥ 7　♦ A109　♣ 107

because we feel this hand is far too strong for a preemptive opening. We would open 1♠. But, if hand (a) qualifies as a non-vulnerable three-level opening in your partnership methods, then you cannot open 3♠ with:

(b)   ♠ QJ98532   ♥ 5   ♦ 87   ♣ J87

What should partner do over your 3♠ opening looking at:

♠ A   ♥ J832   ♦ KQ54   ♣ K932

If the 3♠ bidder holds (a), responder should raise to game and score 10 or 11 tricks depending on the location of the Ace of clubs; opposite (b), it will be a question of how many undertricks your side suffers.

Keeping these four factors in mind, let us now examine 3♣, 3♦, 3♥ and 3♠ openings and various responding tools that you should consider. We will first review several different approaches to 3♣ and 3♦ openings and then move up to the major suit three-level openers.

## 3♣ AND 3♦ OPENINGS

Most partnerships have the same requirements for 3♣ and 3♦ openings as they do for 3♥ and 3♠ openers. Since the openings are all at the three-level, their reasoning goes, one should have the same values for a 3♣ opening as one would hold to open 3♠. Unfortunately, this is a gross oversimplification.

Three-level minor suit openings are actually more closely related to weak two-bids than to 3♥ and 3♠ preempts. Their preemptive value is considerably less than major suit openings at the three-level. When the opening bid is 2♠ or 3♣ the enemy still has almost all of the three-level to work with; the three-level is not available over 3♠. Therefore, we advocate more constructive 3♣ and 3♦ openings than three-level major suit openers.

The following box outlines the guidelines we recommend for the traditional three-level minor suit opening:

# REQUIREMENTS FOR OPENING 3♣ AND 3♦

(1) Vulnerable, a good seven-card suit. Non-vulnerable, a **good** six-card suit is acceptable with sufficient playing strength. An eight-card suit might be opened at the three-level if the suit or hand does not qualify for a four-level minor suit opening.

(2) No more than one Ace or King — not both — outside the trump suit.

(3) 5+ playing tricks at FAVORABLE VULNERABILITY. 6 Playing tricks at EQUAL VULNERABILITY. 7 Playing tricks at UNFAVORABLE VULNERABILITY. (The "Rule of Two, Three and Four.")

(4) No four-card major (you may hold four cards in the other minor).

(5) No void(s).

(6) No more than 10+ HCP (beware Qx or Jx outside your suit).

Following the guidelines for 3♣ and 3♦ openings we have outlined, what would you do as dealer with the following hands?

(a)  ♠ K  ♥ K95  ♦ QJ96532  ♣ Q8   NV vs. NV
PASS. Your suit is adequate for a three-level preempt, but you have far too much strength outside your suit. Remember, singleton King, Queen-doubleton and even Jack-doubleton rarely produce tricks on offense, but often provide unexpected and

even unwanted defense against enemy contracts.

(b) &spades; 7 &hearts; 98 &diams; J107 &clubs; AKJ9852 V vs. V

If you were writing a book on preempts, you
might well include this hand as an excellent
example of a 3&clubs; OPENING. We did.

(c) &spades; J754 &hearts; 7 &diams; J &clubs; AQJ10753 V vs. V

PASS. Textbook suit and strength for a 3&clubs;
opening but the four-card major should
prevent you from preempting 3&clubs;. Partner
would not (and should not) bid 3&spades; over 3&clubs;
holding a hand like:

&spades; AK1092 &hearts; A32 &diams; 976 &clubs; 96

If you were to open (c) 3&clubs;, you might well
find yourself playing in a minor suit partscore when 4&spades; is practically laydown. On
a bad day, you will open 3&clubs; on this hand,
partner will have a great hand with four or
more spades, and the King of clubs will be
onside, making 6&spades; cold!

(d) &spades; 984 &hearts; 4 &diams; J109 &clubs; KQJ985 NV vs. V

OPEN 3&clubs;. This is a good example of a
six-card three-level minor suit opening.
Both your suit and overall playing strength
are more than adequate.

(e) &spades; 7 &hearts; 85 &diams; KQJ9763 &clubs; K109 V vs. NV

OPEN 3&diams;. Typical 3-level preempt at
unfavorable vulnerability.

(f) &spades; A4 &hearts; 7 &diams; 1097 &clubs; AQJ8732 NV vs. V

OPEN 1&clubs;. Following our guidelines, this
hand is far too strong for a favorable preempt. If your partnership refuses to open
such hands 1&clubs;, then you will be forced to
pass.

# RESPONSES TO 3♣ AND 3♦

Responses to 3♣ and 3♦ are quite similar to those we recommended over weak two-bids. There are two notable exceptions: we urge you to adopt the first treatment and suggest you at least consider the second.

The first treatment comes from Dr. George Rosenkranz in his excellent book co-authored by Phillip Alder, <u>Bid To Win, Play For Pleasure</u>. Dr. Rosenkranz recommends that a 3♦ response over the 3♣ opening be played as an artificial bid, asking opener to show a three-card major if he has one. Opener rebids:

| | | |
|---|---|---|
| (1) | 3♥ | with a three-card **spade** suit; |
| (2) | 3♠ | with a three-card **heart** suit; |
| (3) | 4♦ | with BOTH three-card majors; and |
| (4) | 3NT | with NO three-card major. |

This treatment has four advantages. It facilitates locating a 5-3 major suit fit. It allows 5-3 major suit fits to be played from the right side of the table (the strong hand) via the transfer response. It clarifies the 3♥ and 3♠ bids by responder; both promise at least six-card suits (with only a five-card major, responder would start with 3♦). It prohibits the partnership from playing in a poor 5-2 major suit fit.

The second special treatment we suggest you play over three-level openings is suggested by the World Bridge Federation's #1 ranked player, Bob Hamman. The treatment presumes you do not make a three-level opening with outside Aces or voids. It calls for a 4♣ response to 3♦, 3♥ and 3♠ — or a 4♦ response to 3♣ — to be used as an asking bid for second-round control in a side suit (either a King or a singleton). Without a second-round control, opener simply rebids his suit; with a second-round control, opener bids the suit in which he has a control. With a control in the other minor, opener rebids 4NT. If opener shows a singleton or King, responder can bid that suit at a minimum level to ask which opener holds (1st step = singleton; 2nd step = King).

With these two additions in mind, here is an outline of our responses to 3♣ and 3♦ openings:

# RESPONSES TO 3♣ AND 3♦

(1) Single raises are defensive — **not** invitational.

(2) Jump raises may be made with hands that are preemptive or which contain game-going values unsuited for play in 3NT.

(3) 3♦ is conventional over 3♣, asking for a three-card major. Opener rebids:
   3♥ = three **spades**.
   3♠ = three **hearts**.
   3NT = no three-card major.
   4♦ = BOTH three-card majors.

(4) 3♥ and 3♠ are **forcing**. Over the 3♣ opening they promise a six-card major.

(5) 3NT is to play.

(6) 4♣ over 3♦ (3♥ and 3♠), and 4♦ over 3♣ are conventional inquiries asking opener for second-round controls. Opener rebids:
   - The opened minor, denying second-round control in any outside suit.
   - 4♥ with second-round heart control.
   - 4♠ with second-round spade control.
   - 4NT with second-round control in the other minor.

   Next bid by responder in opener's second-round control suit asks whether opener holds a singleton or a King. Opener bids the first step with a singleton; the second step with a King.

(7) 4♥ and 4♠ are to play. (Or you may play them as CABs).

(8) 4NT is Blackwood.

(9) 5NT is the Grand Slam Force.

Using these methods, what would you do over partner's 3♣ opening, both sides vulnerable, holding:

(a)    ♠ KJ76432  ♥ A985  ♦ K5  ♣ —

PASS. Yes, 3♠ could easily be a far better contract than 3♣. That, however, is strictly academic; there is no way you could get to 3♠ AND stay there. Remember, 3♠ is 100% forcing.

(b)    ♠ 8743  ♥ A  ♦ J1095  ♣ KJ74

JUMP TO 5♣. Perhaps the enemy strength will be evenly divided and the opponents will not realize their side's potential. On a good day the 5♣ call will end the auction.

At favorable vulnerability partner opens 3♦. What response would you make holding:

(c)    ♠ A5  ♥ 652  ♦ KQ4  ♣ AKQJ10

RESPOND 4♣. This is an excellent example of the conventional inquiry recommended by Bob Hamman to find out if partner holds a second-round heart control. If your side can avoid two fast heart losers, a diamond slam should be cold.

(d)    ♠ AKJ107  ♥ 8754  ♦ AQ7  ♣ 5

RESPOND 3♠. Dr. Rosenkranz's conventional inquiry to locate 5-3 major suit fits is not available over 3♦. You must make a natural, forcing call of 3♠ which promises at least a five-card suit (since the opening bid was 3♦, not 3♣).

Although the disciplined 3♣ and 3♦ openings we have been discussing may seem quite conservative by today's standards, several experts — and modern bidding systems — advocate even more constructive minor suit three-bids than those we have described. For example, the Precision Club system restricts 3♣ and 3♦ openings to hands that contain the following:

(1)     A semi-solid seven-card suit (with at least two of the top three honors);

(2)     An outside entry (usually an Ace or King);

(3)     8 to 12+ HCP;

(4)     Seven playing tricks — six in trump and one in a side suit.

In addition, your hand should not contain: (5) A four-card major; (6) A void; (7) More than one outside Ace or King. The obvious purpose of these requirements is to permit partnerships using these methods to reach good 3NT contracts with fewer than the normal 25 or 26 HCP. Dr. Rosenkranz and other experts also advocate sound, constructive 3♣ and 3♦ openings. Their specific requirements are a solid or near-solid suit with no outside Ace or King. Here again, three-level minor suit preempts promise a source of tricks for notrump play.

The Crane system, developed by the greatest matchpoint player of all time, Barry Crane, required a very specific suit in order to open 3♣ or 3♦. In first or second seat, Crane demanded a seven-card suit headed by three of the top four honors, which had to include the Ace. This enabled responder — holding as little as a small doubleton — to estimate at least six tricks (and a likely entry in the suit) for notrump play when partner opened three of a minor.

Any of these 3♣ and 3♦ opening strategies can be incorporated into most systems. Which approach to three-level minor suit openings should you use? The answer is to use the methods that you and your partner feel most comfortable playing. The same is true in determining which responding tools to employ.

# 3♥ AND 3♠ OPENINGS

The 3♥ and 3♠ openings we are about to advocate are more preemptive in nature than the 3♣ and 3♦ openings we have been discussing; they describe hands with specific playing strength, and suit length and quality. Here are our recommendations:

# REQUIREMENTS FOR OPENING 3♥ AND 3♠

(1) Vulnerable, a good seven-card suit (the suit should not contain more than two losers, opposite a singleton, assuming normal breaks). Non-vulnerable, an occasional six-card suit may be adequate.
An eight-card suit (rare), may be opened if the hand does not qualify for a four-level opening.

(2) No more than one Ace or King outside the trump suit.

(3) No other four-card major.

(4) 5 playing tricks at FAVORABLE VULNER-ABILITY.
6 playing tricks at EQUAL VULNERABILITY.
7 playing tricks at UNFAVORABLE VULNERABILITY. (The "Rule of Two, Three and Four)"

(5) No void(s).

(6) No more than 9 or 10 HCP (beware Qx or Jx outside your suit).

The key to sound 3♥ and 3♠ openings is the quality of your trump suit. It should provide most, if not all, of your playing strength. Typically, it should be a well-textured suit with good intermediate cards.

Using the standards we have outlined, let us examine a few hands you might consider opening 3♥ or 3♠.

(a)     ♠ K986532   ♥ 5   ♦ A109   ♣ J10     V vs. NV
You should not open this hand 3♠ with such a poor trump suit. Partner could hold a few scattered high cards — enough to prevent

your opponents from making a game — and spade shortness. In such circumstances you might be held to three or four tricks — a disastrous result.

When an opponent opened 3♠ against Sid Grossman in the 1993 Omaha-Nebraska Regional Open Pairs, the consequences were disastrous!

North
- ♠ K986532
- ♥ 5
- ♦ A109
- ♣ J10

West
- ♠ 7
- ♥ A874
- ♦ KJ84
- ♣ AQ63

Board 9
Dlr. - North
Vul. - E/W

East
- ♠ AQJ10
- ♥ K1063
- ♦ 63
- ♣ 852

South
- ♠ 4
- ♥ QJ92
- ♦ Q752
- ♣ K974

| OUR TABLE | | Opening Lead ♦ 6 |
| | | N/S -1100 |

| *Grossman* | | *Andersen* | |
| West | North | East | South |
| — | 3♠ | P | P |
| Dbl. | P | P | P |

It was little consolation to North that perhaps a better defense would have netted 1400, especially since game is unlikely on the East-West cards against reasonable defense.

(b) ♠ K10 ♥ QJ109643 ♦ A109 ♣ K    V vs. NV
OPEN 1♥. Here the objection to opening 3♥ is not the quality of your trump suit (which is fine), but the amount of outside strength you hold. Remember, your strength should be concentrated in the trump suit.

(c) ♠ AJ109864 ♥ 7632 ♦ A ♣ 8    V vs. V
PASS OR OPEN 1♠. Your diamond and spade Aces and four-card heart suit eliminate a 3♠ opening from consideration. This hand would make an excellent dummy for a heart contract, and opening 3♠ could easily prevent your side from locating a good heart fit. Worse, you might end the auction with a 3♠ bid when your side is cold for 6♥.

(d) ♠ KQJ10872 ♥ 4 ♦ 85 ♣ KJ10    V vs. NV
OPEN 3♠. This hand meets all the requirements for a 3♠ opening at unfavorable vulnerability. You can reasonably expect to win seven tricks, even if partner's hand is worthless. Your trump suit is more than adequate.

(e) ♠ 43 ♥ AQJ10985 ♦ 1097 ♣ 5    NV vs. NV
OPEN 3♥. You have a perfect non-vulnerable 3♥ opener: exactly what partner might expect for a three-level preempt.

(f) ♠ AQJ985 ♥ 7 ♦ J1097 ♣ 83    NV vs. V
In first or second seat we would undoubtedly open this hand 2♠. However, we would not object to a 3♠ opening considering the vulnerability, the adequate trump suit and playing strength. We would definitely open 3♠ in third chair.

(g)　　♠ 4 ♥ KJ875432 ♦ J109 ♣ 5　　　V vs. V

OPEN 3♥. A rare example of a 3♥ opening that contains an eight-card suit. As we will discuss in Chapter 5 on major suit preempts, this hand does not meet the requirements of a four-level preempt.

As these examples illustrate, an opening 3♥ or 3♠ bid should say the following: "I have a one-suited hand that is not worth much unless my suit is trump, and I have relatively little or no defensive strength. Even if partner's hand is worthless to me, I am within two tricks of my contract if the vulnerability is unfavorable, three tricks if equal, and four tricks if favorable."

Opening 3♥ or 3♠ with four cards in the other major is inviting disaster (and unless you are unusually lucky at the bridge table, disaster rarely refuses an open invitation). We even shy away from opening 3♥ or 3♠ with a four-card minor. Such hands make excellent dummies when partner has a good fit for your four-card minor and a poor fit for your major.

As a general rule, 3♥ and 3♠ openers should not contain a void. Responder's job of judging the best course of action for his side is often impossible if your preempt might include either 7-3-3-0 or 7-4-2-0 distributions.

Be a good partner. If your hand does not meet all the requirements and guidelines for a three-level major suit opening, simply pass and await developments. Most of the time you will be able to introduce your long suit later, with less risk. This course of action has the added advantage of restricting your opponents at the bridge table to **two** — more than enough for any of us.

## RESPONSES TO 3♥ AND 3♠

When partner opens 3♥ or 3♠ it is usually an easy task for responder to judge whether the partnership assets are in the partscore, game or slam zone. Adding your quick tricks and winners to the number of playing tricks partner has promised will give you an accurate estimate of your side's offensive potential, and will indicate your defensive prospects should your opponents contest the auction. Unlike 3♣ and 3♦ openings, 3♥ and 3♠ openers are not invitations to bid 3NT. As a matter of fact, 3NT is rarely your side's best game after a 3♥ or 3♠ opening. You plan to play in opener's suit since his hand may be totally worthless if your side declares the hand in any other strain.

Due to the level of the opening bid, the small amount of remaining bidding space below game — 3♠ (over 3♥), 4♣ and 4♦ — can best be used exploring for slam, NOT for trying to find a different game contract. This is particularly true playing the disciplined 3♥ and 3♠ openings we advocate. Consequently, over 3♥ or 3♠ we recommend the following simple structure of responses:

---

### RESPONSES TO 3♥ AND 3♠

(1)  3NT is to play.

(2)  Raises to game may be preemptive.

(3)  Game bids in a new suit are to play (except 4♠ over 3♥, which is a CAB).

(4)  4♣, 4♦ and 4♠ (over 3♥) are CABs. Responder's subsequent bids in new suits are also CABs.

(5)  4NT is Blackwood, preferably Keycard for opener's suit.

(6)  Five of the opener's major is preemptive, not slam-going.

(7)  5NT is the Grand Slam Force.

---

Since the playing strength of a 3♥ or 3♠ opening bid is clearly defined, responder should rarely have any problem setting the final contract. Let us consider a few examples.

Partner opens 3♥ and you hold:

(a)     ♠ AJ7653   ♥ —   ♦ K94   ♣ KJ98    NV vs. NV

PASS. It is not clear that you should bid 3♠ even if it were not forcing and you knew partner would pass. Of course, that is not a consideration, since 3♠ is FORCING and cannot be passed. Hope the enemy balances.[1]

(b)     ♠ AK752   ♥ Q   ♦ A1083   ♣ K104    V vs. V

RAISE TO 4♥. This hand should produce four winners for partner; sufficient for game since opener has indicated that he can take six tricks if hearts are trump. Remember, when responding to 3♥ or 3♠, your single-ton Queen is adequate support since partner has shown a **good** seven-card suit. Even playing matchpoint duplicate you should not consider bidding 3NT; partner may have opened 3♥ holding:

    ♠ 4   ♥ AK109853   ♦ 764   ♣ J8

which would make 4♥ almost ironclad while 3NT would be hopeless unless the heart Jack falls doubleton.

(c)     ♠ AJ10   ♥ —   ♦ AKQJ643   ♣ K105    NV vs. V

RESPOND 3NT. Any winners that partner can contribute to 3NT will be overtricks. There is no danger that opener will "correct" to 4♥ because 3NT is not correctable.

(d)     ♠ AKQJ98   ♥ AQ3   ♦ 763   ♣ A    V vs. NV

RESPOND 4♦ (CAB). The final contract will be 4♥ or more — maybe even 7♥ — depending on the number of immediate

---

[1]   Make sure you pass in tempo with this type of hand. Do not telegraph your displeasure of your partner's 3♥ bid to your opponents. Partner isn't entitled to this information either.

diamond losers your side has. Partner's response to 4♦ will permit you to set the final contract accurately. And, you will not even get past 4♥ if opener has three losing diamonds, since his response to 4♦ with no control will be the next step — 4♥!

(e)    ♠ A76   ♥ —   ♦ KJ1098542   ♣ 85   NV vs. NV

PASS. Yes, 4♦ may well be a better contract than 3♥. Unfortunately, you cannot play 4♦. Remember, 4♦ over 3♥ would be a CAB and you would be propelled even higher on your limited partnership assets. If 3♥ doubled is passed back to you, escape to 4♦, which rates to be a more successful contract.

(f)    ♠ AKJ1087   ♥ —   ♦ 7   ♣ AK10982   V vs. V

RESPOND 3♠. Even if opener's hand is relatively worthless unless hearts are trump, a red suit will not be trump when responder holds this hand. 3♠ is forcing and if opener does not raise, you will introduce your other black suit.

Turning our attention to spades, what response to 3♠ would you make holding:

(g)    ♠ 4   ♥ AKQ10875   ♦ AJ7   ♣ 93   V vs. NV

RESPOND 4♥. Game bids in new suits are to play. They are not CABs. Bid what you think you can make.

(h)    ♠ AK5   ♥ A4   ♦ A95   ♣ 109842   NV vs. NV

RESPOND 3NT. Playing rubber bridge or IMPs, this is one of the rare instances where it appears right to play 3NT even though you have an excellent fit for partner. Nine tricks are available in a no-trump contract: seven spades (or six plus partner's outside winner) plus your two Aces. In 4♠ you might have four losers for down one.

(i)    ♠ —  ♥ AKQ  ♦ A8652  ♣ A9432   V vs. NV
RAISE TO 4♠. Partner expects to win seven tricks if spades are trump, assuming normal breaks and a singleton in your hand. Despite your total lack of spade support, your five winners — including first-round control of all side suits — should be enough to give your side ten tricks. It may seem hard to believe, but 4♠ rates to be the only game that will make given partner's opening bid. In fact, even a spade slam is possible if partner has opened with something like
   ♠ KQJ10875  ♥ 4  ♦ 102  ♣ K65.

(j)    ♠ A104  ♥ AKQ10875  ♦ —  ♣ 984   V vs. V
RESPOND 4♣ (CAB). You should be able to make anywhere between four and seven spades, depending on the number of immediate club losers your side has. Partner's response to your control asking bid will enable you to set the final contract precisely.

(k)    ♠ 984  ♥ A109743  ♦ 85  ♣ K2     V vs. V
RAISE TO 4♠. Obey the LAW.

Control Asking Bids (CABs) are often the key to reaching good slam contracts after a 3♥ or 3♠ opening, particularly when your side has considerably fewer than the normally required 32 or 33 HCP for slam.

Consider the following deal played by your authors in the team event at Count Gianfranco Fabbricotti's 1992 tournament in St. Moritz, high in the Swiss Alps.[1]

---

[1] In 1992, Count Fabbricotti was Chairman of the Organizing Committee for the St. Moritz tournament, one of the most glamorous in the world, for the 51st consecutive year; a record that undoubtedly will never be broken.

## North
- ♠ AQ109632
- ♥ 984
- ♦ 96
- ♣ 8

## West
- ♠ J8
- ♥ 653
- ♦ Q1053
- ♣ KJ95

Board 13
Dlr. - North
Vul. - Both

## East
- ♠ 54
- ♥ QJ1072
- ♦ KJ872
- ♣ Q

## South
- ♠ K7
- ♥ AK
- ♦ A4
- ♣ A1076432

OUR TABLE

Opening Lead ♥ Q
N/S +2210

| West | *Andersen* North | East | *Zenkel* South |
|------|------------------|------|----------------|
| —    | 3♠               | P    | 4♣ (a)         |
| P    | 4♥ (b)           | P    | 4NT (c)        |
| P    | 5♦ (d)           | P    | 5♥ (e)         |
| P    | 6♠ (f)           | P    | 7♠ (g)         |
| P    | P                | P    |                |

(a) CAB in clubs.
(b) Second-round control — King or singleton.
(c) Keycard Blackwood.
(d) One keycard.
(e) Asking for the trump Queen.
(f) "I have it, but I don't have any outside Kings."
(g) "We have 13 tricks as long as I can establish my club suit."

Our teammates, Austrian experts Karl Rohan and Kurt Feichtinger, were a bit concerned about their result on this board. Their opponents had reached a 24-point small slam. However, -1460 turned into a 13 IMP gain when compared with our +2210. The CAB was critical in reaching an excellent grand slam.

Your authors also used a CAB to good advantage in a bidding competition conducted by a leading European bridge magazine. Neither side is vulnerable; the scoring is IMPs:

| West | East |
|------|------|
| ♠ 876 | ♠ AKQJ7 |
| ♥ KQ108732 | ♥ AJ5 |
| ♦ — | ♦ 109742 |
| ♣ 1094 | ♣ — |
| *Andersen* | *Zenkel* |
| 3♥ | 4♦ (a) |
| 4NT (b) | 5NT (c) |
| 7♥ (d) | P |

(a)  CAB.
(b)  3rd step = 1st-round control.
(c)  Grand Slam Force.
(d)  "I have two of the top three honors."

Our relatively simple, straightforward auction drew considerable praise from the moderator of the competition. He reported that in the semi-finals of a national team competition in his country, all four pairs holding the East-West cards had failed to reach the virtually laydown grand slam. In fact, one pair did not get beyond the four-level. Admittedly, if you do not play CABs, 7♥ is not an easy contract to reach. With them, it was one of your author's favorite desserts — "A piece of cake!"

Another illustration of the effective use of a CAB over a 3♠ opening took place on the following deal played during the 1990 North American Ladies Swiss Team Championship in Forth Worth, Texas. The problem was not to reach a laydown slam with fewer than the prescribed 32 or 33 HCP, but instead to avoid a hopeless slam when the partnership held 33 HCP.

```
                    North
                 ♠  KQ9
                 ♥  AKQ98
                 ♦  QJ
                 ♣  AKQ

West                          East
♠  5            ┌──────────┐  ♠  74
♥  652         │ Board 23  │  ♥  43
♦  AK932       │ Dlr. - South │  ♦  10654
♣  9763        │ Vul. - Both │  ♣  108542
               └──────────┘
                    South
                 ♠  AJ108632
                 ♥  J107
                 ♦  87
                 ♣  J
```

OUR TABLE                          Opening Lead ♦ K
                                        N/S +650

|  | Sabine Zenkel | | Edith Rosenkranz |
| West | North | East | South |
| — | — | — | 3♠ |
| P | 4♦ (a) | P | 4♥ (b) |
| P | 4♠ (c) | P | P |
| P | | | |

(a)  CAB. Partner's diamond holding will determine whether we play 4♠, 6♠ or 7♠.

(b)  "Sorry, partner, I do not have first- or second-round control of diamonds."

(c)  Too bad. "I wonder if our opponents — holding these cards at the other table — will be able to stop short of slam."

The answer to Sabine's question was **NO**. Against her world champion teammates, Kerri Shuman and Karen McCallum, the final contract was 6♠ down one. This deal was crucial in winning not only this match, but the entire event.

## THIRD AND FOURTH SEAT
## THREE-LEVEL SUIT PREEMPTS

Many leading authorities advocate drastically reducing and relaxing the requirements for three-level preempts in third position. Their reasoning is simple. Once partner is a passed hand, strict adherence to a set of requirements designed to facilitate constructive bidding (when responder has a good hand) becomes a needless restraint (slam is certainly out of the question).

Although we recognize the possible tactical advantages (particularly non-vulnerable) of opening at the three-level in third seat, we urge caution. Remember, even though partner is a passed hand, it will be his job to judge the best course of action should your opponents reach game. What would you open in third chair holding:

(a)  ♠ KQJ953  ♥ —  ♦ J107  ♣ 9854  NV vs. NV
OPEN 3♠. This bid makes life more difficult for your opponents by denying them three levels of bidding space. Although the void is a serious negative, you have both the right playing strength and trump suit for a 3♠ opening. Despite your void and 6-0-3-4 distribution, responder should be able to judge your side's offensive and defensive prospects — a critical factor to consider when you are about to elevate the auction directly to a high level.

(b)  ♠ Q765432  ♥ 107  ♦ —  ♣ AKJ7  NV vs. V
This hand simply is not a 3♠ opening at any vulnerability in any position. If partner holds a maximum passed hand with a fit for spades you will miss a laydown game.

Should your opponents bid to 4♥, partner may take a (phantom) 4♠ save when their game had no play because of your defensive strength. There is also the danger that 3♠ doubled may become the final contract and you will suffer a considerable loss on a deal where your opponents had no play for game. We open 1♠ hoping that if we defend we get the chance to make an opening lead of a club.

(c)     ♠ 7  ♥ J1094  ♦ KQ10973  ♣ J10     NV vs. V
OPEN 3♦ IN THIRD SEAT ONLY. We would never open 3♦ in first or second chair with this hand. However, since partner is a passed hand, 4♥ is very unlikely to make, even though this hand is an excellent dummy for a heart contract. This hand probably belongs to the enemy since partner could not open.

Our advice in determining whether to open a three-bid in third chair with marginal hands is similar to the U.S. National Safety Council's recommendations regarding passing automobiles on the highway, "When in doubt, DON'T."

The expression "fourth chair preempt" is basically a contradiction in terms. After three passes, holding considerably less than the values for an opening one-bid, you should be delighted to pass and get on to the next deal. When you open 3♣, 3♦, 3♥ or 3♠ in first, second or third position, you make it difficult for the opponents to find their optimum contract. This is no longer an objective when you have heard three passes around the table. Now you can keep your opponents from bidding simply by PASSING.

When you open 3♥ or 3♠ in fourth seat, you suggest that your side will go plus by playing the hand at the three-level (you were in a position to pass the deal out for no score). Therefore, you must have more HCP and playing strength to preempt at the three-level in fourth seat than you would have had in any of the other three positions.

You will usually have the values for an opening one-bid — in addition to extra trump length — when you elect to open at the three-level in fourth chair. You make it more difficult for opponents to come into the auction when you open at the three-level. After three passes, consider your opening bid with the following hands:

(a) ♠ AQJ10963  ♥ 7  ♦ A104  ♣ J10    V vs. V
OPEN 3♠. Although you would have opened 1♠ in all first, second or third seat, bidding to 3♠ in fourth chair will give partner a clear picture of both your suit and overall playing strength. It may also prevent your opponents from finding an excellent heart or club fit (and possibly a good sacrifice if your side is cold for game). Bid to the maximum level with this hand.

(b) ♠ J10  ♥ KJ109732  ♦ QJ  ♣ QJ    NV vs. NV
PASS. No score on this deal is better than the minus score you are likely to achieve by opening. Your suit is not shabby, but there is a major problem with this hand. No disrespect for ducks intended, but this hand simply contains too many "Quacks" — Queens and Jacks.

(c) ♠ 7  ♥ AKJ10952  ♦ K1095  ♣ 6    V vs. NV
OPEN 3♥. This bid places partner in an excellent position to judge your chances for game and may prevent the enemy from finding a good sacrifice in either spades or clubs.

(d) ♠ K5  ♥ 7  ♦ J103  ♣ AKJ10754    NV vs. NV
OPEN 3♣. If the enemy could not open the bidding at this vulnerability, the hand rates to belong to your side despite your sparse major suit holdings. If partner can control the red suits, a notrump game is possible.

(e)   ♠ A  ♥ KJ1097532  ♦ Q109  ♣ 5      V vs. V
OPEN 3♥.  Although we would not advise
opening 3♥ with this hand in first or second
position, in fourth position it is perfectly
acceptable.   Remember, you can have an
eight-card suit.   Some aggressive players
would open this hand 4♥ in fourth chair,
but with six losers to be covered opposite a
"passing" partner, we recommend 3♥.


Responding to partner's fourth chair three-level opening is just
as easy as responding to first, second or third seat three-bids.  If you
can contribute 2½ or 3 tricks (fast tricks and controls) and have a
mild fit for opener's suit, you should raise to game.  For example,
suppose partner opens 3♣ in fourth chair and you hold:

(a)   ♠ J1086  ♥ A105  ♦ A985  ♣ J3
RESPOND 3NT.   That is what you think
you can make.   This rates to be a near
perfect responding hand to a fourth chair 3♣
opener — stoppers in all suits, two Aces,
and J3 in opener's good long suit.

(b)   ♠ Q6  ♥ KQJ4  ♦ Q763  ♣ J73
PASS.  Despite your 11 HCP (in "Quacks")
prospects for game are at best remote.  Hope
partner will win nine tricks in clubs.

If partner opens 3♥ in fourth seat, choose your action holding:

(c)   ♠ QJ7  ♥ J7  ♦ QJ65  ♣ KJ92
PASS.  This Aceless 11-count loaded with
"Quacks" does not warrant a raise.  Hope
partner can take nine tricks.

(d)   ♠ A5  ♥ 532  ♦ A10984  ♣J109
RESPOND 4♥.  This control-rich 9-count is
sufficient for a raise to game when partner
makes a fourth-seat preempt.

## THE OPPONENTS COMPETE
## OVER 3♣ AND 3♦

Do you think you are in trouble when the opponents compete with a double over your side's opening three-level preempt? We hope not. With the understandings we have outlined and recommended for 3♣ and 3♦ openings, there is little cause for concern when your opponents compete. Responder has a clear picture of opener's suit, playing strength and limited outside values. You can use most of the responses and rebids available in non-competitive auctions, room permitting, and add the double and redouble.

Since an opponent's takeout double of your three-level preempt consumes no bidding space, it is easy to handle. Keep your non-competitive structure of responses and rebids intact, and add the redouble. We suggest you have the following agreements for the redouble:

---

### REDOUBLES OF 3♣ AND 3♦

(1)   Your side will have the balance of strength.

(2)   You invite opener to double an enemy contract, when appropriate, despite his opening preempt.

(3)   You have sufficient strength to be willing to play partner's suit redoubled at the three-level in case both opponents elect to pass (rare).

Often, responder will also have:

(4)   A poor fit for opener's suit.

(5)   A hand better suited for defense than offense in light of partner's preemptive opening.

---

Overcalls of your side's opening 3♣ or 3♦ bid cause a bit more difficulty since your initial response may be affected. The bidding space consumed by the overcall sometimes denies you the opportunity to make the response you would have made in a non-competitive auction. However, with a few adjustments you can handle overcalls as easily as takeout doubles. Furthermore, you can add the penalty double as a weapon when an opponent makes a bid that is not going to work out well for his side.

The following outlines our recommendations:

---

## RESPONSES TO 3♣ AND 3♦
## AFTER THE OPPONENTS OVERCALL

(1) Raises are non-forcing and typically preemptive in nature.

(2) New suits introduced at the three-level are forcing for one round and show a good five-card (or longer) suit. Opener will rebid as in a non-competitive auction, except 3NT will promise a stopper in the enemy suit.

(3) 3NT is to play.

(4) 4♥ and 4♠ (even when jumps) are to play. They are not CABs.

(5) Doubles are penalty. Opener cannot pull; he must pass.

(6) Cuebids indicate a fit, are forcing to game, and show slam interest.

---

Using this structure, your auctions after partner opens 3♣ or 3♦ should be almost as accurate in a contested auction as they are when the opponents do not compete. Sometimes the bidding space consumed by an opponent's overcall will prove costly. Remember, there will also be times when an enemy overcall will present you with the opportunity to make a lucrative penalty double on a deal when your side might have made only a partscore.

Let us consider a few examples. Suppose partner's 3♣ opening is greeted by RHO with a 3♥ overcall. Choose your action holding:

(a)      ♠ AQJ104   ♥ 86   ♦ AQ75   ♣ Q9    NV vs. NV
RESPOND 3♠. This bid is 100% forcing and promises a good five-card (or longer) spade suit.

(b)      ♠ KQ10974   ♥ Q76   ♦ K74   ♣ 3     V vs. V
PASS. Do not be tempted to compete with 3♠. Remember, a 3♠ response would be 100% forcing and you are far short of the values for a forcing response.

(c)      ♠ AK42   ♥ Q1093   ♦ KQ95   ♣ 6     V vs. V
DOUBLE. Your opponent has made what is likely to be a serious error in contesting the auction. Your defensive prospects are excellent on this apparent misfit.

Your partner opens 3♦ and your RHO bids 3♠. What action would you take with the following:

(d)      ♠ 7   ♥ KQJ10532   ♦ A4   ♣ KJ9    NV vs. NV
RESPOND 4♥. Remember, 4♥ is natural and to play; it is not a CAB.

(e)      ♠ 6   ♥ A109432   ♦ QJ62   ♣ 85     NV vs. V
JUMP TO 5♦. Primarily, this is an advance sacrifice (although if partner held a magic hand such as
     ♠ 754   ♥ 8   ♦ AK109754   ♣ K3
it might actually make); your side is not likely to have much defense against 4♠.

(f)      ♠ KQ1095   ♥ 74   ♦ 3   ♣ KQ1085
PASS. Yes, you will most likely beat 3♠, but do not even think about doubling. Defending 3♠ is likely to be your only chance for a plus score. Do not frighten your opponents into a better spot.

# THE OPPONENTS COMPETE OVER 3♥ AND 3♠

The approach we use in competition over our major suit three-level preemptive openings is quite similar to the recommendations we suggested over competition of 3♣ and 3♦. There is no reason to make any changes to the meaning of either responses or raises, although some CABs may be eliminated by the space consumed by an enemy overcall.

When the opponents make a takeout double of 3♥ or 3♠, they have not consumed any bidding space; therefore, you we have no reason to alter any of our responses. We simply add the redouble to our arsenal of responses. Our requirements for a redouble when the opponents make a takeout double of a 3♥ or 3♠ opening are exactly the same as they were after a 3♣ or 3♦ opening. For reference, they are:

---

## REDOUBLES OF 3♥ AND 3♠

(1) Your side will have the balance of strength.

(2) You invite opener to double an enemy contract, when appropriate, despite his opening preempt.

(3) You have sufficient strength to be willing to play partner's suit redoubled at the three-level in case both opponents elect to pass (rare).

Usually, responder will also have:

(4) A poor fit for opener's suit.

(5) A hand that is better suited for defense than offense in light of partner's preemptive opening bid.

---

Using these guidelines, we would redouble 3♠ doubled with:

(a)     ♠ J   ♥ KJ107   ♦ K1095   ♣ AJ93

(b)     ♠ J2   ♥ AQ108   ♦ KQ109   ♣ K95

With (a) you intend to double anything your opponents bid, at any vulnerability. Game is no certainty for your side and a double of any escape should yield a substantial profit. With (b), you may have more of a problem, depending on your opponent's choice of escape and the vulnerability. If you are at unfavorable (V vs. NV), you might elect to double four of either red suit and bid 4♠ over 4♣. No matter how the auction proceeds, redouble should be your initial action with both hands.

Overcalls of your opening 3♥ and 3♠ bids are more of a problem. The bidding space consumed by the enemy's overcall may deny you the opportunity to make the response you would have made in a non-competitive auction. You cannot bid 3NT after a 4♣ overcall of 3♠, nor can you use a conventional 4♣ response (CAB) after a 4♦ overcall of 3♥. However, like takeout doubles, overcalls do add two additional weapons to your responding arsenal: the penalty double and cuebids.

Consider a few examples. Suppose after partner's 3♥ opening there is a 4♣ overcall. Decide what action you would take holding:

(a)     ♠ AK1052   ♥ Q3   ♦ AJ62   ♣ 108     V vs. V
BID 4♥. Although we would expect to defeat 4♣, prospects for a heart game are excellent, and 4♥ is likely to produce a greater plus than doubling 4♣.

(b)     ♠ AKQ1073   ♥ AJ7   ♦ 8732   ♣ —    NV vs. NV
BID 4♦ (CAB). The enemy overcall has not prevented you from using a CAB in diamonds. Knowing the number of fast diamond losers your side has will enable you to set the final contract in 4♥, 6♥ or 7♥.

Should an opponent double a CAB, we advise the following space-saving revisions in responding: Pass (1st step) = no control;

Redouble (2nd step) = 2nd round control; Next suit (3rd step) = 1st round control. Should an opponent bid a suit over a CAB, we advise: Pass = no control; Double = 2nd round control; Next suit = 1st round control.

After a 4♦ overcall of partner's 3♠ opening, what action would you take holding:

(c)  ♠ 7  ♥ AKJ10832  ♦ 74  ♣ AJ6    NV vs. V
     BID 4♥. A natural signoff as it would have
     been in a non-competitive auction. The
     enemy overcall does not affect your ability
     to sign off in your own suit.

(d)  ♠ 5  ♥ AK1072  ♦ Q1073  ♣ K109    V vs. V
     DOUBLE. You have excellent defense
     against 4♦. Doubling 4♦ should net a
     considerable plus on a deal where your side
     was not destined to score a game. (Note
     that you would have passed 3♠.)

Unfortunately, sometimes an enemy overcall (or the bidding space consumed by that overcall) will prove costly to your side. But there will be times when an overcall will present you with the opportunity to make a profitable penalty double on a deal when your side could make only a partscore.

# DEFENSES AGAINST THREE-LEVEL PREEMPTS

Our approach to defending against opponents' preemptive three-bids is similar to the methods we advised (in Chapter 2) against weak two-bids. However, since the level of the opening bid has risen, the risk and dangers are also elevated. The only compensation is that the opening bidder's hand is likely to be even weaker defensively for a three-level opening than it was for a weak two-bid.

The following box outlines the requirements for, and responses to, takeout doubles when your opponents make a three-level opening.

# REQUIREMENTS FOR DOUBLING
## THREE-LEVEL PREEMPTS

(1) Takeout-oriented hand with at least three-card support for the unbid suits.

(2) Values for a sound opening bid.

(3) The more HCP, the less perfect the support for all the unbid suits need be, but support for any unbid major(s) is essential.

### OR

(4) A hand that is too strong for a simple overcall. You will bid your suit at your next turn.

---

# RESPONDING TO PARTNER'S DOUBLE
## OF THREE-LEVEL PREEMPTS

(1) Simple responses in a new suit are **not forcing** and **non-constructive**.
   If the doubler introduces a new suit over a simple response, he shows a hand that was too strong for an initial overcall.

(2) 3NT, 4♥, 4♠, 5♣ and 5♦ show game values and are to play.

(3) Cuebids are forcing to game. They may be used either to locate the best game or to show strength and possible slam interest.

(4) Pass converts partner's takeout double to a penalty double.

The key to successful overcalls of three-level openings is the **quality** of your suit — as it is with overcalls at most levels. Sound three-level overcalls necessarily contain reasonably good suits. Although AQ763 is a reasonable suit to overcall at the one-level, it is inadequate for a three-level overcall unless you have considerable compensating outside strength. Keeping this in mind, the following outlines our suggestions for overcalling when the opponents start the auction with a three-level opening.

---

## REQUIREMENTS FOR OVERCALLING THREE-LEVEL PREEMPTS

(1)  A good suit.

(2)  Values for a sound opening bid.

(3)  Extra values at the four-level.

(4)  An even stronger hand for a jump overcall.

(5)  3NT shows one of the following:
  • A strong balanced hand with 15+ to 18+ HCP (up to 20 HCP is fine, but begin by doubling with 21 or more).
  • A stopper in the opponent's suit and a long running suit of your own.

(6)  Cuebids in the minors show a good distributional takeout for the majors.

(7)  Cuebids in the majors show a good two-suiter with the other major and an unspecified minor.

---

We are not happy with the range of hands covered by a 3NT overcall. It is not good. To be blunt, it is worse than simply not good. It reminds your authors of Winston Churchill's analysis of democracy when the great British leader observed, "Democracy is the worst system devised by the wit of, except for all the others." We feel similarly toward 3NT overcalls of three-level preempts. But what are you going to do with the following hands when RHO opens 3♦ with both sides vulnerable?

(a)    ♠ K10   ♥ Q104   ♦ AJ7   ♣ AJ1095

(b)    ♠ Q4   ♥ 983   ♦ A5   ♣ AKQ1094

(c)    ♠ KQ2   ♥ AQ   ♦ AQ9   ♣ K6532

(d)    ♠ AQ3   ♥ K   ♦ AJ102   ♣ KQ1094

The three tens and strong intermediates tip the scales in favor of a 3NT overcall on a good 15-count with (a). You might also bid 3NT with hand (b); it is a classic example of a 3NT overcall with a stopper and a source of tricks. Despite the 20 HCP in hand (c), 3NT is your only call. We must confess that we would also overcall 3NT with (d), but only after moving the ♦ 2 next to the ♥ K as a "safety play."

We would not, however, bid 3NT over a 3♦ opening holding:

(e)    ♠ K1095   ♥ K1076   ♦ K2   ♣ AK10

(f)    ♠ AQJ   ♥ KQJ7   ♦ A9   ♣ Q1095

(g)    ♠ 98   ♥ AKJ109   ♦ AK4   ♣ J109

A takeout double is a better description of both (e) and (f) because a 3NT overcall could easily prevent you from reaching your best spot. On (g) we would prefer a 3♥ overcall.

To reach your side's optimum contract after you overcall 3NT with these hands requires more than simply a good bridge partner — you will sometimes need Houdini sitting across the table from you! The lesson in this discussion of 3NT overcalls is this: be sympathetic if partner does not get your side to the best contract after you have overcalled 3NT. Partner is often forced to pass and hope you have come to rest in a reasonable contract.

Responding effectively to high-level overcalls other than 3NT also requires practicality and good judgment. The bidding space consumed by the opponent's preempt usually prevents delicate probing and exploration. At best your partnership will be limited to a few understandings and agreements. We recommend those outlined in the following box:

# RESPONDING TO PARTNER'S OVERCALL OF THREE-LEVEL PREEMPTS

(1) New suits introduced below game after an overcall are **forcing** for one round.

(2) 3NT and other game bids are to play and show game-going values.

(3) Cuebids show slam interest and are generally based on a fit for partner's suit.

(4) Over partner's 3NT: 4♣ is Stayman; 4♦ transfers to hearts; 4♥ transfers to spades; 4♠ is for the minors; 4NT is quantitative with 13 to 15+ HCP; 5♣ is Gerber.

(5) 4NT is Blackwood.

(5) Over partner's major suit cuebid showing the other major and an unspecified minor: 4NT asks which minor.

Using these methods, consider a few examples. Suppose RHO opens 3♦, neither side vulnerable, and you hold:

(a)      ♠ AJ10   ♥ KQJ5   ♦ 3   ♣ AJ1094
DOUBLE. It would be nice if the ♣ 4 were the ♠ 4. You have an adequate takeout double with sixteen working HCP and reasonably good support for all the unbid suits.

(b)      ♠ A985   ♥ Q84   ♦ K4   ♣ KJ72
PASS. Here is a typical illustration of a hand worth a takeout double of 1♦, but not of 3♦. This is an opening bid, but with less than perfect support for hearts and minimum strength, you are best advised to pass. Perhaps partner will take action in the balancing seat if your side belongs in the auction.

RHO opens 3♥, both sides vulnerable. What action would you take holding:

(c)      ♠ AQJ107   ♥ 7   ♦ 3   ♣ AKJ843
CUEBID 4♥. This is an excellent description of your two-suiter. If partner is interested in finding out which minor you hold, he will bid 4NT.

(d)      ♠ AKQ1084   ♥ 32   ♦ K85   ♣ 94
OVERCALL 3♠. You have sound values for a three-level overcall. This is by no means a maximum overcall. In fact, except for the excellent trump suit, it is minimum.

You are vulnerable, they are not. RHO opens 3♣. What do you bid?

(e)      ♠ KQJ75   ♥ AQ10974   ♦ 32   ♣ —
CUEBID 4♣. This is a typical minor suit cuebid after a three-level minor suit opening, asking responder to pick his best major.

(f)      ♠ AKQJ962   ♥ A4   ♦ QJ6   ♣ 8
JUMP TO 4♠. Bid what you think you can make. Remember, a jump overcall is never preemptive — it is always strong — after an opponent's preempt.

In Chapter 1 we noted suit rank as a factor when preempting. You need less to double or overcall when the opponents open 3♣ than you do when they open 3♠. Over 3♣ you can end the auction at the three-level, which will (hopefully) be safe. Over 3♠, however, you have been pushed to the four-level and may find no safe haven anywhere. As Victor Mollo sagely observed, "If you can locate a fit you may be able to avoid the 'chopper' at the three-level, but you will rarely avoid enemy 'bullets' at the four-level when you err in competing against an opponent's preempt."

Both North/South Pairs on Board 28 of the 1993 Vanderbilt final would have done well to heed Mollo's warning:

```
                    North
                    ♠  84
                    ♥  53
                    ♦  KQJ10742
                    ♣  K7

West                                          East
♠  5              ┌─────────────┐             ♠  A10763
♥  Q62           │  Board 28    │             ♥  AK
♦  985           │  Dlr. - West │             ♦  A3
♣  AJ10963       │  Vul. - N/S  │             ♣  Q854
                 └─────────────┘
                    South
                    ♠  KQJ92
                    ♥  J109874
                    ♦  6
                    ♣  2
```

---

CLOSED ROOM                           Opening Lead   ♦9
                                                N/S -1100

| *Lev* | *Sanders* | *Russell* | *Arnold* |
| West | North | East | South |
|------|-------|-------|-------|
| 3♣ | P | 3N | 4♣ |
| Dbl. | 4♦ | 5♣ | P |
| P | Dbl. | Redbl. | P |
| P | 5♦ | Dbl. | 5♥ |
| Dbl. | P | P | P |

Sanders judged well not to bid 3 ♦ over 3♣, believing a three-level overcall should be reserved for a stronger hand. This good decision, however, did not prevent him from having the displeasure of putting his fine seven-card suit down as part of the dummy and recording -1100 against non-vulnerable opponents — whose notrump game would have failed if partner clairvoyantly led a diamond. (The defense against 5♥ doubled was charitably less than perfect.)

Comparatively, minus 1100 was not a bad result! Here was the auction and play that appeared in the Vugraph room:

| OPEN ROOM | | Opening Lead ♠ A | |
| | | | N/S -1700 |
| *Weinstein* | *Fallenius* | *Nagy* | *Nilsland* |
| West | North | East | South |
| 3♣ | 3♦ | 5♣ | Dbl. |
| P | P | Redbl. | 5♦ |
| Dbl. | P | P | 5♥ |
| Dbl. | 6♦ | Dbl. | P |
| P | P | | |

Against the Swedish internationalist, the defense was merciless. Nagy started with the pointed Aces and gave partner a spade ruff. Two rounds of hearts and a diamond exit left declarer with two inescapable club losers for **-1700**.

The lesson of this deal is simple. Dubious action over enemy preempts rarely goes unpunished — and that punishment can easily be a four-digit number.

## BALANCING OVER THREE-LEVEL PREEMPTS

It is reasonable to reduce some of the requirements for most of your competitive weapons of enemy three-bids in the balancing seat. The strength for overcalls and take-out doubles can and should be lowered. Remember, partner may have been forced to pass with considerable values if his hand did not meet the requirements for any direct action. We do not recommend reducing the strength for 3NT; as we discussed earlier, 3NT has a broad enough range already. The key (and safety) to balancing against enemy overcalls is still the quality of your suit. Your support for the unbid suits remains a crucial element of balancing doubles. Keep in mind that it is possible for RHO to have a good hand despite his pass. He might have passed because he had no interest in game after an opening preempt by his partner.

Let us consider a few examples. Suppose LHO opens 3♦, which gets passed around to you. Everybody is vulnerable. What call do you make holding:

(a)      ♠ KJ7   ♥ Q9832   ♦ 7   ♣ AJ85

DOUBLE. In the long run it is a losing proposition to sell out to 3♦ with diamond shortness and moderate strength. It is better to double than overcall with such anemic hearts when you have support for both black suits.

(b)      ♠ 74   ♥ KQJ98   ♦ 63   ♣ A1095

BALANCE WITH 3♥. Although you would not make this call in direct seat, it is dangerous to pass with this hand in balancing position, particularly at matchpoints. We admit that we would bid at all forms of scoring even though we know we may occasionally get too high or go for a "number."

(c)      ♠ AKQ10973   ♥ 96   ♦ 7   ♣ KJ10

BALANCE WITH 4♠. Make the same call you would have made directly over the 3♦ opening.

(d)      ♠ KQJ63   ♥ AQJ84   ♦ 7   ♣ K9

BALANCE WITH 4♦ — the same bid you would have made directly over 3♦.

At the one-level, balancing is far from an exact science. At the three- or four-level, it is even less so. Discretion, good judgment and luck are most often the keys to success in determining the best course of action for your side when the enemy's three-level opening is passed around to you in fourth position. Should you have a choice, choose **luck** — she will produce far better results more consistently.

# CHAPTER 4

# HIGH-LEVEL MINOR SUIT PREEMPTS

## 3NT AND BEYOND

By far the rarest preemptive openings are 4♣, 4♦, 5♣ and 5♦ — which is as it should be.

Because there is little or no room for exploration, it is critical that all four- and five-level openings be completely disciplined. Responder must have a clear picture of opener's trump suit and general playing strength. Without one, responder usually will be forced to take a shot in the dark at his side's best final contract.

At New York's famed Cavendish Club, Adam Meredith — the legendary British player — who was highly regarded on both sides of the Atlantic — was once asked by a new rubber-bridge partner what she might assume if he were to open 4♣ or 4♦ as the dealer. His practical reply was, "Although I believe such openings should be reserved for regular partnerships, you might reasonably assume either that I hold a broken eight- or nine-card suit with no more than a Queen outside, or," returning his wine glass to the side-table, "I have had too much to DRINK!"

Every partnership needs to have firm agreements about minor suit preempts. Requirements for the opening bid and the exact meaning of the limited number of available responses must be clearly established. We will provide you with the foundation for these understandings in this chapter.

# 4♣ AND 4♦ OPENINGS —
# USE 3NT

We recommend using a 3NT opening to describe a preemptive 4♣ or 4♦ opener. There are three reasons for this approach:

(1)     As we shall discuss in the next chapter, this method reserves four-level minor suit openings for strong major suit preempts — NAMYATS.

(2)     In most modern systems, 3NT is not needed to describe balanced hands with 25-27 HCP. The balanced battleships can be shown via a forcing opening followed by a notrump rebid, often conserving bidding space.

(3)     Using 3NT to describe a preemptive 4♣ or 4♦ opening allows responder to convert by passing whenever he holds appropriate values. Obviously, you can no longer play 3NT when partner opens 4♣ or 4♦. Holding a weak hand responder can get out over 3NT by responding 4♣, which opener will pass or correct to 4♦.

Although this approach prevents you from playing the Gambling 3NT opening, this is not a significant sacrifice. The standard gambling 3NT promises a long, solid minor suit with outside stopper(s) by partnership agreement. Such hands can be perfectly described by a simple minor suit opening followed by an appropriate rebid. In addition to avoiding 3NT when your opponents may be able to cash the first five, six, or seven tricks, you gain the often critical advantage of getting to 3NT played from the right side of the table.

The importance of playing 3NT from the right side of the table holding a solid minor was clearly demonstrated on the following deal. It was played by one of your authors with New Jersey expert David Berkowitz in a New York team event. Here is the complete deal with the results from both tables.

```
                        North
                        ♠  A4
                        ♥  7
                        ♦  AKQJ1052
                        ♣  952

West                                        East
♠  Q86          ┌─────────────────┐         ♠  K752
♥  A8632        │   Board 13      │         ♥  QJ104
♦  97           │   Dlr. - North  │         ♦  63
♣  KQ6          │   Vul. - Both   │         ♣  J107
                └─────────────────┘
                        South
                        ♠  J1093
                        ♥  K95
                        ♦  84
                        ♣  A843
```

| OUR TABLE | | | Opening Lead ♥ 3 |
| | | | N/S +630 |

| | *Berkowitz* | | *Andersen* |
| West | North | East | South |
| — | 1♦ | P | 1♠ |
| P | 3♦ | P | 3NT |
| P | P | P | |

| THEIR TABLE | | | Opening Lead ♥ Q |
| | | | N/S -100 |

| West | North | East | South |
| — | 3N (a) | P | P (b) |
| P | | | |

(a)    A textbook gambling 3NT under the methods our opponents
       were playing — seven solid minor suit winners plus an
       outside Ace.

(b)    Delighted to pass holding stoppers in all of the unbid suits.

Admittedly, North-South at the other table were a bit unlucky. They did not have to get a heart honor lead through the King and the Ace of hearts might have been onside. At our table, where I played 3NT, the defense was helpless. East could not gain the lead to put the heart Queen through my unprotected King. In short, the vulnerable game, unbeatable when played by South, had no play from the North chair with the lead through the heart King.

As this deal illustrates, it is our philosophy that you limit your gambling bids and plays to casino gaming tables and avoid them at the bridge table. It has been our experience that opening 3NT on a solid minor with an outside stopper loses far more than it gains. If your side belongs in 3NT, you can get there easily by simply opening the bidding with your suit and then determining whether you have all the suits stopped and who should play the notrump game. Rarely should the player with the solid suit — and little, if any, outside strength — be the declarer in 3NT.

Since an opening bid of 3NT is not needed to describe other types of hands, we use it to show a preemptive 4♣ or 4♦ opening. Our requirements for opening 3NT (a four-level minor suit preempt) are:

## REQUIREMENTS FOR OPENING 3NT

(1)  A reasonable eight- or nine-card broken minor suit (at least two of the top four honors).

(2)  No outside Ace or King.

(3)  6 to 6+ playing tricks at FAVORABLE VULNERABILITY.
7 to 7+ playing tricks at EQUAL VULNERABILITY.
8 to 8+ playing tricks at UNFAVORABLE VULNERABILITY. (The "Rule of Two, Three and Four").

(4)  No four-card major.

Since you cannot have an outside Ace or King when you open 3NT, the quality of your trump suit must be the key to your playing strength. Responder must have this knowledge to accurately determine the best course of action for your side.

Here are a few examples of opening minor suit preempts:

(a) &spades; 5 &hearts; 8 &diams; J107 &clubs; AQ1097542   NV vs. NV
OPEN 3NT. The trump suit and playing strength of this hand are adequate for a preemptive 4&clubs; opening.

(b) &spades; 86 &hearts; — &diams; AQJ107642 &clubs; QJ10   V vs. NV
OPEN 3NT. This hand meets all the requirements of a 4&diams; opening at unfavorable vulnerability.

(c) &spades; Q62 &hearts; 7 &diams; 5 &clubs; AJ865432   V vs. NV
PASS. Although you have two of the top four club honors, neither your trump suit nor your overall playing strength is sufficient for a vulnerable 4&clubs; opening. It is simply too dangerous.

(d) &spades; 52 &hearts; KJ &diams; AQJ106532 &clubs; 5   V vs. NV
OPEN 1&diams;. You cannot open 3NT (as a preemptive 4&diams; bid) with an outside Ace or King. Besides, this hand should qualify as an opening one-bid in your partnership methods.

(e) &spades; 3 &hearts; J10 &diams; 52 &clubs; AJ1098752   NV vs. NV
OPEN 3NT. This is a minimum 3NT opening. If clubs are distributed normally around the table, you will be able to win seven tricks in your trump suit.

The obvious question you may be asking is: when the opening bid is 3NT, how does partner know whether opener's suit is clubs or diamonds? Although responder's hand will usually suggest which suit opener holds, on rare occasions he may not know partner's suit. But, he can easily find out — as we are about to discuss.

## RESPONSES TO 3NT

With appropriate values, responder can make 3NT the final contract by passing, or he may elect to use the following:

---

### RESPONSES TO 3NT

(1) 4♣ is "**pass** or **correct**." Opener passes with a club suit or corrects to 4♦ with a diamond suit.

(2) 4♦ is conventional, and asks for opener's **shortness**. Opener rebids:

    4♥ = ♥ singleton or void.

    4♠ = ♠ singleton or void.

    4NT = singleton or void in the other minor (with no shortness in either major).

    5♣ = shortness in spades and the other minor.

A 4♠ rebid by responder over 4♥ asks if opener has a second short suit. Opener rebids 4NT with no other shortness, or bids five of the second suit in which he is short.

Responder's bid of five of opener's known short suit asks whether opener holds a singleton or void. Opener responds in steps: 1st step = singleton, 2nd step = void. Responder must have a hand that can play in at least a small slam in the minor to initiate this sequence.

(3) 4♥ and 4♠ are to play — opener must pass.

(4) 5♣ is "**pass** or **correct**"; opener passes with clubs or corrects to 5♦.

(continued)

---

# RESPONSES TO 3NT (continued)

(5)   4NT asks about the quality of opener's trump
      suit (Note: This is **not** any kind of keycard
      inquiry).

      Opener rebids:

      5♣ =  Two of the top four hon-
            ors (but not two of the
            top three; i.e., a suit
            headed by AJ, KJ or QJ)

      5♦ =  Two of the top three hon-
            ors — missing the Ace or
            King but promising the
            Queen

      5♥ =  Both the Ace and King

      This conventional 4NT response can also be
      used after a 4♦ inquiry and responses.

      After opener's response to 4NT, new suits
      by responder ask for distributional control
      (shortness) in the suit bid.

      Opener bids the first step with no
      controls; he bids the second step with
      a singleton; the third step shows a
      void.

Using these responses, what action would you take after partner
opens 3NT holding:

(a)   ♠ KJ10732  ♥ AQ105  ♦ 95  ♣ 10   V vs. V
      RESPOND 4♣. "**Pass** or **correct**." Game
      is out of the question. Even if partner holds
      two spades, giving your side an eight-card
      major suit fit, you should play in partner's
      minor. Partner's hand may be totally worth-
      less unless his suit is trump. If you are
      lucky, your high cards will cover two of his
      losers.

(b) &spades; AKQ10973 &hearts; 6 &diams; KQ10 &clubs; 95 NV vs. NV
RESPOND 4&spades;. Although partner's hand
may be of little or no value to you in a
spade game, bid what you think you can
make.

(c) &spades; AQ10 &hearts; QJ107 &diams; AJ9 &clubs; Q107 NV vs. NV
PASS. 3NT is most likely to be the only
game contract your side can make. You
hope partner's suit is clubs; if it is, 3NT will
be laydown. It partner has diamonds, perhaps partner will have help in clubs (you can
hope that Q107 will constitute a stopper).

(d) &spades; AK94 &hearts; 8742 &diams; AKQ &clubs;KJ          V vs. V
RESPOND 4&diams;, asking for shortness. If
opener has a singleton heart, 6&clubs; should be
lay-down. If opener does rebid 4&hearts;, bid 5&hearts;
(asking whether opener's shortness is a
singleton or a void); if opener shows a heart
void, bid 7&clubs; which should be cold. Over
opener's rebid of anything but 4&hearts;, sign off
in 5&clubs; and hope the enemy cannot take the
first three heart tricks.

(e) &spades; J98 &hearts; KQ107632 &diams; Q105 &clubs; —  NV vs. V
RESPOND 4&clubs;. Do not be tempted to bid
4&hearts; with this hand. Partner has promised a
better trump suit and more playing strength
in his suit than you have in yours. Perhaps
your hand will produce a trick for him. His
hand might be totally worthless to you in a
heart contract. (The optimists among you
can hope partner's suit is diamonds; but we
all know opener holds clubs).

The following hand illustrates effective use of these methods.
The ability to ask a few simple questions made it possible for Mark
Feldman and one of your authors to reach the optimum final
contract. The complete deal and auction:

112

North
- ♠ 62
- ♥ 983
- ♦ —
- ♣ AQJ97653

West
- ♠ 10753
- ♥ KQ7
- ♦ 10763
- ♣ 84

Board 29
Dlr. - North
Vul. - Both

East
- ♠ 984
- ♥ J1062
- ♦ AK985
- ♣ 2

South
- ♠ AKQJ
- ♥ A54
- ♦ QJ42
- ♣ K10

Opening Lead ♦ A
N/S +2140

|  | *Andersen* |  | *Feldman* |
| West | North | East | South |
| — | 3NT (a) | P | 4♦ (b) |
| P | 4NT (c) | P | 5♦ (d) |
| P | 5♠ (e) | P | 5NT (f) |
| P | 6♦ (g) | P | 7♣ (h) |
| P | P | P | |

(a)   Typical 3NT opening.
(b)   Conventional, asking for opener's shortness.
(c)   Shortness in the other minor, no shortness in either major.
(d)   Conventional, asking if shortness is a singleton or void.
(e)   "I have no diamonds, partner."
(f)   "How good is your trump suit?" (the Grand Slam Force)
(g)   "I have two out of three top honors, missing Ace or King."
(h)   "Partner has Ace-Queen eighth of clubs. That's 13 tricks."

Sometimes 3NT creates considerable confusion for your opponents, and good result for your side. Consider the following well-publicized deal played in the European Junior Championships.

```
                    North
                    ♠  AJ63
                    ♥  Q9542
                    ♦  —
                    ♣  K952

West                                      East
♠  K854          ┌─────────────┐         ♠  92
♥  AJ763         │ Board 11    │         ♥  K108
♦  AK107         │ Dlr. - South│         ♦  QJ9863
♣  —             │ Vul. - None │         ♣  86
                 └─────────────┘
                    South
                    ♠  Q107
                    ♥  —
                    ♦  542
                    ♣  AQJ10743
```

---

**CLOSED ROOM**  Opening Lead ♦ K

N/S +1190

| West | North | East | South |
|------|-------|------|-------|
| — | — | — | 3NT (a) |
| Dbl. | 4♦ (b) | Dbl. | 5♣ (c) |
| 5♦ | 6♣ (d) | P | P |
| Dbl. | P | P | P |

(a)  Unspecified four-level minor suit preempt.
(b)  In this partnership, 4♦ is "pass or correct."
(c)  "My suit is clubs."
(d)  "Should be a good sacrifice."

In the Open Room, South chose to pass, and his opponents bid up to 4♥ which got doubled by North. The defense did not go well (North gave declarer his 10th trick in spades) and +590 was recorded for East-West.

In the 6♣ "save" South had no difficulty capturing all the tricks when the spade finesse worked. Plus 1190 was worth 18 IMPs — a victory for the confusion that is sometimes created by the 3NT opening.

## 4NT, 5♣ AND 5♦ OPENINGS

Your authors have not always seen eye-to-eye on what constitutes a 5♣ or 5♦ opening bid. Non-vulnerable, Sabine felt that

(a)     ♠ —   ♥ 3   ♦ KQ1087654   ♣ 10974

was more than adequate for a 5♦ opening. Ron, on the other hand, felt that

(b)     ♠ —   ♥ 5   ♦ AKJ106532   ♣ K1093

better met the requirements of an opening 5♦ bid. Despite Sabine's retort that if Ron's declarer play were better, hand (a) would be enough, your authors found a compromise.

The solution was provided by Dr. George Rosenkranz.[1] George knows we are advocates of NAMYATS to describe preemptive and constructive four-level major suit openings. So he suggested we adopt a similar approach to 5♣ and 5♦ openings.

| | | |
|---|---|---|
| 4NT | = | A **constructive** 5♣ or 5♦ opening, like (b) above |
| 5♣/5♦ | = | A preemptive five-level minor suit opening, like (a) above |

---

[1]   The description of the 4NT opening and responses was adopted from Dr. Rosenkranz's excellent book Bid to Win, Play for Pleasure, co-authored by Phillip Alder.

It is no great sacrifice to play that a 4NT opening describes a constructive 5♣ or 5♦ opening. To our knowledge, an opening bid of 4NT is not needed for any other worthwhile purpose.

The requirements for Dr. Rosenkranz's 4NT opening are:

---

## REQUIREMENTS FOR OPENING 4NT

(1)  An excellent eight- or nine-card suit.

(2)  Sound playing values for the five-level (9+ playing tricks).

(3)  No more than **one** loser in any suit.

---

For the (preemptive) 5♣ and 5♦ openings, we recommend:

---

## REQUIREMENTS FOR OPENING 5♣ AND 5♦

(1)  An exceptional eight-or nine-card trump suit. (Never more than one loser in the suit)

(2)  No more than one outside Ace or King, with the understanding that your hand cannot contain two Aces.

(3)  Eight playing tricks NON-VULNERABLE — nine playing tricks VULNERABLE (The "Rule of Two and Three").

---

Knowing that opener cannot hold two Aces is often helpful to responder since Blackwood is no longer available; it can also be useful should the auction be contested. In addition, a hand with two Aces and a near-solid long suit is too strong for a five-level preemptive opening.

Non-vulnerable, we would open 5♣ holding:

(a)      ♠ 6  ♥ 3  ♦ KJ10  ♣ KQJ109762

(b)     ♠ 53   ♥ —   ♦ J103   ♣ AKQ106532

Vulnerable, we would open 5♦ with:

(c)     ♠ A3   ♥ 74   ♦ KQJ876432   ♣ —

(d)     ♠ 96   ♥ —   ♦ AKQ1076532   ♣ 107

These hands do not meet our requirements for a 5♣ or 5♦ bid at any vulnerability; (e) is too weak and (f) is far too strong:

(e)     ♠ 94   ♥ QJ10   ♦ —   ♣ AQ1086532

(f)     ♠ AQ10   ♥ —   ♦ J10   ♣ AKQJ8765

## RESPONSES TO 4NT, 5♣ AND 5♦

When you follow our guidelines for opening five-level preempts in a minor, responder will have enough information to accurately place the contract. Responder will total his side's quick tricks and controls to establish the number of available playing tricks.

---

### RESPONSES TO 4NT

(1)   Pass, hoping to play 4NT (rare!).

(2)   5♣ asks opener to pass with a club suit or correct to 5♦ with diamonds.

(3)   5♥ shows first-round controls in both hearts and the other minor, denying first-round spade control.

(4)   5♠ shows first-round controls in spades and the other minor and denies a first-round heart control.

(5)   5NT shows first-round control in **both majors**, denying a first-round control in the other minor.

---

After these responses, opener signs off in six of his minor without first-round control of the fourth suit. He bids seven of his minor with a void in that suit or 6NT holding the Ace. Here is a sample auction:

| | |
|---|---|
| ♠ 7 | ♠ AQJ86 |
| ♥ 7 | ♥ AKQ |
| ♦ A6 | ♦ KQJ |
| ♣ KQJ1098543 | ♣ A7 |

| Opener | Responder |
|---|---|
| 4NT | 5NT (a) |
| 6NT (b) | 7NT (c) |
| P | |

(a)  First-round control of both majors, not in the other minor.

(b)  "I have the ♦ Ace."

(c)  "Bridge is an easy game — I can count at least 15 tricks!!"

When you begin the auction at the five-level you preempt partner as well as the opponents. The little bidding space below slam must be reserved for exploring grand slam potential in opener's suit — you should not be looking for a better fit at the five-level. Therefore, opener's suit is **always** trump (unless responder jumps directly to a slam in a new suit or notrump). We advise the following responses to a 5♣ or 5♦ opening:

---

### RESPONSES TO 5♣ AND 5♦

(1)  A new suit at the five-level (and 6♣ over 5♦) are CABs (Control Asking Bids). You are committed to bidding six; the only question remaining is whether you can make seven of opener's minor.

(continued)

---

## RESPONSES TO 5♣ AND 5♦ (cont'd)

(2) 5NT is the Grand Slam Force asking about the exact quality of opener's trump suit. Opener's rebids are:

> 6♣ = "I have a trump loser."
> 6♦ = "I have no trump losers; my suit is solid."

(The 5NT inquiry may be used after a CAB. If opener's suit is diamonds, 6♣ may be played as the Grand Slam Force when 5NT is not available because of opener's response to a CAB).

(3) All jumps to slam in new suits are to play.

Using these methods, let us consider a few examples. If partner opens 5♣ non-vulnerable, what action would you take holding:

(a)  ♠ KQJ7  ♥ KQ95  ♦ K107  ♣ J6
PASS. You need Aces, voids and quick tricks to make a slam when partner opens 5♣ or 5♦. Kings, Queens and Jacks that are unsupported by Aces are of dubious value. You will be lucky if this 15-count can produce a game opposite a non-vulnerable 5♣ opening.

(b)  ♠ AK743  ♥ A9865  ♦ 9  ♣ Q4
RAISE TO 6♣. Although a club slam may not be laydown, it should have a reasonable play with your excellent controls, fast tricks and good fit. Queen-doubleton is excellent support for a 5♣ or 5♦ opening. Note that although this hand has only 13 HCP it is worth a raise to slam, while you would pass with (a).

(c)    ♠ 98753   ♥ AK   ♦ AKQ4   ♣ K3

RESPOND 5♠ (CAB). Admittedly, 5♠ is a bit of a calculated risk. However, if partner has no spade losers you will make a grand slam; if he has one spade loser 6♣ will be cold.

What action would you take with the following hands after partner's vulnerable 5♦ opening?

(d)    ♠ AKQ74   ♥ —   ♦ 95   ♣ A76532

RESPOND 5NT. If partner's trump suit is solid, 7♦ should be cold.

(e)    ♠ 8   ♥ AKQ762   ♦ A3   ♣ A1084

RESPOND 5♠ (CAB). 6♦ should be bullet-proof, and a grand slam should be bid if opener has first-round control of spades. If partner bids 6♦ (first-round control), you will rebid 6♠ to find out whether partner has a void or the Ace. If partner holds the Ace, you should bid 7NT instead of 7♦, especially at matchpoints. At any form of the game, 7NT is probably the best contract because it eliminates the possibility that declarer's RHO will ruff the opening lead.

(f)    ♠ 109   ♥ AKQ108752   ♦ —   ♣ K104

PASS. Unfortunately, there is no way to play 5♥ (or better still 4♥) after a 5♦ opening. Remember 5♥ would be a CAB and 5♦ rates to play better than 6♥, which is the first non-conventional call in hearts that responder can make.

Take a look at these methods in practice on a deal your authors played in the 1993 Mixed Pairs Championship in Kansas City:

```
                          North
                       ♠  A84
                       ♥  A1097532
                       ♦  Q102
                       ♣  —

West                    ┌─────────────┐      East
♠  KQ102                │  Board 3    │      ♠  J9763
♥  Q6                   │  Dlr. - South│     ♥  K84
♦  6                    │  Vul. - E/W │      ♦  4
♣  K97632               └─────────────┘      ♣  A854

                          South
                       ♠  5
                       ♥  J
                       ♦  AKJ98753
                       ♣  QJ10
```

Opening Lead ♦ 6
N/S +1440

|       | *Zenkel* |      | *Andersen* |
| West  | North    | East | South      |
|-------|----------|------|------------|
| —     | —        | —    | 5♦         |
| P     | 5♥ (a)   | P    | 5NT (b)    |
| P     | 6♣ (c)   | P    | 7♦ (d)     |
| P     | P        | P    |            |

(a)   Realizing that there was a good possibility her side might be
      cold for a grand slam in diamonds if partner had second
      round control of hearts, responder uses a CAB.
(b)   "I have second-round control in hearts."
(c)   The Grand Slam Force — to cover the unlikely event that
      opener does not hold both the Ace and King of diamonds.
(d)   "I have a near solid trump suit including both the Ace and
      King."

Except for opening 3NT or five of a minor in fourth seat, there are no positional considerations in opening four of a minor (via 3NT) and 5♣ or 5♦. All responses are the same whether partner has opened in first, second, third or fourth chair.

Obviously, when you open with a preempt in fourth seat, you expect to get a plus score; otherwise you would have simply passed the hand out. Consequently, responder should assume that opener has more playing strength when he opens 3NT or five of a minor in the passout seat. A fourth chair 3NT opening might be made on either:

(a)      ♠ —   ♥ 98   ♦ KQ1097632   ♣ A109

or

(b)      ♠ 95   ♥ K4   ♦ 7   ♣ AQ1096532

If the enemy competes over a four- or five-level minor suit preempt, responder may be unable to make the response he would have made in a non-competitive auction. However, the enemy action does not change the meaning of any response he does make. In addition to the responses we have discussed, the redouble and penalty double are automatically added to your responding arsenal. Since the nature and strength of opener's hand are clearly defined and limited, responder is in an excellent position to judge accurately your side's offensive and defensive potential.


## DEFENSES AGAINST 4♣, 4♦ AND 3NT

Should your opponents play them, defending against natural 4♣ and 4♦ preempts is rarely an easy task because you have been denied three complete levels of bidding space. This often proves costly in reaching your optimum contract; little room remains for exploration and probing to find the right strain and level. In addition, errors in judgment which often go unpunished at lower levels frequently prove costly over 4♣ and 4♦.

The following box outlines the simple defensive measures we recommend over 4♣ and 4♦:

# DEFENSES AGAINST 4♣ AND 4♦ PREEMPTS

(1) Double shows a good hand with support for the unbid suits. The less perfect your support for the unbid suits, the more high card strength you should hold, (or the more ability you should have to handle a response in a suit you do not have).

(2) An overcall shows a good suit and a good hand.

(3) A cuebid shows an excellent two-suiter with sufficient playing strength to force the bidding to the five-level.

(4) 4NT is simple Blackwood.

(5) A jump overcall shows a powerful hand with a self-sufficient trump suit containing 10+ tricks. It is strongly invitational to slam.

Following these guidelines, what action would you take over 4♣ holding:

(a)     ♠ AQJ7  ♥ KQ1085  ♦ K4  ♣ A3
        DOUBLE. Your distribution is not ideal but you have too much to remain silent. If partner bids 4♦, you will be forced to correct to 4♥, indicating your lack of diamond support and suggesting a five-card heart suit.

(b)     ♠ AQ7632  ♥ K3  ♦ Q32  ♣ Q7
        PASS. This hand is far short of a 4♠ overcall. Your suit is barely adequate for an overcall at this level and your playing strength is grossly inadequate. This is the type of overcall that goes for a four-digit

number when the enemy might at best have a partscore or even be going minus in 4♣.

(c) ♠ AKQ107 ♥ AKQJ92 ♦ 5 ♣ 3
OVERCALL 4NT (Blackwood). If you cuebid 5♣, you will locate your longest combined major suit. However, you will have no idea whether to raise partner's 5♥ or 5♠ since you will not know if you are off an Ace. After partner's response to Blackwood, you can either sign off in hearts or ask partner to pick the trump suit by making a club cuebid at the right level.

(d) ♠ A10 ♥ AKJ1097 ♦ KJ103 ♣ 7
OVERCALL 4♥. This is a sound four-level overcall, but you could still go for a number if you catch partner with a worthless hand and heart shortness. This "sound" overcall illustrates how dangerous it is to take initial action at the four-level.

(e) ♠ KJ85 ♥ KQ72 ♦ K983 ♣ 7
PASS. This hand would be a perfect double of a diamond opening at the one-level; it would be a minimum double of a preemptive 2♦ bid. At the three-level, it is at best marginal; at the four-level, it is unacceptable. In short, a double of 4♣ or 4♦ must be made of sterner stuff.

"BE PRACTICAL" is our advice when partner competes over a 4♣ or 4♦ opening. You have little or no room for exploration. The only conventional calls available to help you reach the best final contract are 4NT (asking for Aces or Key Cards in accordance with your partnership agreements); cuebids (showing slam interest and suggesting a control in the enemy suit); and (rarely) 5NT (Grand Slam Force). Use these bids with discretion.

It is easier to defend against a 3NT opening which suggests a four-level minor suit preempt than it is to combat natural 4♣ and 4♦ openings. We suggest the following:

---

### DEFENSES AGAINST 3NT
### SHOWING A 4♣ OR 4♦ PREEMPT

(1)    4♣ is a major suit takeout, promising at least five cards in each major.

(2)    Double shows a good hand, typically balanced or semi-balanced, with the approximate strength of a strong notrump (or better). After your double partner will know whether to compete or to allow the opponents to play in a doubled contract.

(3)    Overcalls are natural, showing a good suit and a good hand.

(4)    4NT is Blackwood.

---

Using these methods, we would double 3NT holding:

(a)    ♠ AK75  ♥ KQ10  ♦ 54  ♣ AJ93

We would make a conventional 4♣ call (major suit takeout) with:

(b)    ♠ KJ1095  ♥ AQJ108  ♦ A4  ♣ 2

## DEFENSES AGAINST
## 5♣ AND 5♦

Little has been written about defending against 5♣ and 5♦ openings. Your authors feel this is reasonable, considering how rarely these openings occur. We refuse to contribute substantially to the sparse amount of space in bridge literature devoted to this subject. Our partnership has the following simple understandings when the enemy opens 5♣ or 5♦.

---

## DEFENSES AGAINST 5♣ AND 5♦ PREEMPTS

(1) Doubles are strength showing, indicating sufficient assets to defeat the opponent's contract. Partner is invited to bid with a reasonable long suit. However, partner should pass with most balanced or semi-balanced hands.

(2) 5NT shows a battleship. It asks partner to pick a suit for slam.

(3) Overcalls are natural showing a good suit and a good hand with (typically) 8½ to 9½ playing tricks.

(4) Cuebids show similar battleships with the majors only.

---

We would double 5♦ with either of these hands:

♠ AK3  ♥ KQ107  ♦ 85  ♣ A1093

♠ KJ105  ♥ AJ102  ♦ A  ♣ K1073

Over a 5♣ opening, we would cuebid 6♣ with:

♠ AQJ98  ♥ AKJ107  ♦ A10  ♣ 3

Finally, we would overcall 5♣ with 5♠ holding:

♠ AKQ10765  ♥ K62  ♦ KQ3  ♣ —

# CHAPTER 5

# HIGH-LEVEL MAJOR SUIT PREEMPTS
## 4♥, 4♠ AND NAMYATS

What do the following five hands have in common?

(a)  ♠ AKQJ10752  ♥ —  ♦ J1097  ♣ 3

(b)  ♠ KQJ1042  ♥ 3  ♦ AK1073  ♣ J

(c)  ♠ AQJ10963  ♥ 85  ♦ —  ♣ QJ108

(d)  ♠ AKQ10963  ♥ 6  ♦ A109  ♣ J10

(e)  ♠ J1098532  ♥ K5  ♦ AKQ7  ♣ —

In a world championship, all these hands were opened 4♠ in first or second seat! Despite the differences in distribution, trump quality, outside values and playing strength, all five of them have features that merit a four-level opening bid. There are two reasons for opening four of a major:

(1)      You want to preempt the bidding with a good long suit. You want to describe your playing strength while depriving the opponents of a great deal of potentially valuable

bidding space. In short, you want to make life difficult for your opponents (while risking little).

(2)    You have a good one-suited hand, exceptional trump, and excellent playing strength. Although you are preempting several levels of bidding, you wish to make a constructive — as opposed to a strictly preemptive — opening bid. Far from being a sign-off, such openings encourage responder — with a few quick tricks and controls — to move in the direction of slam.

Responding to a 4♠ opening bid can pose serious problems when opener can have either (1) or (2). You would need to be clairvoyant to judge the best course of action for your side most of the time. In this chapter, we will outline methods you can use to solve this problem.

## 4♥ AND 4♠ OPENINGS

The requirements for opening 4♥ and 4♠ are similar to those described for 3♥ and 3♠ openings in Chapter 3. The only real difference is the quality of the trump suit and your general playing strength; since you are one level higher, you must have compensating playing strength. However, that additional playing strength must come from your trump suit, not outside high-cards. The need for additional playing strength is due to the fact that you are more apt to get doubled for penalty in a game contract at the four-level than you are in a partscore at the three-level.[1]

Therefore, we recommend the following for preemptive 4♥ and 4♠ openings:

---

[1]    Since you are more likely to get doubled at the game level, we recommend the "Rule of Two and Three" (rather than the "Rule of Two, Three and Four") for required playing strength.

# REQUIREMENTS FOR OPENING 4♥ AND 4♠

(1) A good seven- or eight-card suit. Non-vulnerable the suit occasionally may contain two losers. Vulnerable, the suit should never have more than one loser opposite a possible singleton in partner's hand, assuming normal breaks.

(2) At most one Ace **or** King outside the trump suit.

(3) Seven playing tricks NON-VULNERABLE; eight playing tricks VULNERABLE (the "Rule of Two and Three").

---

Like all other preemptive openings we have discussed, 4♥ and 4♠ openers are based on trick-taking potential (almost exclusively in your proposed trump suit). They are not based on high-card points or a long suit.

Here are a few examples for you to consider:

(a) ♠ KQ109852   ♥ A7   ♦ K109   ♣ 3     NV
OPEN 1♠, not 4♠. Although your playing strength meets the requirements for a 4♠ opener and the trump suit is acceptable (given the vulnerability), you have far too much outside strength. You have second-round control (or better) in all three side suits. Remember, you cannot have more than one Ace or King outside the trump suit.

(b) ♠ AKQJ1074   ♥ 7   ♦ 4   ♣ KJ109     NV
This hand is far too strong for a preemptive 4♠ opener non-vulnerable because it has nine sure winners. We will discuss what you should open with this type of hand later in this chapter.

(c) ♠ 3 ♥ KQJ108652 ♦ KJ10 ♣ 8    V
OPEN 4♥. You have eight winners (seven of them in your trump suit) with an excellent eight-card heart suit.

(d) ♠ A6 ♥ KQJ10743 ♦ KJ10 ♣ 7    V
OPEN 1♥, not 4♥. Even vulnerable, you should never have more than one Ace or King outside your trump suit.

(e) ♠ KQ1097643 ♥ — ♦ 74 ♣ AJ10    V
OPEN 4♠. Your trump suit should not be weaker for a vulnerable 4♠ opening. Your playing strength is more than adequate.

(f) ♠ AKQ1095 ♥ KQJ43 ♦ 98 ♣ —    V
OPEN 1♠. As a general rule, four-level major suit openings should be made with one-suited hands. Your side could easily belong in hearts (perhaps in slam) when partner would pass your 4♠ opening.

# RESPONSES TO 4♥ AND 4♠

By following the recommended guidelines, responder will have a clear picture of partner's trump suit and limited outside strength when the opening bid is 4♥ or 4♠. Remember, an opening 4♥ or 4♠ bid says, "Partner, I have a one-suited hand that may not be worth much unless my suit is trump. Even if your hand is worthless to me, I am within two tricks of my bid if we are vulnerable and within three tricks if we are non-vulnerable. Should we defend, I have no more than one defensive quick trick outside my suit."

Due to the level of the opening bid, the small amount of bidding space below the slam level should be reserved for exploring slam in opener's suit, not finding a better game contract. Like responses to 5♣ and 5♦, you should presume that opener's suit is trump unless responder jumps directly to slam in a new suit or notrump.

# RESPONSES TO 4♥ AND 4♠

(1)   A new suit at the five-level — as well as 4♠ in response to 4♥ — is a CAB.
      After opener's response, new suits introduced by responder are also CABs.
      When opener's response to a CAB shows a control, rebids in the "asked" suit by responder ask whether the control shown was a high card or distributional. Opener rebids: 1st step = distributional; 2nd step = high card.

(2)   4NT is Keycard Blackwood for opener's suit.

(3)   Direct raises to five of opener's suit are slam tries. They ask about the quality of opener's trump suit. Opener's responses:
      • Pass shows more than one trump loser.
      • Six of the major shows only one trump loser.
      • Cuebids show a second-round control in a side suit with no trump losers.

(4)   5NT is the Grand Slam Force. Opener responds:

      6♣ = Missing two of the top three trump honors.

      6♦ = Missing either the Ace or King of trumps; promises two of the top three honors.

      6♥ = Promises both the Ace and King of trumps, missing the Queen (enabling you to bid a grand slam missing the Queen of trumps but with compensating length).

      6♠ = Promises Ace, King, AND Queen of trump.

Responding to 4♥ or 4♠ rarely involves more than adding your quick tricks and controls to the number of playing tricks opener has promised. This should give you an accurate estimate of your side's offensive potential, as well as defensive prospects if your opponents contest the auction.

Using the methods we have outlined, what action would you take if partner opened 4♥ non-vulnerable when you hold:

(a)    ♠ AQ109632   ♥ —   ♦ K1074   ♣ J10
PASS. Even if 4♠ were a natural signoff (which it is not), 4♠ would be an inexcusable "shot in the dark." Your high cards should be of some value to opener, but his hand might be totally worthless to you in a spade contract. Following our guidelines, his trump suit has to be better than yours.

(b)    ♠ AKQJ92   ♥ KJ3   ♦ Q532   ♣ —
RESPOND 5♦ (CAB). Partner's diamond holding will determine whether you bid 5♥, 6♥, or 7♥.

Partner opens 4♠ vulnerable. What do you bid holding:

(c)    ♠ K7   ♥ KQJ10   ♦ AK73   ♣ AQ2
RESPOND 4NT. If partner has one Ace you intend to sign off in 6NT; if he holds two you plan to jump to 7NT. The reason for playing in notrump, even at the six level, is that you want to be declarer in order to protect your AQ of clubs.

(d)    ♠ 2   ♥ AK84   ♦ A9843   ♣ AKQ
RAISE TO 5♠. You would like to be in slam if partner has no more than one potential loser in his trump suit. Partner will carry on to slam with good spades.

The responding tools we have been discussing proved most beneficial to your authors on the following deal, played at the 1990 Proton International Friendship Tournament in Taipei.

```
                        North
                    ♠  —
                    ♥  AQJ109832
                    ♦  942
                    ♣  86

West                                      East
♠  KJ753        ┌─────────────┐           ♠  AQ862
♥  7            │  Board 1    │           ♥  54
♦  KQ86         │  Dlr. - North│          ♦  J105
♣  1073         │  Vul. - None │          ♣  542
                └─────────────┘
                        South
                    ♠  1094
                    ♥  K6
                    ♦  A73
                    ♣  AKQJ9
```

OUR TABLE                          Opening Lead ♦ K
                                          N/S +1510

|        | *Zenkel* |      | *Andersen* |
|--------|----------|------|------------|
| West   | North    | East | South      |
| —      | 4♥ (a)   | P    | 4♠ (b)     |
| P      | 5♦ (c)   | P    | 5NT (d)    |
| P      | 6♦ (e)   | P    | 7♥ (f)     |
| P      | P        | P    |            |

(a)  Typical 4♥ opening — seven tricks non-vulnerable.
(b)  CAB.
(c)  "I have a first-round control."
(d)  Grand Slam Force.
(e)  "Two of top three trump honors, missing the Ace or King."
(f)  "Rates to be a claim after the opening lead."

This converted to an 11-IMP pickup because N/S only reached the small slam in the other room.

A disciplined preempt, two simple questions and the answers to the two questions led to a laydown grand slam. At the other table, the opening bid was the same but N/S were not playing our methods, so South just gambled and jumped to 6♥. The "bet" was won, but the 11-IMP loss was hardly a triumph.

# NAMYATS 4♣
# AND 4♦ OPENINGS

At the outset of this chapter, we saw that there are two different types of 4♥ and 4♠ opening. First, the preemptive type. We have already studied those hands where opener has a relatively weak hand (particularly non-vulnerable) with a long suit that will produce several tricks. We open those hands 4♥ and 4♠.

Now we will discuss the constructive type of hand where opener holds a solid, long trump suit, and maybe an outside trick or two. New York expert Victor Mitchell, who is regarded as one of the world's great players, designed an approach to four-level major suit openings which gives us a bid for these hands. It is commonly called either the Mitchell Transfer or NAMYATS[1]. Playing NAM-YATS, an opening bid of 4♣ is a strong 4♥ opener and 4♦ is a strong 4♠ opener. In contrast, opening bids of 4♥ or 4♠ are primarily preemptive rather than constructive.

Some partnerships insist on very strict requirements for the 4♣ and 4♦ openings. They insist that a 4♣ or 4♦ opening include a solid seven-card suit (AKQxxxx or better) with an outside Ace or King; or, a solid eight-card suit without an outside trick. Although such methods (or agreements) are playable, we prefer requirements which are less restrictive.

Our requirements for a NAMYATS opening are:

---

[1]   "NAMYATS" is STAYMAN spelled backwards. Sam Stayman and Victor Mitchell enjoyed one of the most successful partnerships in the world for many years, and it was during that time that the convention was devised.

## REQUIREMENTS FOR OPENING
## 4♣ AND 4♦ NAMYATS

(1) 4♣ and 4♦ are constructive, showing hearts and spades respectively.

(2) The trump suit is always self-sufficient and never contains more than **one** loser. It is at least seven cards in length, frequently eight.

(3) No more than one Ace or King (but not both) outside the trump suit.

(4) Eight or nine playing tricks.

In general, opening 4♣ or 4♦ suggests that you are within a trick or trick and a half of your contract, and **never** more than two tricks away. Consequently, your decision of whether or not to open 4♣ or 4♦ is never affected by the vulnerability — getting doubled is not a concern as it is with 4♥ and 4♠ openings.

We would open 4♣ with either of the following hands:

(a)  ♠ 7  ♥ AKJ108754  ♦ K104  ♣ 9

(b)  ♠ —  ♥ AKQ109654  ♦ J1075  ♣ 6

4♦ would be our opening call holding:

(c)  ♠ KQJ10875  ♥ —  ♦ J10  ♣ KQ109

(d)  ♠ AKQ10973  ♥ 7  ♦ A107  ♣ 62

## RESPONSES TO NAMYATS

Since opener's suit, outside strength and playing strength are clearly defined, responder's task is usually simple over NAMYATS. Holding fewer than three or four fast tricks, slam is out of the question; responder should sign off in opener's suit. With three or four tricks and sufficient controls, responder can probe for slam.

## RESPONSES TO 4♣ AND 4♦

(1) The bid of opener's real suit is to play — opener must pass.

(2) The bid of the intermediate suit (4♦ over 4♣ and 4♥ over 4♦) shows slam interest and asks opener to:
- Bid an outside first-round control — Ace or void.
- Bid 4NT with an outside King (responder's rebid of 5♣ asks "which King").
- Bid his real suit without an outside first-round control or an outside King.

(3) A change of suit other than the intermediate suit (including the intermediate suit at the five-level) is a CAB.

Subsequent bids of new suits are also CABs.

(4) 5NT asks opener to bid seven of his suit with a completely solid trump suit.

---

Using these methods, what action would you take over partner's 4♣ opener holding:

(a) ♠ A8  ♥ 74  ♦ 109763  ♣ AKQ5
JUMP TO 5♦. You have ample values for slam if your side can avoid two immediate diamond losers. Use a CAB to find out.

(b) ♠ KQJ  ♥ J7  ♦ KQ1072  ♣ KQ9
RESPOND 4♥. You have 17 HCP but there is almost NO chance for slam. Partner would have to have both an outside Ace and a void — three controls — which is almost impossible. Remember, only responder's

fast tricks — Aces, voids and controls — produce slams when partner makes a four-level major suit opening.

Partner opens 4♦. What response would you make with:

(c)     ♠ 94   ♥ KQ10   ♦ AQ63   ♣ AQJ5
RESPOND 4♥. A bid of the intermediate suit is a perfect slam try with this hand. If opener rebids 4♠, you will pass. Any encouraging rebid will propel you toward slam.

(d)     ♠ —   ♥ AK752   ♦ AK4   ♣ A9843
JUMP TO 5NT. If opener's trump suit is completely solid, 7♠ should be cold.

Competition over a four-level major suit opening may prevent you from making the response you would have made in a non-competitive auction. However, it does not change the meaning of your responses. The redouble and penalty double are automatically added to your responding arsenal. Since the nature and strength of opener's hand are clearly defined and limited, responder is in an excellent position to make an accurate judgment about your side's offensive and defensive potential.

# KANTAR 3NT

An alternative to NAMYATS that serves a slightly different purpose is the Kantar 3NT opening. The Kantar 3NT convention is an opening bid of 3NT based on a solid seven- or eight- card major suit with no side suit Aces and with at most one King outside the solid major. Using this device, 4♥ and 4♠ openings deny solid suits. The convention, developed by California expert Edwin Kantar, is designed to remove the ambiguity of four-level major suit preempts as to suit quality and outside strength; it facilitates evaluating slam prospects and slam exploration.

The Kantar 3NT opening has this added advantage; responder can pass if he feels that 3NT is the partnership's best game. This can easily be the case when opener holds a solid heart or spade suit with little outside strength. If responder is certain which suit opener holds (i.e., responder has a top honor in one of the majors) and wishes to play game in opener's major he can bid it himself. Otherwise, responder is forced to use the conventional 4♦ call which asks opener to bid his suit.

If responder's aspirations are beyond the game level, he may make any of a number of asking bids to solicit additional information from the 3NT opener. A 4♣ response, for example, asks opener to bid a side suit in which he has a King. Lacking a King, opener simply returns to his long suit. If opener shows a King, a jump to 6♣ by responder asks opener to bid six of his major, protecting his outside King. Responder must "know" opener's suit to make the 4♣ inquiry — otherwise opener's rebid may be ambiguous.

Since 4NT is not needed as either Blackwood or a Keycard inquiry, Kantar recommends using 4NT to ask for Queens outside opener's long suit. It can be used either directly over the 3NT opening or after the response to the conventional 4♣ bid. If the opener has one queen, he bids it. With two outside queens, he jumps to the six-level as follows: 6♣ shows the Queen of diamonds and the other major; 6♦ shows the Queen of clubs and the other major; 6♥ shows both minor suit Queens. With no Queens, opener simply bids five of his major.

A 5NT response to a 3NT opening is a form of Grand Slam Force which asks opener to bid a grand slam in his suit if that suit can play for no losers opposite a void (presuming normal breaks).

Playing the Kantar 3NT opening, suppose that opener and responder pick up the following hands.

| Opener | Responder |
|--------|-----------|
| ♠ 109 | ♠ AQ85 |
| ♥ AKQJ762 | ♥ 5 |
| ♦ 42 | ♦ A83 |
| ♣ Q5 | ♣ AK1097 |

The bidding might proceed:

| | |
|-----------------|------------------|
| 3NT | 4♣ (Kings?) |
| 4♥ (No Kings) | 4NT (Queens?) |
| 5♣ (♣ Queen) | 7♥ |

Knowing that opener has a solid heart suit, responder wants to bid 7NT if opener holds the spade King; he will take 7 heart tricks, 3 spades, 1 diamond and 2 clubs, adding to 13. If opener holds the club Queen, responder will be happy to play in 7♥ with 7 heart tricks, 2 Aces and 4 likely club winners. As one of your author's high school football coaches was fond of saying after a touchdown by the good guys: "Just like we drew it up on the chalkboard!"

# DEFENSES AGAINST 4♥ AND 4♠

According to The Official Encyclopedia of Bridge:

> " Against an opponent's opening bid at the four level it is standard to use the calls of double and 4NT in a variety of ways, depending on the suit of the opening bid.... Against a 4♥ opening, a double is for takeout and guarantees spade support. The prevailing agreement is that a 4NT bid is takeout for the minors. Against a 4♠ opening a double is used for penalties. Hence a 4NT bid is for takeout."

These methods were standard practice for years and are still used by several fine pairs throughout the world. If they are the methods that your partnership feels most comfortable using, by all means continue to use them as your defense against four-level major suit openings. However, we recommend, and believe you should consider, the suggestions in the box on the following page.

Although doubles of both 4♥ and 4♠ are described as takeout doubles, they are converted to penalty doubles far more often than their lower-level brethren. The reason is simple. Lacking genuine prospects for going plus by playing the hand, the partner of a player who makes a takeout double of 4♥ or 4♠ will simply pass and hope to go plus knowing that partner has a good hand. Sometimes the penalty for your bid will be more expensive than the score for four of a major doubled, making. Four or five tricks are often available on defense when 10 or 11 are not available on offense.

# DEFENSES AGAINST 4♥ AND 4♠ PREEMPTS

(1) Double of 4♥ is takeout, guaranteeing support for spades.

(2) Double of 4♠ is takeout, showing support for the unbid suits.

(3) 4NT shows a two-suited hand and is for takeout.

(4) Overcalls are natural, promising a good hand with a good suit.

4NT in response to a takeout double of 4♥ or 4♠ is best played as a request for partner's minor, not as a conventional request for Aces (Blackwood). It is a useful tool for locating the best strain when responder holds both minors. We would bid 4NT over a takeout double of 4♥ with:

(a) ♠ 54  ♥ 7  ♦ KQ1053  ♣ Q9852

and might bid 4NT over partner's double of 4♠ holding:

(b) ♠ 532  ♥ 4  ♦ KQ107  ♣ A9832

depending on the vulnerability. Remember, with a good hand partner may not have perfect — or even near perfect — distribution when he makes a takeout double of 4♥ or 4♠. Use 4NT to locate your best trump suit.

## DEFENSES AGAINST NAMYATS

Actually, it is easier to defend against 4♣ (as a strong 4♥ opening) and 4♦ (as a strong 4♠ opening) — NAMYATS — than it is to combat natural 4♥ and 4♠ openings. The small amount of additional space (and the ability to pass and then act) often proves most helpful. In addition, you have a four-level cuebid of opener's real suit available.

Paul Soloway and Bobby Goldman, one of the world's best pairs, have a relatively simple defense against NAMYATS 4♣ and 4♦ openings that your authors like and use. The Soloway-Goldman defense is:

---

## SOLOWAY-GOLDMAN DEFENSE
## OVER 4♣ AND 4♦ NAMYATS

(1) A double of 4♣ or 4♦ shows a distributional takeout of opener's real suit. It does not show great high card strength.

(2) A double of 4♣ or 4♦ followed by a double of opener's suit shows a strong takeout.

(3) Pass of 4♣ or 4♦ followed by double of opener's suit is penalty-oriented.

(4) 4♥ over 4♣ shows a two-suiter with spades and a minor, at least 5/5. 4♠ over 4♦ shows a two-suiter with hearts and a minor, at least 5/5.

   Partner bids 4NT to locate the minor.

(5) 4NT over 4♣ or 4♦ shows the minors.

(6) Pass of 4♣ followed by 4♠ over 4♥ shows four spades and a longer minor.

(7) Overcalls are natural, showing a good hand with a good suit.

---

Using these conventional methods, the only thing you give up is the lead-directing double of 4♣ and 4♦, which is of dubious value and well compensated for by the scheme of doubles advocated by Soloway-Goldman.

Let us consider a few examples using this defense against NAMYATS. Suppose RHO opens 4♣ showing a strong 4♥ opening and you hold:

(a)     ♠ KJ107   ♥ 6   ♦ QJ106   ♣ AJ103

DOUBLE. A good illustration of a distributional takeout of hearts. The hand may belong to your side or you may have an economical sacrifice depending on the vulnerability.

(b)     ♠ AQ1097   ♥ 5   ♦ KQJ985   ♣ 7

BID 4♥. Typical "cuebid" of opener's real suit showing the other major and a minor.

RHO opens 4♦ (showing a strong 4♠ opener) and you have:

(c)     ♠ 3   ♥ AKQ1097   ♦ KJ95   ♣ 109

BID 4♥. A simple, natural four-level overcall which this hand and suit are worth.

(d)     ♠ 5   ♥ 7   ♦ AQ10652   ♣ KQ1094

BID 4NT. This is unusual for the minors.

Suppose your LHO opens 4♣ (showing a strong 4♥ opener), partner passes, RHO bids 4♥ and it is your turn. You are in essentially the same position you would have been if the opening bid had been 4♥, except you are armed with additional information about opener's hand, responder's hand (you know he does not have a slam try), and even partner's hand (to the limited extent that he could not act over 4♣). In this position, we recommend using the methods we suggested over 4♥ and 4♠ openings.

As we have said before, and no doubt will say again since it is worth repeating, competing effectively against your opponents' preemptive openings requires good judgment and firm partnership understandings. We added a third factor which often is equally as important as the two we just mentioned — a bit of luck. We have tried to assist you with the first two factors, and hope you are in possession of the third. You will need all three to successfully compete against your opponent's four-level major suit openings.

# CHAPTER 6

# OTHER PREEMPTIVE WEAPONS
## COMPLETING YOUR PREEMPTIVE ARSENAL

Our discussion of preemptive methods and tactics so far has been confined to opening bids.  There are many other situations when you can use preemptive methods to make life difficult for your opponents — the prime objective of all preemptive bids.

1. Preemptive Jump Overcalls:  when the enemy opens the bidding and you have a weak hand with a long suit;

2. Preemptive Jump Raises:  when partner opens the bidding at the one-level and you have an excellent fit for partner's suit with a weak hand;

3. Preemptive Jump Shifts:  when partner opens the bidding at the one-level and you have a weak hand with a long suit; and,

4. Preemptive Jump Shifts and Raises in Competition:  when partner overcalls and you hold a weak hand with a good fit for partner's suit or a good, long suit of your own.

It is just as important to have effective preemptive methods in these situations as it is when you have the opportunity to make a preemptive opening bid. The modern trend toward reducing strength requirements for opening bids makes this increasingly important.

In this chapter we will deal with preemptive methods and tactics after one-level openings by either side. First, we will consider various preemptive calls made after the enemy opens with a bid of one of a suit. Then we will review preemptive responses and rebids when your side opens the bidding at the one-level. Finally, we will briefly consider preemptive ploys when partner has intervened after an opponent opens the bidding.

## TWO-LEVEL PREEMPTIVE JUMP OVERCALLS

Preemptive jump overcalls are not a product of the modern bridge era. According to The Official Encyclopedia of Bridge, preemptive jump overcalls were an innovation of the Four Aces in the 1930s and credited to Oswald Jacoby.

Despite their nearly universal acceptance today, preemptive jump overcalls have not always been popular. For years, strong jump overcalls were advocated by Charles Goren and his legion of followers. Subsequently, intermediate jump overcalls (showing a good suit and the values for a sound opening bid) were in vogue. Eventually, however, the double value of the preemptive jump overcall — describing a hand clearly and simply in one bid while depriving opponents of potentially valuable bidding space — caused Goren and other experts to incorporate preemptive jump overcalls into their bidding systems.

Originally, a preemptive jump overcall showed the equivalent of an opening weak two-bid: approximately 6-12 HCP and a six-card (or perhaps even seven-card) suit. Most experts discarded these lofty requirements years ago, considering them too restrictive.

Experts today continue to make preemptive jump overcalls on hands that would qualify for opening weak two-bids. Preemptive jump overcalls no longer require good six-card suits, and they almost never contain the upper range of the traditional 6-12 HCP.

Opposite a passed partner, however, especially at unfavorable vulnerability, upper range tactical preemptive jump overcalls can be quite effective.

The factors to consider when contemplating a preemptive jump overcall are almost exactly the same as those for an opening preempt.

(1)     Suit length and quality.
(2)     Vulnerability.
(3)     Level.
(4)     Position.
(5)     Playing strength.
(6)     High cards outside your suit.
(7)     Partnership agreements and understandings.
(8)     Partner and opponents.
(9)     State of your game or match.

These elements combine to determine whether the odds favor, or are against, a preemptive jump overcall (add the "luck" factor and you have the true odds).

Your authors favor the modern trend toward aggressive attacking preemptive jump overcalls. The benefits of such tactics outweigh the relatively rare disaster. These advantages include:

(1)     Taking away potentially valuable bidding space from the enemy when the hand most likely belongs to their side;

(2)     Describing a weak one-suited hand;

(3)     Alerting partner immediately to your lack of defense. This may enable him to disrupt the opponent's orderly exchange of information while allowing you to find an economical sacrifice.

(4)     Narrowing the range of your simple over-calls, since you no longer make simple overcalls with weak one-suited hands.

We recommend the following requirements for two-level preemptive jump overcalls:

# REQUIREMENTS FOR TWO-LEVEL PREEMPTIVE JUMP OVERCALLS

(1)   A reasonable six-card suit. Non-vulnerable, and particularly at favorable vulnerability, a good five-card suit, by partnership agreement.

(2)   Typically 2-8 HCP.

(3)   A one-suited hand.

(4)   At most one Ace or King outside your suit.

(5)   Preferably, no Aces and no voids.

Using these guidelines, what action would you take over a natural 1♣ opening at favorable vulnerability holding:

(a)   ♠ AK10652  ♥ 7  ♦ J1094  ♣ 86
OVERCALL 1♠. This is **not** a preemptive jump overcall, particularly non-vulnerable versus vulnerable. You could easily miss a game by bidding 2♠ with this hand. This is a sound, one-level overcall.

(b)   ♠ KQJ98  ♥ 7  ♦ J1098  ♣ 542
OVERCALL 2♠. Here is a good example of a reasonable preemptive jump overcall made with a five-card suit. All conditions are ideal: vulnerability, position, internal trump strength, lack of outside defensive strength and maximum space consumption.

(c)   ♠ QJ109652  ♥ 6  ♦ 52  ♣ QJ10
OVERCALL 3♠. Your suit is ideal and your outside strength is acceptable for a jump overcall. At favorable vulnerability, you have enough playing strength to bid at the three-level.

Responding to a two-level preemptive jump overcall is quite similar to responding to partner's opening weak two-bid. In fact, as the following box outlines, we recommend almost an identical responding structure.

---

## RESPONSES TO TWO-LEVEL PREEMPTIVE JUMP OVERCALLS

(1) 2NT is a conventional inquiry, asking partner for a further description of his hand. Overcaller responds via Ogust.

      3♣ = minimum strength; poor suit.
      3♦ = maximum strength; poor suit.
      3♥ = minimum strength; good suit.
      3♠ = maximum strength; good suit.
      3NT = solid suit (UNLIKELY!).

(2) 3♣ asks partner to bid his short suit. He responds by bidding:

• His suit if he has no outside shortness.
• A new suit, showing shortness.
• 3NT with club shortness.

(3) Simple raises are preemptive; they are not invitations to game.

(4) Jump raises in response to 2♥ and 2♠ may be either preemptive or bid to make. Jump raises to the four-level in the minors are preemptive.

(5) New suits are natural and **non-forcing**.

(6) Jumps to 3NT or game in new suits are to play.

---

An aggressive preemptive jump overcall coupled with these responses helped your authors finish second in the 1993 North American Mixed Pairs Championship. Here is the complete deal and our auction:

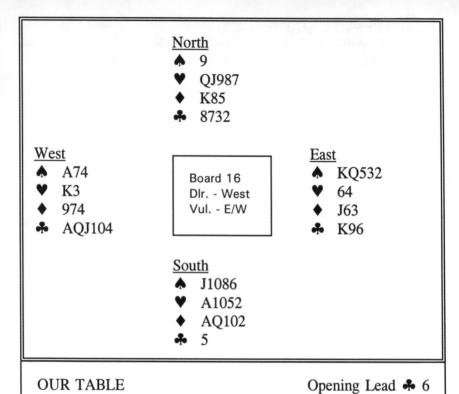

North
- ♠ 9
- ♥ QJ987
- ♦ K85
- ♣ 8732

West
- ♠ A74
- ♥ K3
- ♦ 974
- ♣ AQJ104

Board 16
Dlr. - West
Vul. - E/W

East
- ♠ KQ532
- ♥ 64
- ♦ J63
- ♣ K96

South
- ♠ J1086
- ♥ A1052
- ♦ AQ102
- ♣ 5

OUR TABLE

Opening Lead ♣ 6
N/S +420

| West | *Zenkel*<br>North | East | *Andersen*<br>South |
|------|-------------------|------|---------------------|
| 1♣ | 2♥ (a) | Dbl. (b) | 3♣ (c) |
| Dbl. | 3♠ (d) | Dbl. | 4♥ (e) |
| P | P | P | |

(a)   A "weak" jump overcall in ideal conditions playing match-points (which excuses a multitude of sins and excesses).
(b)   Negative double.
(c)   Conventional inquiry asking for shortness (not a cuebid).
(d)   Shortness in spades.
(e)   "BINGO!" Just what South hoped for when he bid 3♣.

Plus 420 was an excellent score on a deal where several N/S pairs did not enter the auction.  The keys were North's jump overcall based on a five-card suit and South's conventional 3♣ inquiry.

# HIGHER-LEVEL PREEMPTIVE
# JUMP OVERCALLS

As the level of your preemptive jump overcall is elevated, so must the length and quality of your suit increase. Vulnerability becomes a more important factor and playing strength must be considered.

As with preemptive openings, the recommended playing strength for preemptive jump overcalls should come from your suit, not outside high card strength. Your partnership needs to have clear understandings about what constitutes a simple jump overcall, and double- and triple-jump overcalls. Here are our suggestions:

---

## REQUIREMENTS FOR PREEMPTIVE JUMP OVERCALLS AT THE THREE-LEVEL AND BEYOND

(1)   Your suits should be six cards in length at the three-level; and you need a good seven-card (or frequently an eight-card) suit to preempt at the four-level.

(2)   Your playing strength, determined by the level and vulnerability, must be agreed upon by your partnership.

(3)   ALL preemptive jump overcalls should be made with one-suited hands (possible exceptions are the rare jumps to 4♥ and 4♠).

(4)   Your strength outside trumps should never include more than one Ace or King and should never include an outside void when bidding below 4♥.

(5)   All preemptive jump overcalls should be avoided with outside "Quacks."

---

Using these guidelines, what action would you take over an opening 1♦ bid at favorable vulnerability holding:

   (a)    ♠ 7632  ♥ KQJ9852  ♦ 2  ♣ 5

OVERCALL 3♥, at least. We would not be critical of a 4♥ bid with this hand. If you are concerned about the four-card spade suit, don't be. Your spades are weak; this is a one-suited hand.

   (b)    ♠ KQJ1097  ♥ 7  ♦ J1095  ♣ 85

OVERCALL 3♠ — at this vulnerability. If you bid 2♠ you have missed the boat regarding the advantages of aggressive preempts. (We also recommend that you read Chapter 8 on Bergen Preempts while lying down, and only after consulting with your cardiologist.)

   (c)    ♠ KQ76532  ♥ K  ♦ QJ  ♣ Q105

OVERCALL 1♠. Much as we like to preempt, making a jump overcall on this type of hand is most likely to give you **three** opponents: RHO, LHO and partner! You simply have too much outside strength, (particularly the "Quacks"), to consider anything other than a simple overcall.

Now consider a few examples after a 1♥ opening with both sides vulnerable. In second seat you hold:

   (a)    ♠ K1087  ♥ 54  ♦ 7  ♣ KQJ1087

OVERCALL 2♣. We might venture 3♣ if partner were a passed hand, but it is far too dangerous to preempt in front of partner with this type of hand; you might miss a spade game. Although most two-level vulnerable overcalls typically contain more strength, the advantages of bidding outweigh the disadvantages. A 3♣ bid would be more attractive after a 1 ♦ opening (although we would still advise bidding a simple 2♣).

(b)    ♠ J1098543  ♥ 3  ♦ 7  ♣ QJ109
OVERCALL 3♠. The 10-9-8 of spades and 10-9 of clubs tip the scales in favor of an aggressive double-jump overcall.

On the following hands the vulnerability is unfavorable and RHO opens 1♠. Choose your overcall holding:

(a)    ♠ 7  ♥ QJ10962  ♦ J1074  ♣ J10
Discretion being the better part of valor, we sadly confess that we would PASS. Bidding 3♥ rates to produce a minus 800: a "toll-free" number. A 3♥ bid alerts the opponents to the distribution around the table, and may keep them out of a hopeless slam. Spades outranks hearts; do not start a bidding war you cannot win.

(b)    ♠ 6  ♥ 7  ♦ AQJ10965  ♣ J1095
OVERCALL 3♦. Yes, on a bad day 3♦ would be a "toll-free" number. But even if the enemy can get you for 800, it is far from clear that they actually WILL. This looks like a preemptive jump overcall at unfavorable vulnerability, so make one.

Responding to three- and four-level preemptive jump overcalls does not require conventions, special treatments or sophisticated methods. It requires discretion, good judgment and a bit of luck. Our advice is to be practical. The partner of the player who has made a preemptive jump overcall will usually pass. With a fit, and appropriate values, raise partner's preempt immediately to the highest possible level (keeping the LAW in mind). Without a fit, beware of introducing your own suit at a high level if you will need help from partner: chances are he will not have it. Reserve penalty doubles for hands that require only that partner "follow suit" (e.g., not revoke) in order to defeat the enemy contract.

This concludes our discussion of preemptive jump overcalls. Add them to your arsenal of preemptive weapons with many of the (responding) agreements you have for opening preempts.

## PREEMPTS WHEN YOUR SIDE OPENS THE BIDDING

The strength required for one-level openings has been considerably reduced over the years. As a result, the possibility that the hand belongs to the side that does not open the bidding has increased dramatically. Therefore, preemptive measures are often most useful to the side that opens when responder has little overall strength but either a long suit or good fit for opener's suit.

A good illustration of a popular preemptive tool by the side that opens is the inverted minor suit raise. Playing inverted minor suit raises, a single raise in a minor is constructive and forcing for at least one round, and a jump raise to three of opener's minor is preemptive. The illustration of a non-vulnerable inverted raise to a 1♣ opening given in The Official Encyclopedia of Bridge is:

♠ 653   ♥ 82   ♦ 93   ♣ J97643

The article continues, "if vulnerable, the bidder should have a singleton." Disciples of the LAW would agree to make a jump raise holding six-card support; even if opener has only three clubs, the partnership has at least a nine-card fit, putting the LAW on their side.

The founding fathers of bridge decreed that jump raises of major suit openings promised a fit and a minimum of game-forcing values. Subsequently, (after considerable debate), limit jump raises of 1♥ and 1♠ openings showing a fit and invitational values were universally accepted in the world of tournament bridge. Today, the concept of preemptive jump raises of major suit openings is becoming increasingly popular.

There are two reasons for the almost universal acceptance of inverted minor suit raises and increasing popularity of preemptive jump major suit raises by experts. Other vehicles are available and often are more effective to describe stronger raises. There is an increasing recognition of the importance of being able to preempt the bidding when responder has a weak hand and a good fit for opener's suit.

Playing preemptive jump raises of major suit openings, we would raise 1♠ to 3♠ (irrespective of the vulnerability) with:

(a)    ♠ J1095  ♥ 7  ♦ J109542  ♣ 85

(b)    ♠ QJ103  ♥ 109652  ♦ 2  ♣ 542

If you like the concept of playing preemptive jump raises over 1♥ and 1♠ openings, the obvious question is: "How does responder show a limit or forcing raise?" The most popular scheme of raising major suits that includes preemptive jump raises is the following:

---

## BERGEN RAISES OF MAJOR SUIT OPENINGS

Over an opening bid of 1♥ or 1♠:

(1)    A single raise shows 7-10 HCP with three-card support.

(2)    3♣ shows 7-10 HCP with four-card (or more) support.

(3)    3♦ shows a limit raise with four-card (or more) support and typically 10+ to 11+ points in support of the major.

(4)    An initial forcing notrump followed by a jump raise shows a limit raise with three-card support.

(5)    A direct jump raise is preemptive, promising four-card support (or more) with 0-6 HCP.

(6)    2NT is a forcing raise with at least four-card support and at least game-forcing values. (Jacoby 2NT).

---

The Goldman-Soloway partnership plays preemptive jump raises in the majors with simpler responses showing hands that have limit or strong values in support of opener's suit. Since they prefer to retain 2NT as a natural notrump call, (instead of as a conventional raise), they play that 3♣ over a 1♥ or 1♠ opening is a strong forcing raise, and 3♦ over the one-level major suit opening shows a limit raise. They also play various splinter bids.

Either of these approaches, as well as several others, are perfectly playable. They all enable you to play preemptive jump raises in the majors while retaining the ability to describe stronger hands with support for partner's major in simple fashion.

The concept of jump raising opener's major suit opening with a good fit and a poor hand is not new. In the 1930s, the vast majority of players used jump raises over 1♥ and 1♠ openings as preemptive after an enemy takeout double. Similarly, most expert partnerships today play jump raises of partner's 1♥ or 1♠ openings as preemptive after their opponents have intervened with an overcall. The same is true for many good partnerships after an overcall of a 1♣ or 1♦ opening: jumps to the three-level in opener's minor are preemptive as they would be in non-competitive auctions playing inverted minor suit raises.

We urge you to adopt preemptive jump raises of partner's opening bid after overcalls and takeout doubles. There are simple ways to show limit or stronger raises of opener's suit after intervention, cuebids being the most obvious and widely-used choice.

We have seen that when you have a weak hand and a fit for partner, a preemptive jump raise is effective in making life difficult for your opponents. Now let us turn to hands where you do not have a fit.

You pick up one of the following at favorable vulnerability:

(a)  ♠ QJ10965  ♥ 7  ♦ J1074  ♣ J2

(b)  ♠ KJ1098  ♥ 3  ♦ J87  ♣ 10984

(c)  ♠ 5  ♥ KJ109762  ♦ 1097  ♣ 94

(d)  ♠ K107  ♥ QJ109754  ♦ 5  ♣ 109

If you were the dealer, you would most likely venture a preemptive 2♠ bid with (a) or (b) and commence the bidding with 3♥ holding (c) or (d). (All are in accord with our previous discussions of such openings). If RHO were the dealer and opened 1♣, you would have no trouble with any of these hands playing preemptive jump overcalls. With (a) or (b) you would jump to 2♠ over 1♣; with (c) or (d) our choice over 1♣ would be 3♥.

Now we are going to complicate things a bit. Suppose it is partner, not RHO, who opens the bidding with 1♣, and RHO passes. Lacking the methods we recommend and are about to describe, you most likely would respond 1♠ with (a) or (b) and 1♥ with (c) or (d). Unfortunately, the relatively "unlimited" responses of 1♥ or 1♠ over 1♣ do not disclose your weakness or reveal your long suit. There is a way to inform partner immediately of both: **preemptive** jump shift responses. Playing preemptive jump shift responses, you can respond 2♠ with (a) or (b) and jump to 3♥ with (c) or (d) over partner's 1♣ opening.

When you describe the exact nature of your hand to opener immediately, he can determine the best course of action for your side quickly and easily. In addition, you have the advantage of preempting your opponents, which may be important, particularly if the hand belongs to their side.

The usual question that arises regarding preemptive jump shift responses is: "How weak can a preemptive jump shift response be?" Our answer is: "WEAK"! To be more specific, a Preemptive Jump Shift (hereafter abbreviated to PJS) is generally made with responding hands containing less than the time-honored standard of six points required for a simple one-level response to an opening one-bid. Therefore, the precise high-card strength shown by a PJS is zero to five (and we do mean zero).

Miami expert Janice Seamon picked up the following hand:

♠ 1087542   ♥ 7   ♦ 9842   ♣ 96

(which could make several good Cribbage hands) and made what turned out to be a devastatingly effective PJS response to a 1♦ opening bid made by one of your authors. Here is the complete deal, auction and result at both tables.

```
                         North
                         ♠  QJ
                         ♥  Q96
                         ♦  65
                         ♣  A87432

West                  ┌─────────────┐      East
♠  K963               │  Board 12   │      ♠  1087542
♥  1032               │  Dlr. - West│      ♥  7
♦  AQJ10              │  Vul. - N/S │      ♦  9842
♣  K10                └─────────────┘      ♣  96

                         South
                         ♠  A
                         ♥  AKJ854
                         ♦  K73
                         ♣  QJ5
```

---

OUR TABLE                                Opening Lead ♥ K
                                                    N/S +50

| *Zenkel* |  | *Seamon* |  |
|---|---|---|---|
| West | North | East | South |
| 1♦ | P | 2♠ (a) | 3♥ |
| 4♠ (b) | P (c) | P (d) | P (e) |

(a)  Minimum HCP for any hand.
(b)  Unable to take a joke, and taking advantage of the vulnerability with an excellent fit.
(c)  Not quite enough to bid; the Queen-Jack doubleton of spades is more than likely to be worthless on defense and offense.
(d)  "I hope my insurance is paid."
(e)  Conservative, but any action is far from 100%.

At the other table (hand repeated for convenience):

```
                      North
                   ♠  QJ
                   ♥  Q96
                   ♦  65
                   ♣  A87432

West                                      East
♠  K963          ┌─────────────┐         ♠  1087542
♥  1032          │  Board 12   │         ♥  7
♦  AQJ10         │  Dlr. - West│         ♦  9842
♣  K10           │  Vul. - N/S │         ♣  96
                 └─────────────┘
                      South
                   ♠  A
                   ♥  AKJ854
                   ♦  K73
                   ♣  QJ5
```

---

THEIR TABLE                    Opening Lead ♥ 2
                                      N/S +710

|       | *O'Grady* |       | *Moore* |
|-------|-----------|-------|---------|
| West  | North     | East  | South   |
| 1♦    | P         | P     | Dbl.    |
| P     | 2♣        | P     | 2♥      |
| P     | 3♥        | P     | 4♥      |
| P     | P         | P     |         |

The 12 IMPs Zenkel and Seamon picked up on this board were decisive in winning the seven-board match against the leaders. Our team went on to win the 1992 Fort Lauderdale Regional Ladies Teams.

---

Note that Seamon's 2♠ response to the 1♦ opening bid made life extremely difficult for the opponents. They had to settle for a paltry +50. When East made an initial pass at the other table, our teammates had an unobstructed road straight to a cold game (which happened to be a cold slam due to a passive opening lead and a fortuitous lie of the cards).

When responder makes a preemptive response to the opening bid, opener rarely has a tough decision. Armed with considerable knowledge about responder's hand, he will usually know what is best for his side.

There is one remaining preemptive tactic available to the side that opens the bidding at the one-level that many partnerships fail to utilize. Consider the following auction playing matchpoints:

| West | North | East | South |
|------|-------|------|-------|
| 1♥ | P | 2♥ | P |
| P | ??? | | |

It does not require the judgment of an Al Roth, the aggressiveness of Meck-Well, or the knowledge of the "Law of Total Tricks" possessed by Larry Cohen or Marty Bergen, for North to balance. Even at other forms of scoring, it is rarely right to permit your opponents to play at the two-level after they have clearly found a fit; you probably have one also.

Consequently, it is best to play **preemptive re-raises** in these auctions. A preemptive re-raise is a three-level rebid by opener in his own suit which has been raised by responder. It is not an effort to reach game, but is used to make it harder for the opponents to bid. Responder is expected to pass this rebid irrespective of the strength of his initial raise. On the following auction, 3♥ is a preemptive re-raise, not a game try:

| West | North | East | South |
|------|-------|------|-------|
| 1♥ | P | 2♥ | P |
| 3♥ | | | |

For his bid, West might hold something like:

♠ 7  ♥ AQJ872  ♦ KJ52  ♣ 76

and it is not inconceivable that the hand actually belongs to the enemy. The opponents could score nine, ten or eleven tricks in spades or clubs, so even -50 in 3♥ rates to be a very good result.

With a different hand and invitational values, West would have to find a different call to invite East to continue on to game. This is rarely a hardship since with invitational values opener can usually find a better and more helpful game try than a simple re-raise of his own suit.

## PREEMPTIVE RESPONSES TO OVERCALLS

For even more (and better) reasons than those we used to advocate preemptive jump raises of opening one-bids, we urge you to play preemptive jump raises of overcalls. The only difference we recommend in their treatment is that the preemptive jump raise of an overcall should be a bit stronger than a preemptive jump raise of an opening bid. The reason is simple. An overcall, particularly at the one-level, may be based on considerably less strength than even a minimum opening bid.

Although we would make a sporting preemptive jump raise of partner's 1 ♠ opening (particularly non-vulnerable) on as little as:

(a)　　♠ Q1095　♥ 76　♦ 109842　♣ 85

or

(b)　　♠ 98732　♥ 85　♦ 92　♣ Q1094

we recommend a bit more for a preemptive jump raise of an overcall. By a bit more, we do not necessarily mean more HCP; a singleton would do at favorable vulnerability. Remember, the more aggressive your overcalls, the more partner must have for a jump raise of your overcall.

The danger in attacking your opponents with preemptive jump raises of overcalls is not simply that you will get doubled and suffer a large set (although that is a possibility). There is also the danger that you will buy the hand undoubled and go for more than the enemy partscore. This is particularly true when you are vulnerable and -200 hits the recap sheet playing matchpoints. To avoid these traps, we recommend the following requirements for a preemptive jump raise of partner's overcall:

# REQUIREMENTS FOR MAKING
## A PREEMPTIVE JUMP RAISE
## OF PARTNER'S OVERCALL

(1)   Four-card (or longer) trump support.   The better your trump support, the less outside strength you need.

(2)   One VALUE outside of your trump support; often a distributional value (preferred).

(3)   NEVER more than an Ace or King outside trumps, even at unfavorable vulnerability.

(4)   Preferably, no outside Ace.

(5)   Preferably, no "Quacks."

(6)   Preferably, an unbalanced hand with a side five-card suit.

Depending on the vulnerability, the minimum requirements for a preemptive jump raise of an overcall are fairly clear:  good trump support and an outside "value" (not necessarily a high card, often distributional).  The maximum strength for a preemptive jump raise of an overcall should also be clearly defined.   We favor the following understanding:  **A jump raise of an overcall is always weaker than a distributional limit raise of an opening bid.**  With a distributional limit raise of partner's overcall, make a jump cuebid in opener's suit.

When both sides are vulnerable or your side is at unfavorable vulnerability, the additional values required for a preemptive jump raise should not come from outside high card strength; the additional strength should be in trump support or distributional assets.

To put theory into practice, consider a few examples of potential preemptive jump raises after partner's overcall.  With neither side vulnerable, partner overcalls LHO's opening 1♦ bid with 1♥ and RHO passes.  You hold:

(a) ♠ 72  ♥ QJ74  ♦ 83  ♣ Q10954

RESPOND 3♥.  In support and playing strength, this hand is not a disappointment. We would be delighted if partner always held something like this when making a preemptive jump raise of our overcalls.

(b) ♠ 7  ♥ Q10952  ♦ A43  ♣ J1095

RESPOND 3♦.  This is a perfect illustration of a distributional limit raise:  five trump, a singleton, and seven potentially useful HCP.  This hand is far too strong for a preemptive jump raise to 3♥, particularly when not vulnerable.  (If we did not play that a jump cuebid of 3♦ was a distributional limit raise of an overcall, we would raise to 2♥.  We would bid 4♥ if we desperately needed a good result, but we would never bid 3♥).

With both sides vulnerable, partner overcalls 2♣ after a 1♦ opening, and RHO passes.  You hold:

(a) ♠ 7  ♥ K1095  ♦ 873  ♣ Q10542

RESPOND 4♣.  The enemy rates to have at least an eight-card spade fit and few club losers.  Make it difficult for them to get together by jumping to 4♣.  Note that preemptive jump raises DO apply over two-level minor suit overcalls.

(b) ♠ K104  ♥ 52  ♦ K1098  ♣ 8732

RESPOND 3♣.  A preemptive jump raise could easily take you past your side's only makeable game contract, 3NT.  The danger of the opponents successfully getting together is not nearly as great as it was with the previous hand.  This hand has more defensive potential against an enemy contract than (a).

Now let us consider a couple of examples at unfavorable vulnerability. LHO opens 1♦, partner overcalls 1♠ and RHO passes. You hold:

(a)  ♠ J1094  ♥ 7  ♦ 76  ♣ AJ10953
RESPOND 3♦. Do not even consider making a preemptive jump raise with this hand. Your choices are between showing a distributional limit raise (via a jump cuebid of 3♦) and jumping directly to game. With a conservative partner it is probably best to jump directly to 4♠.

(b)  ♠ Q9832  ♥ 7  ♦ 652  ♣ QJ109
RESPOND 3♠. Despite the vulnerability, this hand appears to have all the essential features for a preemptive jump raise. You have 5 trumps, a singleton, a side suit with concentrated values, good offense and little defense.

Preemptive jump raises are not affected when RHO bids over partner's overcall. For example, 3♠ is preemptive in both of the following auctions:

| West | North | East | South |
|------|-------|------|-------|
| 1♦ | 1♠ | Dbl. (neg.) | 3♠ |

| West | North | East | South |
|------|-------|------|-------|
| 1♥ | 1♠ | 2♣ | 3♠ |

Preemptive jump raises of overcalls are actually more useful when RHO bids, since that increases the likelihood that the hand belongs to the enemy. When you preempt on these auctions, it is quite likely that you are denying your opponents the valuable bidding space they may require to reach their optimum contract.

Our final recommendation of a useful preemptive tactic after partner overcalls requires very little discussion. In the following auction, South's 2♠ or 3♦ bids would be preemptive:

| West | North | East | South |
|------|-------|------|-------|
| 1♣ | 1♥ | P | 2♠/3♦ |

For the 2♠ bid, South might hold:

♠ QJ10873   ♥ 74   ♦ J1085   ♣ 3

Since the level is higher, South's 3♦ call might look like:

♠ 76   ♥ J3   ♦ KQ107652   ♣ 83

The same guidelines and considerations apply here that we discussed at the beginning of this chapter regarding preemptive jump overcalls. If the quality of your suit is reasonable, there is less danger in making a preemptive jump shift after partner overcalls, since partner rates to have a useful card or two.

This concludes our discussion of standard preemptive openings, responses and rebids, as well as preemptive tactics when the enemy opens the bidding. We have come a long way since we considered 2♥ and 2♠ openings in Chapter 2. We hope this has been a useful trip so far and that you now have:

(1)   An idea or two that you can profitably add to your preemptive arsenal;

(2)   A better understanding of your opponents' traditional preempts, and how to defend against them; and

(3)   Sufficient cause to look forward to the second part of this book which addresses modern preemptive tactics.

Speaking of PART TWO of this book, we are ready, if you are.

# PART TWO

## NON-TRADITIONAL
## PREEMPTIVE OPENINGS

Having reviewed and updated the traditional two-, three-, four- and five-level openings — as well as preemptive overcalls, responses and rebids — it is time to turn our attention to the non-traditional preemptive openings that are increasing in number and popularity. We will not attempt to see how many non-traditional preempts we can present; that would be neither practical nor particularly useful. Our goal is to present those preemptive vehicles that have either stood the test of time or have been accepted and endorsed by experts on both sides of the Atlantic.

To accomplish this objective, we will begin with the most popular and widely-accepted non-traditional preempt: MULTI. It has stood the test of time, and variations have been developed which are currently being played throughout the world. Our discussion will continue with Two Under preempts and Two-Way Two-Level preempts. We will conclude with a look at the new breed of artificial preemptive openings designed to describe both one- and two-suited hands with limited strength.

All the bids, responses and rebids that will be discussed in Part Two are for experienced, well-established partnerships. They require considerable study and practice, in addition to clearly understood partnership agreements. Without these ingredients, the methods described in Part Two will be as effective as a recipe for mayonnaise without eggs. As any good cook or chef can tell you, for really good mayonnaise you have to break some eggs!

Should you elect to adopt any of the openings presented in the following chapters, make sure they are allowed in the event in which you are playing. Several may only be played in the major events at North American Championships or in international tournaments. Others are permitted at lower levels. For your protection, check with a tournament director (or tournament organizer) for the restrictions regarding conventions.

Even if you decide not to adopt any of the methods presented in Part Two, these chapters contain much useful information. If you play in North American Championships, ACBL open events or in the international arena, you will be confronted with an increasing number of non-traditional preempts. We have presented counter-measures to most of the artificial preemptive openings discussed and you will find this knowledge quite helpful.

One observation before you embark on Part Two: since much of the material may be new to you, or less familiar than the subjects discussed in the first six chapters, you will find more examples and illustrations in the following chapters. Carefully consider the various examples and illustrations; they will simplify and clarify the guidelines we present.

# CHAPTER 7

# MULTICOLORED TWO DIAMOND OPENINGS

## "MULTI"

Outside North America, a Multi 2♦ opening is frequently used to describe a weak two-bid in hearts or spades. Multi was devised in Great Britain in the 1960s by the great British expert Jeremy Flint. It is called Multi because the opening bid can have several different meanings, with subsequent calls indicating which type of hand the opener holds. In general, a 2♦ opening bid shows a strong balanced hand, a 4-4-4-1 (any singleton), or (most frequently) a weak two-bid in either hearts or spades, with strength in accord with partnership agreement. You would open 2♦ with any of the following hands:

| | | |
|---|---|---|
| ♠ KQ10975 ♥ 5 ♦ J109 ♣ 874 | (weak 2♠) |
| ♠ 85 ♥ AQJ1093 ♦ 74 ♣ 632 | (weak 2♥) |
| ♠ KQJ2 ♥ KQ104 ♦ AK105 ♣ 7 | (4-4-4-1) |
| ♠ KJ10 ♥ AQ104 ♦ KQ75 ♣ AQ | (strong balanced hand) |

The Multi 2♦ opening permits partnerships to use opening bids of 2♥ and 2♠ for other purposes and often transfers the play in opener's suit to responder. In addition, it has the advantage of being far more difficult to defend against than a simple weak two-bid. The only disadvantages of the Multi 2♦ opening are that responder: (1) does not know immediately which suit opener has if he holds a preemptive two-bid, and (2) will not know immediately whether or not partner holds a strong hand. However, this convention has plenty of advantages to compensate for its relatively short list of disadvantages.

As Flint's original Multi 2♦ opening became popular, several modifications and improved responses were designed. In this chapter we will review both the comparatively simple versions of the Multi 2♦ opening and the more complex ones. We will begin with the least complicated, appropriately called the Mini-Multicolored 2♦ opening.

## MINI-MULTICOLORED 2♦

The Mini-Multicolored (hereafter called Mini-Multi) 2♦ opening uses the opening bid of 2♦ to show a weak two-bid in hearts or spades. It describes no other hand types.

In theory, the Mini-Multi 2♦ opening, like all multicolored 2♦ openers, is forcing. Responder should not pass unless he holds a very long diamond suit, very poor support for either major, and no interest in game.

The requirements for a Mini-Multi 2♦ opening are exactly the same as your partnership's agreements for a simple preemptive two-bid.

If your partnership favors a more aggressive approach for an opening two-bid, then your requirements for a Mini-Multi 2♦ opening will be correspondingly reduced.

If your partnership favors a sound, conservative approach to weak two-bids, then the following box (similar to the one that appeared in Chapter 2) describes your requirements:

# REQUIREMENTS FOR CONSERVATIVE MINI-MULTI 2♦ OPENING

(1) A good six-card suit with at least two of the top four honors.

(2) 5-11 HCP, with a majority of the points in the suit opened.

(3) A one-suited hand. You may occasionally have a four-card minor, but **never** four cards in the other major.

(4) Preferably, no more than one Ace or King outside your real suit.

(5) Preferably, no void(s).

Following these guidelines, the following hands are good examples of conservative Mini-Multi 2♦ bids.

(a)     ♠ KQJ984  ♥ 52  ♦ K109  ♣ 85

(b)     ♠ 7  ♥ AKJ1073  ♦ 865  ♣ J104

After a 2♦ opening, responder bids 2♥ if he has no interest in getting beyond the two-level in either major. If responder is interested in going further in spades but not hearts, he temporizes by responding 2♥. If opener bids 2♠, responder may raise invitationally to 3♠ or jump to game with appropriate values.

If responder is willing to play on the three-level when partner's suit is hearts, he responds 2♠. With a minimum weak two-bid in hearts, opener will bid 3♥; with a maximum he can make a game try without bypassing 3♥.

With sufficient strength for an invitation to game, partner responds 2NT, inquiring about opener's hand strength and suit. Opener's scheduled responses are outlined in the following box. This structure often enables the strong hand to be declarer, a major advantage:

169

## RESPONSES TO THE 2NT INQUIRY OVER MINI-MULTI 2♦

(1)   3♣ = minimum weak two-bid in hearts.

(2)   3♦ = minimum weak two-bid in spades.

(3)   3♥ = maximum weak two-bid in hearts.

(4)   3♠ = maximum weak two-bid in spades.

A direct 3♣ or 3♦ response to a Mini-Multi 2♦ opening can be natural and forcing, invitational, or a sign-off. Although it is probably best to play 3♣ and 3♦ as either invitational or "to play" with matchpoint scoring, we favor making these responses forcing when playing IMPs where the emphasis is on reaching close games. This is especially true for 3♦ since responder always had the option of passing your 2♦ opening when he was looking at a long diamond suit with no interest in the majors and no interest in game.

Jumps to 3♥ and 3♠ in response to the Mini-Multi 2♦ opening are subject to various partnership agreements. Most partnerships play that 3♥ and 3♠ responses are "**pass** or **correct**," depending on opener's suit. This treatment enables responder to preempt with appropriate strength and a fit for partner (a jump to 4♥ over 2♦ can carry the same meaning). Alternatively, your partnership may elect to play jumps to the three-level in a major over 2♦ as natural and forcing.

Using the simple responding guidelines we have provided for the Mini-Multi 2♦ opening bid is easy. Consider the following hands and choose your response after partner opens 2♦:

(a)   ♠ KJ4   ♥ 7   ♦ A109652   ♣ A103
BID 2♥. You do not want to get higher than the two-level if opener's suit is hearts (which it probably is). When partner's suit is spades, he will correct 2♥ to 2♠. You will then make the appropriate raise to game.

(b)    ♠ J94   ♥ KJ   ♦ AJ1062   ♣ AJ7

BID 2NT. Ask partner to show his suit and describe his strength. Then you can set the final contract accurately.

(c)    ♠ 98   ♥ 109   ♦ AQ6543   ♣ A95

BID 2♥. Do not be tempted to pass 2♦. Your high cards will be useful with partner's suit as trump but partner's hand may be totally worthless for playing a diamond contract.

(d)    ♠ J   ♥ K74   ♦ KQ1085   ♣ A1052

BID 2♠. If partner's suit is hearts, game is likely; if opener's suit is spades, you do not want to play beyond the two-level. Over your 2♠ response, partner will pass with spades and correct to 3♥ with hearts (which you intend to raise). You have the advantage of actually bidding the enemy suit when partner holds hearts. This may prevent the opponents from bidding when they might have competed, or sacrificed, in spades.

Like the Mini-Multi 2♦ opening, the responses we have discussed are simple. Now let us move on to slightly more complicated methods.

# MECK-WELL MINI-MULTI 2♦

Prior to playing with David Berkowitz in the 1990 resumption of the <u>London Times</u> Invitational, one of your authors contacted Meck-Well regarding their recommendations for playing the Mini-Multi 2♦ opening when it is limited to describing a major suit weak two-bid. The following box is based on Meck-Well's suggestions:

# MECK-WELL'S REQUIREMENTS FOR OPENING A MINI-MULTI 2♦

Generally 4 to 10 HCP with a five, six or seven-card suit, depending on suit quality and vulnerability.

NONVULNERABLE:

(1)   4 to 9 HCP (poor 10 acceptable).

(2)   ANY hand with a six-card major and less than four cards in the other major.  No freak distributions (6-5 or greater).

(3)   Weak hands with weak seven-card suits that are unsuitable for a three-level opening.

(4)   A hand with a five-card suit that is at least QJ8xx in strength, as long as the hand does not have another suit that is substantially stronger.

VULNERABLE:

(1)   4 to 10 HCP.

(2)   Most hands with six-card suits, but not if the hand and suit are both weak.  In close decisions, the texture of the suit is the determining factor — Q86532 is a terrible suit whereas Q109875 is perfectly acceptable.

(3)   Seven-card suits where the hand and suit quality are unsuitable for a three-level preempt.

(4)   Strong five-card suits — QJ1098, KQ1097, KQJ87 or AKJ65.  Overall hand quality should also be reasonable.

Using Meck-Well's approach, 2♦ openers are made with a broad range of hands.  Vulnerability plays a larger role in determining whether a hand qualifies for a preemptive two-bid than it did in the approach described in Chapter 2. Using these guidelines, here are some examples Meck-Well gave:

(a)    ♠ A10   ♥ J97643   ♦ 985   ♣ 74
      OPEN 2♦ — Non-vulnerable only.

(b)    ♠ 72   ♥ QJ9432   ♦ A107   ♣ 85
      OPEN 2♦ — Any time.

(c)    ♠ AQ832   ♥ 7   ♦ K762   ♣ 983
      OPEN 2♦ — Non-vulnerable only.

(d)    ♠ 5   ♥ AQ1097   ♦ 754   ♣ K1093
      OPEN 2♦ — Any time.

(e)    ♠ Q976532   ♥ 7   ♦ Q104   ♣ 95
      OPEN 2♦ — Any time. (Vulnerable versus non-vulnerable your authors would recommend opening 2♦ only with an understanding partner.)

(f)    ♠ Q1098743   ♥ 7   ♦ QJ10   ♣ J10
      OPEN 2♦ — Vulnerable.
      OPEN 3♠ — Non-vulnerable.

(g)    ♠ Q5   ♥ KJ732   ♦ J85   ♣ 1093
      PASS. Your 5-3-3-2 distribution and the internal weakness of your heart suit tip the scales against opening.

(h)    ♠ 7   ♥ QJ954   ♦ AQ109   ♣ 984
      PASS. Even with favorable vulnerability you should pass; your diamond suit is much too strong relative to your hearts.

(i)    ♠ AQ1098   ♥ Q1076   ♦ 7   ♣ J104
      PASS. Your spade suit is perfectly acceptable for a 2♦ opening at any vulnerability. The problem is your four-card heart suit; you cannot afford to risk missing an excellent heart fit by telling partner you have a weak two-bid in spades.

(j)     ♠ KQJ1052   ♥ 7532   ♦ 87   ♣ 7

OPEN 2♦. Do NOT be a slave to rules. This is a classic weak two-bid, except for your four little hearts. "If you cannot bring yourself to open a two-bid in spades via 2♦ with four hearts, do what the authors of this book would do — put the ♥2 next to the ♦7 and THEN open 2♦," Eric suggested with a twinkle in his eyes.

Before reviewing the Meck-Well responding arsenal, consider a few principles that are important to keep in mind when partner has opened 2♦. These principles are:

(1)    Perfection in constructive bidding is not possible playing Meck-Well Mini-Multi 2♦. You must accept this principle or these 2♦ openings are not for you and your partnerships. You will generate an exceptionally high percentage of good results when you open 2♦; however, you will not always reach your optimum contract after a 2♦ opening when the hand belongs to your side.

(2)    The responses to 2♦ are designed to make the opening 2♦ bidder DUMMY as often as possible. This is a priority!

(3)    When responder has a strong hand and needs to know opener's major to determine the best final contract, he usually begins with the conventional 2NT inquiry.

(4)    The most frequent responses to 2♦ are based on the principle of "**pass** or **correct**."

(i)    When you open 2♦ and partner responds 2♥ (with the opponents silent), pass if your weak two-bid is in hearts and bid 2♠ if your suit is spades.

Partner's 2♥ bid informs you that he has no desire to go beyond the two-level if hearts was your suit (but he may be interested if you have spades).

(ii) When you open 2♦, LHO passes and partner bids 2♠, you will pass if your weak two-bid is in spades and take other action (described in the box that follows) if it is hearts. You must play in at least 3♥.

Keep these principles in mind while examining the following "**pass** or **correct**" responses Meck-Well recommend:

---

### MECK-WELL "PASS OR CORRECT" RESPONSES TO MINI-MULTI 2♦ OPENINGS

(1) Pass with long diamonds. You have **no** interest in either major and therefore — even with a good hand — no game interest.

(2) Bid 2♥, "**pass** or **correct**," showing a hand which would have passed an opening 2♥ bid. Partner will correct to 2♠ if his weak two is in spades.

(3) Bid 2♠, "pass or correct," showing NO INTEREST in spades and INTEREST in hearts (you would have bid 2♥ lacking interest in both majors). Opener then rebids:
- Pass with a weak two-bid in spades.
- 2NT with a minimum weak two-bid in hearts.
- 3♣ with a medium strength weak 2♥ bid.
- 3♦ with a maximum strength weak 2♥ bid.

---

Partner opens a Mini-Multi 2♦. What would you respond holding:

(a)     ♠ 85   ♥ J7   ♦ K1065   ♣ AK1043
        BID 2♥, intending to pass 2♠.

(b)     ♠ 7   ♥ QJ106   ♦ AK542   ♣ K95
        BID 2♠. If partner corrects, (which would
        be a pleasant surprise), you will bid 4♥
        even if opener shows a minimum.

With game interest, responder begins with 2NT when he needs to
know opener's suit and hand quality; opener's rebid often determines
the level and strain the partnership will reach. Opener's rebids are:

---

## MECK-WELL RESPONSES TO A 2NT INQUIRY AFTER A 2♦ MINI-MULTI OPENING

(1)   3♣ = minimum weak two-bid in light of the
      vulnerability. Responder bids:

    3♦ = Game Forcing, asking
      opener to bid the major
      he does **not** hold; opener
      rebids 3♥ with spades
      and 3♠ with hearts.

    3♥ = Opener should "**pass** or
      **correct**"

    3♠ = Opener should "**pass** or
      **correct**"

(2)   3♦ = a medium strength heart preempt.

(3)   3♥ = a medium strength spade preempt.

(4)   3♠ = a maximum strength heart preempt.

(5)   3NT = a maximum strength spade preempt.

Note that (2) through (5) make the strong hand declarer.

Responder's new suit bids after the 2NT inquiry are game
forcing.

---

Using these methods, choose your response to partner's 2NT inquiry after you have opened a Mini-Multi 2♦ holding:

(a)  ♠ AQ9832   ♥ J108   ♦ 85   ♣ 72
REBID 3♥. Show your medium strength weak two-bid in spades. At unfavorable vulnerability you might decide this looks like a minimum two-bid and respond 3♣.

(b)  ♠ AKJ984   ♥ 5   ♦ J109   ♣ 984
REBID 3NT. This is a maximum weak 2♠ bid, no matter what the vulnerability.

(c)  ♠ KJ1095   ♥ 7   ♦ J1065   ♣ 632
REBID 3♣. This is a minimum! If partner bids 3♦, a conventional game force, you show your spades by bidding 3♥.

(d)  ♠ 7   ♥ Q1076432   ♦ KJ2   ♣ 74
REBID 3♦. The seventh heart makes this a medium weak two-bid, not a minimum.

There is rarely a problem after a Mini-Multi 2♦ opening when responder wants to play in opener's suit or notrump. Most problems take place when responder has a suit of his own that he wishes to make trump. Responder has some options when he has his own suit.

With clubs, responder has two choices. He can bid 2NT and introduce clubs later, natural and game forcing, after partner's conventional response. Or he can bid 3♣ to play.

When responder holds diamonds, he also has two choices. He can pass the opening bid. To force, bid 3♦ over 2♦, natural.

With hearts, responder has three choices. To play at the lowest possible level, start with 2♥. If opener corrects to 2♠, sign off in 3♥. To invite, bid 2♥ and over partner's expected 2♠ rebid, bid 3♦, enabling opener to decline the game try by bidding 3♥. To play 4♥, begin with 2NT, then jump to 4♥.

With spades, responder also has three choices. To play at the lowest possible level, start with 2♠. If opener corrects to 3♥, sign off in 3♠. To invite, bid 3♠ directly over 2♦. To play 4♠, jump there immediately if that is where you want to play no matter what hand partner holds.

Three- and four-level responses to a Mini-Multi 2♦ are:

---

## RESPONSES TO MINI-MULTI 2♦

(1) 3♣ is non-forcing (similar to passing 2♦, but you have clubs, not diamonds and therefore must play at the three-level).

(2) 3♦ is natural and forcing to game.

(3) 3♥ is "**pass** or **correct**" and is preemptive in nature.

(4) 3♠ is natural and invitational in spades.

(5) 3NT is to play. You don't care about opener's suit or hand strength.

(6) 4♣ asks opener to TRANSFER into his major. You want to play the hand.

(7) 4♦ asks opener to bid game in his major.

(8) 4♥ is "**pass** or **correct**."

(9) 4♠ is to play.

---

What would you respond when partner opens a Mini-Multi 2♦?

(a)    ♠ AKJ10954  ♥ 7  ♦ KQ104  ♣ 3
JUMP TO 4♠. Bid what you think you can make.

(b)    ♠ AKJ7432  ♥ 2  ♦ Q87  ♣ 94
RESPOND 2♠. When partner conventionally corrects to 3♥ via 2NT, 3♣ or 3♦, rebid 3♠ — sign-off. Tells opener that you want to play spades although he has hearts.

(c)    ♠ 7  ♥ KQ109854  ♦ AQ10  ♣ 92
RESPOND 2♥. When partner corrects to 2♠, rebid 3♦ to show invitational values

with long hearts. Opener will sign off or accept your invitation by jumping to 4♥.

(d)   ♠ Q85  ♥ —  ♦ KQJ54  ♣ Q7652
RESPOND 2♥. Good partners correct 2♥ to 2♠. Unfortunately, most partners will hold hearts when you have this hand and you will have nowhere to go. Alternatively, you might consider passing the 2♦ opening, which is a fair gamble since opener cannot hold a strong hand (as he could playing other Multi 2♦ openings).

(e)   ♠ 6  ♥ J  ♦ QJ762  ♣ AQJ872
RESPOND 3♣. This hand rates to play better in clubs than in partner's major. It is likely the opponents will compete in the major opener does not hold. Bid clubs now to get your partnership off to a good defensive beginning.

(f)   ♠ Q106  ♥ K832  ♦ K1054  ♣ 83
JUMP TO 3♥. You want to preempt the auction to the three-level whether opener holds spades or hearts. (Needing a swing or good result in a team event you might even gamble with a 4♥ bid, "**pass or correct**.")

(g)   ♠ A1094  ♥ K1098  ♦ 7  ♣ 10985
JUMP TO 4♥ — "**pass or correct**". This is a perfect illustration of a hand worth preempting to the four-level in opener's suit. It does not matter which major partner holds; you want to play in game.

(h)   ♠ A109  ♥ KJ4  ♦ AQJ  ♣ K542
JUMP TO 4♣. Opener will transfer to his major by bidding 4♦ with hearts and 4♥ with spades, and you will be happy to play the appropriate major suit game. Four of opener's major rates to play far better from

your side of the table with the lead coming up to your tenaces.

(i)     ♠ A65  ♥ A983  ♦ 85  ♣ AK62
        JUMP TO 4♦. Partner will bid his major. This is a rare example of when the hand rates to play better from opener's side of the table.

(j)     ♠ 72  ♥ 9  ♦ QJ10873  ♣ AJ105
        PASS. If you get to play 2♦, your prospects for an excellent score are good.

Competition over your Meck-Well Mini-Multi 2♦ opening is not significantly different than competition over your natural two-level preemptive openings. We recommend retaining the meaning of your responses in non-competitive auctions as much as possible. If available, 2NT should continue to be a conventional inquiry, asking opener to describe his hand. In addition, bids that would have been "**pass** or **correct**" in non-competitive auctions should carry that meaning when the enemy competes.

Add partnership agreements for doubles and redoubles to your competitive weapons and you should be prepared to deal with most auctions after your side begins with the Mini-Multi 2♦ and the enemy competes.

Competition over a Mini-Multi 2♦ opening often causes more trouble for the side that competes than the side that opens. Consider the following North-South hands from the 1990 London Times tournament:

North
        ♠ 1085  ♥ AKJ6  ♦ KJ4  ♣ KQ10

South
        ♠ J6  ♥ Q107  ♦ AQ95  ♣ AJ97

After a 2♠ opening by West, it would be difficult to imagine that two fine players holding the North-South cards would not reach a makeable game. Yet with three vulnerable games laydown, our distinguished opponents went -200 with these cards. Here is how it happened.

## North
- ♠ 1085
- ♥ AKJ6
- ♦ KJ4
- ♣ KQ10

## West
- ♠ AKQ972
- ♥ 54
- ♦ 632
- ♣ 84

Board 12
Dlr. - West
Vul. - N/S

## East
- ♠ 43
- ♥ 9832
- ♦ 1087
- ♣ 6532

## South
- ♠ J6
- ♥ Q107
- ♦ AQ95
- ♣ AJ97

---

OUR TABLE

Opening Lead ♠ A
N/S -200

| *Berkowitz* | *Svarc* | *Andersen* | *Shapiro* |
|---|---|---|---|
| West | North | East | South |
| 2♦ (a) | Dbl. | 2♥ (b) | 3NT (c) |
| P | P | P | |

(a) Mini-Multi: showing a weak two-bid in hearts or spades.

(b) "**Pass** or **correct**" — as it would have been in a non-competitive auction.

(c) Not an unreasonable bid — practical considering that this was not a regular partnership.

In retrospect, it is easy to question Boris Shapiro's 3NT call. Nevertheless, the 2♦ opening bid deserves credit for giving the enemy problems they would not have had over a 2♠ opening.

This concludes our discussion of the Mini-Multi 2♦ opening recommended by Jeff Meckstroth and Eric Rodwell. The pressure such openings put on the opponents and the excellent responding arsenal designed to complement this broad range of hands combine effectively to make the opponents miserable as often as possible.

## SIMPLIFIED MULTICOLORED 2♦

A slightly more complicated Multi 2♦ opening uses 2♦ to show either a weak two-bid in hearts or spades, OR a balanced strong hand with approximately 20-22 high card points. Since the Simplified Multicolored 2♦ opening includes the possibility of a balanced battleship, it is absolutely forcing (unlike the Mini-Multi 2♦ openings previously described). Responder may not pass unless he is willing to play 2♦ opposite a balanced 20-22 HCP battleship.

When responder is willing to play at the three-level (or higher) if opener is preempting in hearts, but not in spades, he bids 2♠. Opener passes if his suit is spades (which is fine with responder); if opener's suit is hearts, he bids 3♣ with a medium hand, 3♦ with a maximum and 3♥ with a minimum. Responder then passes 3♥ or bids them at the appropriate level.

When responder is interested in game if opener's preemptive two-bid is in spades, but not if it is in hearts, he simply bids 2♥. If opener corrects to 2♠, responder then either invites to game by raising to 3♠ or jumps to 4♠ with appropriate values.

Your partnership may choose to use either 2NT or 3♥ as a suit and strength inquiry in response to the Simplified Multi. If you choose 2NT, opener responds as follows:

3♣ = Maximum weak two-bid in hearts.
3♦ = Maximum weak two-bid in spades.
3♥ = Minimum weak two-bid in hearts.
3♠ = Minimum weak two-bid in spades.

The bids that are less space-consuming are used to show maximum weak two-bids in order to leave more room for exploration opposite a strong responding hand.

If you choose to use 3♥ as invitational, you give up the "**pass or correct**" meaning of this bid. Then, opener's responses are:

P = Minimum weak two-bid in hearts.
3♠ = Minimum weak two-bid in spades.
4♥ = Maximum weak two-bid in hearts.
4♠ = Maximum weak two-bid in spades.

If opener rebids notrump over any action by responder, he shows the balanced strong hand rather than the preemptive opening. After opener shows this strong hand, the partnership should bid according to their methods over 2NT openings (e.g., Stayman; Jacoby; Blackwood).

## CLASSIC MULTI 2♦

The classic Multi 2♦ (hereafter simply called Multi) opening is more complex than the Multicolored 2♦ openings we have been discussing. It is used to describe four different types of hands.

---

### REQUIREMENTS FOR OPENING A CLASSIC MULTI 2♦

An opening Multi 2♦ shows **one** of the following:

(1)  A balanced strong notrump with 20-22 HCP;

(2)  Any 4-4-4-1 with 17-24 HCP in your three suits (some partnerships limit the high card strength to 18-21);

(3)  A weak two-bid in hearts;

(4)  A weak two-bid in spades.

---

As previously noted, you cannot pass 2♦ when partner opens the bidding with Multi — he may have a battleship. You may bid 2♥, "**pass** or **correct**," as you would over any multicolored 2♦ opening. The responses are as follows:

---

## RESPONSES TO CLASSIC MULTI 2♦

(1)    2♥ is "**pass** or **correct**."

(2)    2♠ is to play opposite a weak two-bid in spades **or** (at least) invitational if partner's suit is hearts.

Note: both 2♥ and 2♠ responses ask opener to "**pass** or **correct**" unless he holds one of the strong Multi 2♦ openings.

(3)    2NT is your forcing inquiry with definite game interest opposite a major suit weak two-bid.

(4)    3♣ and 3♦ are natural and non-forcing.

(5)    3♥ is "**pass** or **correct**," preemptive in either major, assuming partner has a weak two-bid.

(6)    3♠ is natural and invitational in spades. Opener may not correct.

(7)    3NT is to play, typically based on a minor suit as a source of tricks.

(8)    4♣ and 4♦ are natural and game forcing.

(9)    4♥ is "**pass** or **correct**," to play in partner's major at the four-level if opener has the expected weak two-bid.

(10)  4♠ is to play.

---

Notice that 4♥ directly over 2♦ is "**pass** or **correct**." Therefore, in order to play 4♥, responder must first bid 2♥ over 2♦ and then bid 4♥ over partner's expected 2♠ rebid. If you fear that partner may pass 2♥ when you hold long hearts, begin with the forcing 2NT and rebid 4♥ over opener's rebid.

Using these responses to the Classic Multi 2♦, what response to partner's non-vulnerable opening 2♦ bid would you make holding:

(a)    ♠ 32 ♥ 7 ♦ AQJ985 ♣ J1093
RESPOND 3♦. You might have passed 2♦ playing a simpler Multi that is not used to describe strong hands as well as preemptive two-bids, but remember, you cannot pass a Classic Multi 2♦ opening. Partner may have a battleship. Make it tough for the enemy to find their major suit fit and get your lead-director in.

(b)    ♠ A104 ♥ KJ10 ♦ KQJ1043 ♣ 7
RESPOND 4♥. "**Pass** or **correct**." You want to play game in opener's major. Should partner hold a battleship and bid 4NT showing a strong balanced hand, or have a 4-4-4-1 (bidding the suit below his singleton at the five-level), you will proceed toward slam.

(c)    ♠ KQJ10952 ♥ 82 ♦ 6 ♣ A105
RESPOND 4♠. This is not "**pass** or **correct**." It is a sign-off, stating that you desire to play 4♠ if partner holds the expected preemptive two-bid in hearts.

(d)    ♠ K109 ♥ QJ10 ♦ AJ764 ♣ 94
RESPOND 3♥. "**Pass** or **correct**." You are, in effect, making a preemptive raise in whichever suit opener holds; similar to raising a traditional 2♥ opening to 3♥ or 2♠ to 3♠.

Opener has no trouble telling partner if he has a weak two-bid or a battleship, either balanced or unbalanced, over partner's initial response to his Multi 2♦ opening. The following boxes outline the most common methods of describing your Multi 2♦ opener after 2♥ and 2♠ responses:

## RESPONDING TO PARTNER'S 2♥ RESPONSE WHEN YOU OPEN CLASSIC MULTI 2♦

(1) Pass with a weak two-bid in hearts.

(2) Rebid 2♠ with a weak two-bid in spades.

(3) Rebid 2NT with a strong balanced notrump.

(4) Rebid 3♣, indicating specifically 4-4-1-4.

(5) Rebid 3♦ indicating specifically 4-1-4-4.

(6) Rebid 3♥ indicating specifically 1-4-4-4.

(7) Rebid 3♠ indicating specifically 4-4-4-1.

## RESPONDING TO PARTNER'S 2♠ RESPONSE WHEN YOU OPEN CLASSIC MULTI 2♦

(1) Pass with a weak two-bid in spades.

(2) Rebid 2NT with a strong balanced notrump.

(3) Rebid 3♣ indicating specifically 4-4-1-4.

(4) Rebid 3♦ indicating specifically 4-1-4-4.

(5) **3♥ = minimum weak two-bid in ♥s.**

(6) Rebid 3♠ indicating specifically 4-4-4-1.

(7) **Rebid 3NT indicating specifically 1-4-4-4.**

(8) **4♥ = maximum weak two-bid in ♥s.**

**Note that opener usually bids the suit below his singleton**. This permits a partnership to agree on a conventional inquiry when responder bids the next suit (opener's shortness). After opener's rebid showing a strong unbalanced hand, the most commonly played inquiry by responder — particularly if your HCP range is 17-24 — asks about opener's strength.

When opener's rebid is 2NT, responder can use the methods the partnership has agreed to play over strong notrump openings.

Rebids by opener over responder's forcing 2NT are:

---

## RESPONDING TO PARTNER'S 2NT RESPONSE WHEN YOU OPEN CLASSIC MULTI 2♦

(1)  Rebid 3♣ with a maximum weak 2♥ bid.

(2)  Rebid 3♦ with a maximum weak 2♠ bid.

(3)  Rebid 3♥ with a minimum weak 2♥ bid.

(4)  Rebid 3♠ with a minimum weak 2♠ bid.

And if opener has a good hand, too:

(5)  Rebid 3NT with a strong balanced notrump
     Responder uses the methods agreed to
     over strong notrump openings.

(6)  Jump to the four-level to show strong unbalanced hands (any 4 by 1). Bid the suit below your singleton.

---

Using these responses to the 2NT inquiry, opener shows a maximum weak two-bid via 3♣ or 3♦. If responder bids the next higher suit, the bid is conventional and by partnership agreement should ask either for shortness or the quality of opener's trump suit. (Playing sound Multi weak two-bids, it is probably best to use the next suit to ask for shortness, since opener has already suggested a reasonable suit. Playing Meck-Well type two-bids you are probably best advised to use the next suit as a conventional inquiry concerning the quality of opener's suit, since opener may have a maximum with a relatively poor suit.)

Once opener has shown the strong unbalanced hand via any of the above sequences, responder may ask him to define his point count by bidding opener's short suit. Opener answers in four steps:

## DESCRIBING YOUR STRONG UNBALANCED HAND

(1)  1st step = 17-18 HCP.

(2)  2nd step = 19-20 HCP.

(3)  3rd step = 21-22 HCP.

(4)  4th step = 23-24 HCP.

Over these step responses, responder can (for the second time) bid opener's singleton, requesting opener to show how many controls he has (Ace = 2, King = 1).  Opener responds in steps (notrump is a step) as follows:

If opener has shown 17-20 HCP:
1st step = 4 controls
2nd step = 5 controls
3rd step = 6 controls
4th step = 7 controls
5th step = 8 or 9 controls

If opener has shown 21-24 HCP:
1st step = 6 controls
2nd step = 7 controls
3rd step = 8 controls
4th step = 9 controls
5th step = 10 controls

Over these step responses, for partnerships with exceptional memories, responder can (for the third time) bid opener's singleton, requesting opener show how many Queens he holds in his three suits.  Opener responds in steps as follows:

1st step = no Queens
2nd step = 1 Queen
3rd step = 2 Queens
4th step = all 3 Queens

Using these sophisticated inquiries, assume that opener and responder hold these hands:

| Opener | Responder |
|---|---|
| ♠ AJ85 | ♠ K1042 |
| ♥ 7 | ♥ AQ94 |
| ♦ AKJ8 | ♦ Q3 |
| ♣ AJ103 | ♣ KQ6 |

The auction might proceed as follows:

| Opener | | Responder | |
|---|---|---|---|
| 2♦ | (Multi) | 2NT | (Inquiry) |
| 4♦ | (4-1-4-4) | 4♥ | (HCP?) |
| 4♠ | (17-18 HCP) | 5♥ | (Controls?) |
| 6♦ | (7 controls) | 6♥ | (Queens?) |
| 6♠ | (No Queens) | Pass | (High enough; no ♠ Queen) |

It's easy when you have the right tools!

## COMPREHENSIVE MULTI TWO-LEVEL OPENINGS

It is possible to play a far more complicated version of Multicolored openings than those we have described in this chapter. Comprehensive Multicolored Two-Bids, for example, are designed to allow a partnership to show either (1) a weak two-bid in a major suit, (2) an ACOL-style two-bid in any suit, (3) a balanced hand with 22 or more HCP, or (4) a three-suited hand with 19 or more HCP.

Playing Comprehensive Multicolored two-bids, an opening bid of 2♣ shows either a preemptive two-bid in hearts, an ACOL two-bid in clubs, or a balanced hand with 20 to 21 OR 25 or more HCP, depending on the level of opener's notrump rebid.

An opening bid of 2♦ shows either a weak two-bid in spades, an ACOL two-bid in diamonds, or a hand with 4-4-4-1 distribution (with the short suit unspecified) with 19 or more HCP.

This leaves 2♥ and 2♠ openings available to describe ACOL two-bids in the suit bid, or a multitude of other 2♥ and 2♠ openings, which will be described in Chapters 9 and 10. An opening 2NT shows a balanced hand with 22-24 HCP, filling in the partnership notrump ladder of strength.

If, after a 2♣ opening, responder has a hand that is not worth a game invitation opposite a 2♥ preempt, he bids 2♥. This response does not indicate that responder has heart support; actually, he might be void in hearts. If opener has the preemptive 2♥ bid, he will pass. If he has the 25+ HCP balanced hand, he will rebid in notrump. Any other rebid by opener is natural and shows an ACOL-type two-bid with clubs as the predominant suit. If opener has, for example:

    (a)    ♠ 85  ♥ AKJ10  ♦ 7  ♣ AKQ1093

the auction might begin 2♣-2♥-3♥.

When responder has a hand worthy of a game invitation, he begins with 2♦ inviting opener to clarify his hand. Opener rebids 2♥ to verify a weak two-bid, bids 2♠ to show a two-suited hand with clubs and spades, bids 2NT with a balanced hand with 25+ HCP and bids 3NT with an ACOL-type hand with five clubs and four hearts. Any other rebid is natural and shows an ACOL-type two-bid with clubs as the dominant suit. Over opener's 2♥ rebid (showing the weak 2♥ bid), responder's 2NT rebid asks opener for further description. We recommend the structure of responses described in Chapter 2 (2NT Ogust, 3♣ asking for shortness).

Now we will discuss opener's 2♦ bid. If responder has a hand that is not worth a game invitation opposite a 2♠ preempt, he bids two spades. Again, this response does not show spade support — in fact, responder may have no spades at all. If opener has the weak 2♠ bid, he passes. If he has the 4-4-4-1 (any singleton) hand, he rebids 2NT. With the ACOL-type hand with five diamonds and four spades, he rebids 3NT. Any other rebid is natural showing an ACOL-type hand with diamonds as the predominant suit.

When responder has a hand worthy of a game invitation opposite an opening 2♦ bid (presumably weak in spades), he responds 2♥, asking opener for further information. Opener rebids

2♠ with the spade preempt (responder simply uses the partnership methods over weak two-bids to get more information); he rebids 2NT with the 4-4-4-1 (any singleton) hand (responder bids clubs to ask opener to identify his short suit, opener bids his singleton at the three-level [3NT shows short clubs]); and rebids 3NT with four spades and five diamonds and an ACOL type hand. Any other rebid is natural and shows an ACOL-type hand with diamonds as the predominant suit.

If there is an overcall or a double before responder has had an opportunity to bid over a 2♣ opening, a double or a redouble by responder means that he would have bid 2♦ without the interference. If the opening bid was 2♦, the double or redouble means that responder would have bid 2♥.

All suit bids by responder are natural and non-forcing. They are made on the reasonable assumption that opener has a preemptive hand. When opener has the expected preempt, he simply passes any non-forcing response made by partner. If opener has another type of hand, he will bid again, describing a stronger hand.

## DEFENSES
## AGAINST MULTI

Your defensive methods against Multi 2♦ openings are based on the premise that opener holds a weak two-bid in hearts or spades. Remember, no matter how many types of strong hand opener might hold, the opening bid will be based on a weak two-bid most of the time. Consequently, your defensive measures should be similar to those you would use against a standard weak two-bid in the suit(s) suggested by the opening bid.

Your authors favor the defense against Multi 2♦ suggested to them by their friend Tony Forrester, Great Britain's leading player. Tony's defense is simple (which we find to be a definite PLUS). It provides an immediate takeout of either hearts or spades before opener has revealed his suit (obstructing a preemptive call by responder to the 2♦ opening).

# FORRESTER DEFENSE AGAINST MULTI 2♦

(1) Double is a takeout double of hearts, or potentially a hand too strong for a direct 2NT overcall.

(2) 2♥ shows a takeout double of spades (with a weak hand and hearts, partner can pass). If your side ends up playing the hand, you will be playing it from the correct side.

(3) 2♠ is a natural overcall showing spades.

(4) 2NT shows a strong notrump (15+ to 18 HCP). Partner can bid Stayman, transfers, Gerber, etc.

(5) 3♣ and 3♦ are natural overcalls.

(6) 3♥ and 3♠ are strong jump overcalls in the suit bid.

(7) 3NT is to play and typically shows a good minor as a source of tricks.

(8) 4♥, 4♠, 5♣ and 5♦ are natural and to play.

(9) As an option, you can play that 4♣ shows a minimum strength hand with both minors and 4♦ shows a maximum strength hand with both minors, or they can be played as natural.

Pass followed by competitive action shows fewer values than direct intervention.

---

Using these methods, what action would you take over a Multi 2♦ opening holding:

(a)      ♠ AQ104   ♥ 7   ♦ KJ105   ♣ KQ74
DOUBLE. A perfect takeout double of hearts. Classic!

(b)  ♠ AKJ1095  ♥ 2  ♦ KQJ3  ♣ K4
JUMP TO 3♠. We would not argue strongly against 4♠. We think a strong jump overcall to 3♠ describes this hand reasonably well.

(c)  ♠ 6  ♥ 7  ♦ KJ10953  ♣ KQJ94
JUMP TO 4♣. A good description of this "unusual" notrump with limited high card strength. Partner should be well placed to decide what the best course of action is for your side.

(d)  ♠ 74  ♥ K5  ♦ AKJ1097  ♣ J107
OVERCALL 3♦. This is a natural overcall, not a cuebid. Although your overall strength is not exceptional, your suit quality is excellent for a three-level overcall.

(e)  ♠ AQ  ♥ K105  ♦ KJ1093  ♣ K94
OVERCALL 2NT. You have the values for a strong 1NT opening (15+ to 18 HCP). Remember, over a 2NT overcall there is no reason not to use the same responding tools you employ over a strong 1NT opening.

(f)  ♠ 7  ♥ Q1095  ♦ K10932  ♣ AJ10
PASS. Hope that partner will compete or that you can make a balancing double of spades later in the auction.

(g)  ♠ 9  ♥ KQ105  ♦ AJ105  ♣ KJ98
OVERCALL 2♥. This shows a perfect takeout double of spades (if partner remembers). Partner is permitted to pass holding a weak hand with hearts.

(h)  ♠ K5  ♥ A10  ♦ AKQ10972  ♣ J4
JUMP TO 3NT. This hand illustrates a typical 3NT overcall. You have a long minor as a source of tricks and stoppers in both majors.

When LHO has opened Multi, partner has passed and RHO bids, most of your bids carry the same meaning they would have conveyed directly over 2♦. For example, LHO opens 2♦, partner passes and RHO bids 2♥. Your double is a takeout double of hearts, 2♠ is a natural overcall, 2NT shows a strong notrump and 4♣ would be for the minors with limited strength.

Of course, sometimes responder's call will prevent you from making the bid you would have made had you been sitting directly behind the 2♦ opener. In such cases you simply have to make the most descriptive call available to you.

When responding to takeout doubles at the two-level, it is probably best to use Lebensohl responses, which are described in Chapter 2. Lebensohl allows you to more clearly define the limit of your hand in response to partner's takeout double.

Meck-Well advocate a defense against Multi 2♦ openings that is a bit more sophisticated and complex. The essential features of their methods are outlined in the following box:

---

## MECK-WELL DEFENSE VERSUS MULTI 2♦ IN DIRECT SEAT

(1) Double shows 13-15 HCP, relatively balanced, OR a strong hand.

(2) Pass followed by double is takeout.

(3) Simple overcalls are natural.

(4) 2NT shows 16-18 HCP.

(5) A jump overcall shows a good intermediate hand with a good suit.

(6) Pass followed by a new suit is weaker than an initial overcall.

(7) Pass followed by notrump is takeout for the minors.

---

Actions when LHO has opened Multi, partner has passed, and RHO either bids or passes are similar in concept:

---

## MECK-WELL DEFENSE VERSUS MULTI 2♦ IN FOURTH CHAIR

The opponents make a "**pass** or **correct**" response (2♦-P-2♥):

(1) Pass followed by double is takeout of spades.

(2) Double is takeout of hearts.

(3) 2NT shows 15-18 HCP.

(4) 3NT is to play.

(5) 2♠, 3♣ and 3♦ are natural.

(6) 3♥ can be played to show hearts, OR it can be played as Michaels.

(7) 3♠, 4♣ and 4♦ show strong one-suited hands.

The opponents make a "**pass** or **correct**" response (2♦-P-2♠):

(1) Pass followed by double is takeout of hearts.

(2) Double is takeout of spades.

(3) 2NT shows 15-18 HCP.

(4) 3NT is to play.

(5) 3♣, 3♦ and 3♥ are natural.

(6) 3♠ can be played to show spades, OR it can be played as Michaels.

(continued)

---

The opponents make an artificial response (2♦-P-2NT):

(1)     Double shows cards.

(2)     Pass followed by double is takeout.

(3)     3NT shows 19-21 HCP.

(4)     Double followed by 3NT shows 17-18 HCP.

(5)     Overcalls are natural.

If responder passes 2♦:

(1)     Double shows 13-15 balanced HCP or a big hand with a strong suit.

(2)     Two of a major is natural.

(3)     Any other bid is natural.

Using the Meck-Well defense against Multi 2♦ openings, what action would you take over 2♦ holding:

(a)     ♠ KJ10  ♥ AKJ  ♦ Q10542  ♣ J10
DOUBLE. Show your balanced 13-15 HCP.

(b)     ♠ 6  ♥ 94  ♦ AQ943  ♣ KJ1074
PASS. Maybe you can bid notrump later, showing both minors.

(c)     ♠ K10  ♥ AQ95  ♦ KJ103  ♣ A105
OVERCALL 2NT with this strong balanced notrump opening.

(d)     ♠ AKQJ763  ♥ 7  ♦ A109  ♣ J10
JUMP TO 3♠. A jump overcall of a Multi 2♦ opening shows a fine suit and hand.

It is useful to have some agreements about partner's bids when you have interfered over the opponent's Multi openings. Meck-Well suggest the following:

---

## RESPONDING TO PARTNER'S DOUBLE OF A MULTI 2♦ OPENING

The auction proceeds 2♦-Dbl.-2♥ or 2♦-Dbl.-2♠ ("**pass or correct**"):

(1) Pass shows a willingness to defend their contract, undoubled, presuming partner has 13-15 balanced HCP.

(2) Double shows cards and is invitational or better opposite partner's expected 13-15 HCP.

(3) 2NT is Lebensohl.

(4) Other bids can be played Lebensohl-style. You can play 3♥ over 2♥ and 3♠ over 2♠ as natural, OR you can play them as cuebids.

The auction proceeds 2♦-Dbl.-3♣ (or higher):

(1) Double is penalty.

(2) New suits below game are constructive on the three-level.

(3) New suits below game are forcing on the four-level.

---

Suppose the auction goes 2♦-double-2♥ and you hold:

(a)     ♠ 72   ♥ QJ108   ♦ J1063   ♣ 984
        PASS. You are willing to defend 2♥ undoubled if opener has a weak 2♥ bid.

(b)     ♠ K105   ♥ K10   ♦ K873   ♣ J1065
        DOUBLE. Inform partner that the hand belongs to your side.

# RESPONDING TO PARTNER'S OVERCALL OF MULTI 2♦ OPENINGS

The auction proceeds 2♦-2♥-P or 2♦-2♠-P:

(1)     2NT is natural and invitational.

(2)     New suits, **except 3♣**, are a one-round force..

(3)     3♣ is an artificial cuebid.  If you rebid 4♣, it is natural and non-forcing.  You must be prepared for partner to jump to 4♥ over 3♣.

(4)     A bid of three of partner's major is a weak raise with 7-9 HCP.

(5)     Jumps to new suits, **except 4♣**, are splinter bids.

(6)     4♣ is natural and forcing.

The auction proceeds 2♦-2NT-P:

Use whatever methods you play over other 2NT overcalls.

The auction proceeds 2♦-3♣-P or 2♦-3♦-P

New suits are forcing.  Cheaper minor is a cuebid.

---

The key to successful defense against Multi 2♦ openings is similar to the key to success in defending against other preemptive openings (discussed in Part One of this book).  Accept the thesis that you will not always be able to obtain the **best possible result** when an opponent starts the bidding with Multi 2♦.  Using discretion and good judgment, simply try to get the **best result possible**.

# CHAPTER 8

# BERGEN PREEMPTS
## "TWO UNDER"

Zia Mahmood is one of the world's great players and leading personalities. Commentating on a Vugraph presentation at a North American Championship which featured the Marty Bergen-Larry Cohen partnership, Zia observed, "What Al Roth is to the sound opening bid, Marty Bergen is to the modern style of preempting in North America." We agree. For years, Marty has led the fight in North America for reducing traditional requirements for preemptive openings and for improving techniques and responses to two-, three- and four-level openings.

Conservative critics have suggested that many of Marty's tactics work only in weak fields against inexperienced, unsuspecting opponents. We disagree. Consider the following deal played against opponents who hardly qualify as either inexperienced or unsuspecting. With the courage of his convictions, Marty opened one of the most spectacularly successful weak two-bids in the history of North American Championships. The scene was the fourth quarter of the 1983 Spingold final in New Orleans. His opponents were your author's teammates — Bob Hamman and Bobby Wolff — one of the world's great partnerships. The vulnerability was unfavorable. Sitting East, down 40 IMPs, Marty was first to speak holding: ♠ 87642 ♥ J93 ♦ AK3 ♣ 104.

The effect of Marty's 2♠ opening (via 2♦) surpassed his wildest dreams. Here was the complete deal, auctions in both rooms, and results.

---

**North**
- ♠ AQ953
- ♥ K75
- ♦ 972
- ♣ Q3

**West**
- ♠ —
- ♥ Q642
- ♦ J108654
- ♣ J86

Board 22
Dlr. - East
Vul. - E/W

**East**
- ♠ 87642
- ♥ J93
- ♦ AK3
- ♣ 104

**South**
- ♠ KJ10
- ♥ A108
- ♦ Q
- ♣ AK9752

---

OPEN ROOM

Opening Lead ♦ J

N/S -100

| *L. Cohen* West | *Hamman* North | *Bergen* East | *Wolff* South |
|---|---|---|---|
| — | — | 2♦ (a) | 2NT (b) |
| P (c) | 3NT | P | P |

(a)    2♦ = weak two-bid in spades (a Bergen Two Under preempt).

(b)    A practical overcall showing a good strong notrump with spades (opener's real suit) stopped.

(c)    Grateful for Wolff's overcall considering the vulnerability and lack of support for Marty's suit.

In the other room:

| | | | |
|---|---|---|---|
| **CLOSED ROOM** | | Opening Lead ♦ J | |
| | | N/S -50 | |
| *Goldman* | *Goldfein* | *Soloway* | *M. Cohen* |
| West | North | East | South |
| — | — | P | 1♣ |
| P | 1♠ | P | 3♣ |
| P | 3♠ | P | 4♥ |
| P | 6♣ | P | P |
| P | | | |

You will note that one slam cannot be defeated on the North/South cards: 6♠! It is difficult to fault Hamman and Wolff for failing to reach this "obvious" contract after Marty's Two Under 2♦ opening showing spades!! Three notrump had no chance when Larry Cohen failed, with good reason, to lead his partner's "real" suit and elected to lead his own long suit.

In the closed room, Paul Soloway saved a 14-IMP loss for our team by finding the critical spade switch at trick two after winning Goldman's diamond lead. By beating the reasonable club slam, Soloway reduced our loss on the board to a mere two IMPs.

We believe Marty's unorthodox, yet devastatingly effective, preempt, deserved a greater reward. Without the 2♦ opening, Hamman and Wolff would never have reached the hopeless notrump game and might well have come to rest in 4♠ or 6♠ for a substantial gain. This deal illustrates that even great partnerships can go wrong when confronted with an aggressive preemptive opening.

# TRANSFER PREEMPTS

When making a Bergen preempt, opener bids two steps below his long suit, except for 2♥ (which is a 2♥ preempt) and the special cases of 3♥ and 3♠ openings. A 2♠ opening shows a club preempt and 2NT is a preempt in diamonds. In case you are wondering, 2♥ is natural because the suit two below it is clubs; the opening 2♣ bid is reserved for strong hands. This works well: 2♥ is two-under 2NT and therefore is not needed as a two-under opening.

Bergen Two Under preempts have a number of advantages. Some of their more important benefits are:

(1)     The weak hand with the long suit often becomes the dummy, keeping responder's stronger hand concealed as declarer.

(2)     Exploration is possible below opener's real suit.

**Bergen transfer preempts are not played in all four positions. They are played only in first, second and fourth seat. In third chair, it is best to play natural preempts; there is no need for the In-between Inquiry because game is out of the picture and you might as well take up the extra bidding space.**

The quality of opener's suit for a preemptive opening varies considerably depending on the vulnerability (primarily), the level, and position at the table. The preempt previously described against Hamman-Wolff, made on 8-7-6-4-2 of spades, is not a typical weak two-bid at any vulnerability, in any position, playing Bergen preempts. That preempt was motivated by the state of the match. However, playing Bergen preempts, two-level bids with five-card suits are common. Non-vulnerable, opener might bid 2♦ holding either of these (poor) suits:

(a)     ♠ Q10984

(b)     ♠ J97632

Vulnerable, opener would be expected to hold one of the following suits to open 2♥:

(c)     ♥ KQ1065

(d)     ♥ QJ8754

The key ingredient to all Bergen preempts is aggression. Bergen preempts are designed to "attack" the opponents and make life difficult for them. They require a great deal of discipline to be effective. For example, at favorable vulnerability, do not consider opening 2♦ with:

(a)        ♠ AQJ1095  ♥ 7  ♦ K107  ♣ 984

(showing a 2♠ preempt). Similarly, do not open 2♥ with:

(b)        ♠ A3  ♥ KQJ874  ♦ 9843  ♣ 2

Both these hands are far too strong for a Bergen weak two-bid at favorable vulnerability; partner would never play you for this good a hand.

According to Larry Cohen, the chief disciple of Bergen preempts, the minimum suit for a non-vulnerable three-level opening should be ♦ J109653. Vulnerable, opener would be expected to hold a minimum of ♥ QJ10953 for a Two Under 3♣ opening. Your authors suspect that, under ideal circumstances (or if need dictated), a Two Under preempt might be made on a slightly weaker suit.

Obviously, even playing Bergen preempts, the quality of opener's suit climbs as the level of the preempt rises. An opening (Three Under) 3♥ bid showing a four-level club preempt, or an opening 3NT bid showing a four-level diamond preempt, would typically be based on a reasonable broken eight-card suit.

Position is also a factor in Bergen preempts. In second seat, after an opponent has passed, Bergen preempts (like standard preemptive openings) tend to be made on sterner stuff than first chair preempts. In fourth seat opener must have a reason to believe the hand belongs to his side and must expect to go plus when he preempts. Remember, in third seat, all preemptive openings are natural, they are NOT Two Under bids.

Before considering specific Bergen transfer preempts, let us outline a few general guidelines for responder when opener makes a transfer preempt. These guidelines must be followed if your Two Under opening preempts are going to be as effective as possible, while avoiding as many risks and dangers as possible. They apply to all Two Under preempts.

(1)      After a Two Under preempt, the next step (suit or notrump) is artificial and conventional, asking opener for a further description of

his hand. We call it the In-between Inquiry. This conventional response always shows a good hand and should never be psyched.

(2)     After responder makes a conventional In-between Inquiry and opener shows a minimum, responder's new suit rebids are non-forcing.

(3)     After responder makes a conventional In-between Inquiry and opener shows a maximum, the partnership is in a 100% game force.

(4)     Non-vulnerable, new suits by responder (other than the conventional In-between Inquiry) are non-forcing. When vulnerable, all new suits bid by responder are forcing for one round.

(5)     A bid of 4♣ by responder (4♦ if clubs are trump) is always a Keycard inquiry.

Larry Cohen explains that Bergen Two Under preempts are made on very weak hands with very weak suits for one simple reason: it is good to preempt a lot. Cohen then cautions that Two Under preempts are easy to defend against because they allow the opponents to bid their suit at a lower level than traditional preempts. Your major advantages, therefore, in playing these preempts are: they often right-side the contract, and they give you the maximum opportunity to preempt because they are made on a wide range of hands.

Now let us consider the various Two Under Bergen preempts.

## 2♦ SHOWING SPADES

Our review of Bergen preempts starts with 2♦, which shows an opening 2♠ preempt. The following box outlines the responses and rebids to Two Under 2♦ openings:

# RESPONSES AND REBIDS TO A 2♦ OPENING SHOWING SPADES

(1)   Pass is to play in diamonds.

(2)   When responder bids 2♥ as a conventional In-between Inquiry, opener rebids:

> 2♠ = minimum weak 2♠ opener. (2NT by responder asks again.)
>
> 2NT = five or more spades, three or more hearts, maximum hand.
>
> 3♣ = five or more spades, maximum hand, denies three hearts.
>
> 3♦ = six good spades, minimum hand.
>
> 3♥ = six good spades, medium hand.
>
> 3♠ = six good spades, maximum hand.
>
> 3NT = solid spade suit (AKQxxx or better).
>
> 4♣, 4♦ and 4♥ = any non-minimum with a six-card spade suit and four cards in the suit bid.

Responder's other bids:

(3)   2♠ is to play.

(4)   2NT shows clubs, invitational or better.

(5)   3♣ shows diamonds, invitational or better.

(6)   3♦ shows hearts, invitational or better.

(7)   3♥ shows hearts and is to play.

(8)   3♠ is a preemptive spade raise, to play.

(9)   4♣ is a Keycard inquiry in spades.

(10)  4♥ and 4♠ are to play.

Responding to 2♦ is relatively easy, provided responder remembers that opener could have a relatively poor suit and worse hand. To be "LAW-abiding," responder should count on opener for a five-card suit. A preemptive raise — or 3♠ call in competition — usually contains four-card support (three-card support is customary opposite a two-bid).

How weak should responder play opener to be? To answer this question, consider another illustration of a spectacular result generated by a Bergen 2♦ opening that took place in the 1985 North American Team Trials. The Hamman-Wolff partnership was again involved; this time holding Marty Bergen and Larry Cohen's East-West cards at the other table.

Facing one of North America's strongest partnerships, Lew Stansby and Chip Martel (and a considerable deficit on the scoreboard), Marty picked up this hand, favorable, in first chair:

♠ J10872   ♥ 87652   ♦ Q6   ♣ 7

Most players would not consider opening this pitiful hand with a weak two-bid. Bergen is not most players! To him this was a weak two-bid; admittedly a minimum, but a two-bid nonetheless. So, using his Two Under methods, he opened 2♦ (after all, the conservative sages of the past advised against opening a weak two-bid with four cards in a side major; they said nothing about holding a side *five-card* major)!!

On the other side of the table, Cohen heard partner open 2♦ showing a preemptive two-bid in spades. This was momentarily a pleasant surprise because Larry had picked up 19 of the finest:

♠ A53   ♥ A   ♦ AK542   ♣ A965

Looking at Larry's hand opposite a 2♠ preempt, most pundits would conclude that game in spades was a certainty. Some optimists (not unreasonably) would like their prospects of making a spade slam. Wrong!

After using the conventional In-between Inquiry (2♥) and getting a negative 2♠ response, Larry did not venture beyond the two-level! That proved to be a profitable decision because he was about to collect 1100 and win 15 IMPs.

Here is the complete deal, auctions and results from both rooms:

```
                     North
                  ♠  Q64
                  ♥  KQJ943
                  ♦  J83
                  ♣  J

West                                        East
♠  A53          ┌─────────────┐           ♠  J10872
♥  A            │  Board 18   │           ♥  87652
♦  AK542        │  Dlr. - East│           ♦  Q6
♣  A965         │  Vul. - N/S │           ♣  7
                └─────────────┘
                     South
                  ♠  K9
                  ♥  10
                  ♦  1097
                  ♣  KQ108432
```

| OUR TABLE | | Opening Lead ♦ A | |
| | | N/S -1100 | |

| *Cohen* | *Martel* | *Bergen* | *Stansby* |
| West | North | East | South |
|---|---|---|---|
| — | — | 2♦ (a) | P |
| 2♥ (b) | P | 2♠ (c) | P |
| P!! (d) | 3♥ (e) | P | P |
| Dbl. | P | P | 4♣ (f) |
| Dbl. | P | P | P |

(a)  Two Under preempt showing a weak two-bid in spades.

(b)  Conventional In-between Inquiry.

(c)  Minimum (without a doubt).

(d)  Obviously having seen Marty's weak twos at favorable vulnerability before.

(e)  Not unreasonable.  Martel has seen Bergen's weak twos also.

(f)  Not unreasonable.  Could easily have been right.

Hand repeated for convenience:

```
                        North
                        ♠  Q64
                        ♥  KQJ943
                        ♦  J83
                        ♣  J

West                  ┌─────────────┐          East
♠  A53                │  Board 18   │          ♠  J10872
♥  A                  │  Dlr. - East│          ♥  87652
♦  AK542              │  Vul. - N/S │          ♦  Q6
♣  A965               └─────────────┘          ♣  7

                        South
                        ♠  K9
                        ♥  10
                        ♦  1097
                        ♣  KQ108432
```

THEIR TABLE                              Opening Lead ♥ K
                                                  N/S +50

| *Wolff* | | *Hamman* | |
| West | North | East | South |
| --- | --- | --- | --- |
| — | — | P | 3♣ |
| 3♦ | P | P | P |

So much for the Two Under 2♦ opening describing a preemptive two-bid in spades. If we report one more triumph, everyone will give up standard weak two-bids and Part One of this book will become obsolete.

Since 2♣ openings are reserved to describe strong hands, the only way to show a two-level heart preempt playing Bergen preempts is to open 2♥; crude, old fashioned, but necessary. Play your choice methods over standard weak twos when you open 2♥.

# 2♠ SHOWING CLUBS

Now consider an opening 2♠ bid which shows a 3-level club preempt.

---

### RESPONSES AND REBIDS TO A 2♠ OPENING SHOWING CLUBS

(1) Pass shows a desire to play in spades.

(2) When responder bids 2NT as a conventional In-between Inquiry, opener rebids:

> 3♣ = all minimum hands. Responder rebids:
> - 3♦ conventional. Opener rebids 3♥ with three spades; 3♠ with three hearts; 3NT denying a 3-card major.
> - 3♥ and 3♠ are natural and non-forcing.
> - 4♣ is invitational.
> - 4♦ is a Keycard inquiry in clubs.
>
> 3♦ = maximum with a side four-card major.
> - 3♥ asks which major. Opener rebids 3♠ with 4 hearts; 3NT with 4 spades.
>
> 3♥ = Maximum with 3 spades; game force.
> 3♠ = Maximum with 3 hearts; game force.
> 3NT = Maximum without a three-card major.

(continued)

---

# RESPONSES AND REBIDS TO A
## 2♠ OPENING SHOWING CLUBS (continued)

(3)   3♣ is to play; opener can **never** raise.

(4)   3♦ and 3♥ are non-forcing "corrections" non-vulnerable.

(5)   3♦ and 3♥ are forcing "corrections" vulnerable.

(6)   3♠ is natural and invitational non-vulnerable.

(7)   3♠ is natural and forcing vulnerable.

(8)   3NT is to play.

(9)   4♣ is a preemptive raise of opener's suit.

(10)  4♦ is a Keycard inquiry in clubs.

(11)  4♥ and 4♠ are to play, even in competition.

At favorable you open 2♠ (showing clubs). What do you bid over partner's conventional 2NT In-between Inquiry holding:

(a)   ♠ J109  ♥ 5  ♦ 652  ♣ KQ9854
      REBID 3♥. This shows a maximum 3♣ opener and three spades. (Conservatives may question whether this hand qualifies as a maximum.) Note that the strong hand will be declarer in clubs or spades.

(b)   ♠ 2  ♥ 6532  ♦ K5  ♣ QJ10652
      REBID 3♦. Tell partner that you have a maximum with a four-card major. If partner inquires via 3♥, rebid 3♠ to show hearts.

(c)   ♠ 9843  ♥ 5  ♦ 6  ♣ J1095432
      REBID 3♣. Reveal your minimum 3♣ opener; you cannot show your four-card major immediately without a maximum.

## RESPONSES AND REBIDS TO A
## 2NT OPENING SHOWING DIAMONDS

(1) When responder bids 3♣ as a conventional In-between Inquiry, opener rebids:

      3♦ = all minimum hands.

      3♥ = maximum with three or four spades, game force.

      3♠ = maximum with three or four hearts, game force.

      3NT = Maximum without a three- or four-card major.

(2) 3♦ is a sign-off.

(3) 3♥ and 3♠ are non-forcing "corrections" non-vulnerable.

(4) 3♥ and 3♠ are forcing "corrections" vulnerable.

(5) 4♣ is a Keycard inquiry in diamonds.

(5) 4♦ is a preemptive raise of opener's suit.

(6) 4♥ and 4♠ are to play, even in competition.

If partner opens 2NT (three-level diamond preempt) at favorable vulnerability, what would your response be holding:

(a)    ♠ KJ1043  ♥ K965  ♦ —  ♣ Q1076

     RESPOND 3♦. You have nothing else to bid. Good partners do not preempt in diamonds when you hold this hand. Be grateful for the favorable vulnerability. Hope that partner believed he was vulnerable when he opened 2NT and therefore has an exceptional suit — he will need it opposite your void.

(b)　　♠ AKQ1093　♥ 74　♦ K2　♣ AK10
RESPOND 4♠. If 3♠ were forcing, that would clearly be our choice. Unfortunately, non-vulnerable, a simple natural change of suit is not forcing. So, bid what you think you can make.

(c)　　♠ 7　♥ AK　♦ KJ102　♣ AKQ1093
RESPOND 4♣. The number of keycards partner holds will determine whether you sign off in 5♦, bid on to bid 6♦ or pursue the grand slam. Remember, 4♣ always asks partner for keycards except when opener's suit is clubs (then 4♦ would be the keycard inquiry).

(d)　　♠ A10932　♥ 42　♦ J985　♣ K6
RESPOND 4♦. This is a typical preemptive raise of opener's suit. Consume as much bidding space as you safely can. The opponents may not be able to mention their heart suit at the four-level.

(e)　　♠ KQ1097　♥ AQ1095　♦ 3　♣ A4
RESPOND 3♦. Do not be tempted to get higher. Forget about your two fine major suits.

## 3♣ SHOWING HEARTS

Playing Bergen Two Under preempts non-vulnerable, would you open 3♣ holding:

(a)　　♠ 10963　♥ QJ10985　♦ J107　♣ —
YES. You may always open a Bergen Two Under preempt with four cards in the other major (or even a void). Your trump suit is more than adequate for a Bergen three-level preempt.

(b) ♠ A4 ♥ KQ109854 ♦ J104 ♣ 4
NO. An author's mother would consider this hand worth a 3♥ opening. Ergo it is far too strong for a Bergen Two Under preempt.

(c) ♠ 7 ♥ J108754 ♦ QJ109 ♣ 65
YES. Despite the anemic six-card trump suit, this is better than a minimum non-vulnerable three-level heart preempt.

Responding to Bergen 3♣ openings is similar to the responses we discussed for 2NT openers.

---

## RESPONSES AND REBIDS TO A 3♣ OPENING SHOWING HEARTS

(1) Pass is to play in clubs.

(2) When responder bids 3♦ as a conventional In-between Inquiry, opener rebids:
   3♥ = minimum.
   3♠ = maximum, 6-card suit.
   3NT = maximum, 7-card suit.

(3) 3♥ is a sign-off.

(4) 3♠ is non-forcing non-vulnerable.

(5) 3♠ is forcing vulnerable.

(6) 3NT is to play.

(7) 4♣ is a Keycard inquiry in hearts.

(8) 4♥ and 4♠ are to play.

---

The key response to 3♣ openings (as it is to most Bergen preempts) is the conventional In-between Inquiry. It is a critical tool for accurately bidding games and slams when responder has a battleship.

# 3 ♦ SHOWING SPADES

The requirements for a 3 ♦ opening showing spades are exactly the same as those for a 3 ♣ opening holding hearts.

---

## RESPONSES AND REBIDS TO A 3 ♦ OPENING SHOWING SPADES

(1)   Pass is to play in diamonds.

(2)   When responder bids 3 ♥ as a conventional In-between Inquiry, opener rebids:
      3 ♠ = minimum.
      3NT = maximum, 6-card suit.
      4 ♣ = maximum, 7-card suit.

(3)   3 ♠ is a sign off.

(4)   3NT is to play.

(5)   4 ♣ is a Keycard inquiry in spades.

(6)   4 ♥ and 4 ♠ are to play.

---

At favorable partner opens 3 ♦ showing spades and you hold:

(a)   ♠ J   ♥ KQJ   ♦ QJ9532   ♣ KQJ
RESPOND 3 ♠.   Sixteen HCP and the prospects for game are practically nil.  Sign off in 3 ♠ and hope you can go plus.

(b)   ♠ 10965   ♥ AK10962   ♥ A2   ♣ 7
RESPOND 4 ♠.  This prime 11-count with four-card trump support for opener's long suit rates to produce a game.

(c)   ♠ 4   ♥ AK10   ♦ AKQJ96   ♣ A105
RESPOND 3NT.  Any tricks partner's hand contributes should be overtricks.

Hands (a) and (b) illustrate a point we made in the first part of this book. Points do not take tricks; quick tricks, controls and good fits do. Hand (c) might produce a slam opposite the right maximum standard preempt; facing a Bergen preempt at favorable it will not.

## 3♥ SHOWING CLUBS

Vulnerable, we would open 3♥ as a club preempt with:

(a)     ♠ 7  ♥ 3  ♦ J107  ♣ KQ1087532

(b)     ♠ 85  ♥ —  ♦ QJ9  ♣ KJ986532

Hand (a) is just about the hand partner should expect for a vulnerable 4♣ opening. Both your suit and playing strength are adequate. Hand (b) is not perfect, but if you preempt only with ideal hands, the methods advocated in this chapter most likely are not for you.

We would not, however, open 3♥ with this hand:

(c)     ♠ —  ♥ KJ109  ♦ 85  ♣ K1097652

This hand has poor clubs and a multitude of flaws.

---

### RESPONSES AND REBIDS TO A 3♥ OPENING SHOWING CLUBS

Note: This is a "**Three Under**" preempt; it shows a four-level preempt in clubs.

(1)   Pass is to play in hearts.

(2)   When responder bids 3♠ as a conventional In-between Inquiry, opener rebids:
        3NT = maximum.
        4♣ = minimum.
Note the inversion of responses. You do not want to bypass 3NT opposite a maximum.

(continued)

---

# 3♠ SHOWING A GAMBLING 3NT

Another advantage of Bergen preempts concerns the gambling 3NT opening.  Bergen preempts allow an opening bid of 3♠ to describe a gambling 3NT opening.  Transferring the play to partner's hand when opener has a long suit without any outside strength is often quite useful.

These hands would be acceptable 3♠ openings playing Bergen preempts:

- (a)      ♠ J105   ♥ 7   ♦ AKQJ754   ♣ 85

- (b)      ♠ 5   ♥ 4   ♦ Q43   ♣ AKQ98652

The following outlines the responses to a Bergen 3♠ opening:

## RESPONSES TO A 3♠ OPENING
## SHOWING A GAMBLING 3NT

(1) Responder may pass the opening 3♠ bid with a long spade suit and no interest in game only if he believes 3♠ will play better than four of opener's minor.

(2) 3NT is to play from the right side of the table.

(3) 4♣ is "**pass** or **correct**".

(4) 4♦ asks opener for shortness. Opener bids:
4♥/4♠ with shortness in the suit bid.
4NT with no shortness.
5♣ with shortness in the other minor.

(5) 4♥ and 4♠ are to play.

(6) 4NT is the same as whatever agreements you and your partner had when you played a standard gambling 3NT.

(7) 5♣ and 6♣ are "**pass** or **correct**". Opener passes with clubs and bids 5♦ over 5♣ (or 6♦ over 6♣) with diamonds.

(8) 5NT asks opener to bid a grand slam in his minor if he holds the eight-card suit.

Suppose partner opens 3♠. Choose your response.

(a)     ♠ AKQJ  ♥ 6532  ♦ A986  ♣ 3
RESPOND 4♦. If partner shows heart shortness, bid 6♣ which will be laydown.

(b)     ♠ KQJ10763  ♥ 4  ♦ AQ9  ♣ 74
RESPOND 4♠. Bid what you think you can make facing seven or eight solid clubs.

(c)   ♠ K84   ♥ K63   ♦ AQ9754   ♣ 3

RESPOND 3NT. You are delighted to have right-sided the contract.

## 3NT SHOWING DIAMONDS

The final Bergen Two Under preempt we will discuss is 3NT, which describes a four-level diamond preempt. The use of 3♥ to describe a 4♣ opening and 3NT to show a 4♦ bid leaves 4♣ and 4♦ openings available to describe other hands:

---

### RESPONSES AND REBIDS TO A 3NT OPENING SHOWING DIAMONDS

(1)   Pass converts the diamond preempt to a no-trump game.

(2)   When responder bids 4♣ as a conventional In-between Inquiry, opener rebids:
> 4♦ = minimum.
> 4♥ = maximum, 1 keycard, no Queen of diamonds.
> 4♠ = maximum, 1 keycard, plus the Queen of diamonds.
> 4NT = maximum, 2 keycards, no Queen of diamonds.
> 5♣ = maximum, 2 keycards, plus the Queen of diamonds.

(3)   4♦ is a sign-off.

(4)   4♥, 4♠, 5♣ and 5♦ are to play.

(5)   4NT is a Keycard inquiry in diamonds.

---

One of the advantages of using 3♥ and 3NT to describe four-level minor suit preempts is that responder can convert these conventional preemptive calls to 3NT with appropriate values.

(Obviously, you cannot bid 3NT over a 4♣ or 4♦ opening.) For example, we would pass a Bergen 3NT with both these hands because it rates to be the only makeable game:

(a)     ♠ KJ10  ♥ AK10  ♦ KQ6  ♣ J1095

(b)     ♠ A94  ♥ Q10543  ♦ AJ3  ♣ A4

One of the keys to the effectiveness of Bergen preempts is the conventional In-between Inquiry.  This critical responding tool enables Two Under preempts to be made on a broad range of suit length and strength.

Several advocates of Bergen preempts use the "next step" over the conventional In-between Inquiry to inform partner that opener holds a SUBSTANDARD (or sub-minimum) preempt, not simply a minimum.  When you have the understanding that the next step shows a substandard preempt, your rebid when partner responds 2♥ to your 2♦ opening at favorable vulnerability would be 3♥ showing a medium hand with a good six-card suit:

♠ KQ10985  ♥ 76  ♦ 652  ♣ 109

In other words, the first step after partner's inquiry shows the subminimum.  You treat all minimum hands as if they were medium strength hands and make the same responses we have previously discussed.

## RESPONSES TO TRANSFER PREEMPTS

Once you have memorized the responses to the conventional In-between Inquiry and the various other responses and rebids, responding to Bergen preempts is not much different from responding to standard preempts.  Remember that opener's suit is very likely to be shorter and weaker when playing Bergen preempts than when playing standard preemptive methods.

How short and weak is partner's suit likely to be when he opens a Two Under preempt?  That depends on the vulnerability, position at the table, and the state of your game or match.  For example, at favorable vulnerability in first or third seat, a preemptive two-bid using the Bergen approach is usually based on a five-card suit. Therefore, you should count on partner for only five — not six — hearts (via 2♥) or spades (via 2♦) when he begins with a two-level preempt.

At the three-level with favorable vulnerability, opener is likely to have a six — not a seven — card suit. When he does have seven, his suit is probably so weak that it looks like he only has six.

As a general rule, the length and strength of your suit for a Bergen non-vulnerable preempt is a card shorter and considerably weaker than what you were originally taught and probably play now, even vulnerable. Only at unfavorable vulnerability at higher levels do Bergen preempts approximate the standards of old-fashioned preemptive openings. Note that we said "approximate" — even under adverse conditions, they are weaker than the standards dictated by most authors and experts.

Consequently, when playing Bergen preempts you will need to adjust your thoughts regarding responses. For example, suppose you pick up the following strong notrump:

(a)     ♠ A74   ♥ KQ107   ♦ AQ54   ♣ J7

and partner opens 2♠ (a Two Under preempt in clubs) at favorable vulnerability. Playing the "standard" way, 3NT is a good proposition when you hold a hand like this and hear partner preempt with three of a minor. You have stoppers in the unbid suits and honor doubleton in partner's minor. Forget this maxim when playing Bergen preempts. Simply sign off in 3♣ and hope that partner has enough for you to score nine tricks in clubs. Nine tricks in notrump will happen only in your very best dreams. Partner could have as little as King-sixth of clubs and no outside values.

Another maxim has to be discarded when responding to Bergen three-level major suit preempts. When partner preempts 3♣ or 3♦ (showing a major) at equal vulnerability, you probably believe that you are cold for a game when you have 3 to 3½ cover cards (or 3 to 3½ quick tricks) and a modicum of support. Playing Bergen Two Under major suit three-level preempts, your raises had better be made of sterner stuff.

Neither side vulnerable, partner opens 3♣ (showing hearts).

(b)     ♠ KQ107   ♥ 4   ♦ A9852   ♣ K107

Do not even think about bidding a game. Your hand is not even worth a game try at this vulnerability.

Do not commit to game over an opening 3♣ with this hand either:

(c)    ♠ A5  ♥ Q7  ♦ KQ872  ♣ A1095

Bid 3♦ (conventional In-between Inquiry) if you wish. However, if partner shows a minimum by bidding 3♥, you must pass. (Opposite one of your authors' mother's 3♥ openings, you could easily make a slam holding this hand, but she has been a bit conservative since the market crash of '29.)

The following hand, however, is worth a 4♥ bid over an equal vulnerability Bergen 3♣ opening:

(d)    ♠ AK5  ♥ J10  ♦ AQ105  ♣ A954

But do not expect Lloyd's of London to insure your major suit game when you hold this hand opposite a minimum preempt. Take our word for it — 4♥ will not always make when you hold this hand opposite a Bergen style three-level preempt.

As you might expect from the leading North American proponent of the "Law of Total Tricks," Bergen recommends using the LAW when raising a Bergen preempt (or any preempt for that matter). Remember, you cannot count on the standard suit length for preemptive openings when you play the Bergen methods. For example, do not count on your partner for more than a five-card suit for a non-vulnerable weak two-bid (particularly at favorable vulnerability). Three-level openings do not promise seven-card suits at any vulnerability. When using the LAW to determine how high to raise partner's preempt, use opener's most likely minimum number of cards in his suit and then add your support.

Using the LAW as a guide, we would raise a 2♦ preempt (showing spades) to 3♠ at favorable vulnerability holding:

(a)    ♠ J965  ♥ 43  ♦ A10954  ♣ Q4

The reason: opener is most likely to have only a five-card suit at this vulnerability; with a good six-card suit he might have opened with a three-level preempt. Therefore, your side is likely to hold only nine trumps — not 10. The three-level rates to be the limit for your side. In addition, the danger of raising opener's preempt to

4♠ is that your opponents, loaded with HCP, may simply double you for a telephone number at the four-level. Remember our earlier counsel: high-level preempts are more likely to be doubled for penalty.

If partner opens a Two Under 3♣ Bergen preempt with neither side vulnerable, a jump to game, (following the LAW), would be our choice holding:

(b)        ♠ A10952   ♥ 9843   ♦ 7   ♣ K105

Even if doubled, 4♥ rates to be an excellent sacrifice. Our side has a 10-card heart fit if partner holds the expected six-card suit. If partner has a seventh heart, 4♥ is an even better proposition if we are able to buy the contract.

You may have noticed that we have not spent much time discussing constructive auctions after Bergen preempts. There are several reasons for this.

Bergen preempts are designed to make life difficult for your opponents, period. They are not made for delicate, probing constructive auctions. The more conservative preempts played by an author's mother are appropriate for delicate precision auctions. However, Bergen preempts lend themselves more to the meat cleaver technique of a Jack the Ripper. It is the initial aggressive preemptive blow that most often does the damage to the enemy, not responder's action or subsequent bidding.

You cannot have your cake... when it comes to Bergen preempts. If you want to reap the benefits of being able to preempt more often — due to the wide range of suits and strength — you must pay the price when responder has the battleship. Accept it.

As we stated earlier, the most important contribution to responding accurately to Bergen preempts is a clear partnership understanding of the minimum and maximum suits and strength opener can have. Consider the vulnerability, position, etc., when you make a preemptive bid. As long as you have what partner is expecting, and your approach is consistent, you will achieve great results. Without proper understandings, you will be using bows and arrows against guns and rifles.

# THE OPPONENTS COMPETE
## OVER TRANSFER PREEMPTS

Because of the strength, (or more accurately the lack of strength), of most Bergen preempts, you must be prepared for frequent intervention after your side opens with one. It is particularly important to know your agreements when the opponents double:

---

## COMPETITION OVER OUR
## OPENING TRANSFER PREEMPTS

When the opponents double a Two-Under preempt:

(1) Pass shows playability; responder must run without five cards or more in the suit artificially opened.

(2) The next suit by responder is natural (and an attempt to find a safe place to play). It is **not** the conventional In-between Inquiry.

(3) Redouble is the In-between Inquiry. When the auction proceeds 2♦-Dbl.-**Redbl.**, the redouble is the In-between Inquiry.

> Opener rebids the next step (2♥) with a minimum. Opener never rebids his suit (2♠); this allows the strong hand to declare. Opener's rebids above his suit (2NT and beyond) are the same as we have already presented.

When the opponents overcall a Two-Under preempt, use your choice of methods over a natural preempt of opener's real suit.

When the opponents cuebid opener's real suit, responder doubles to show a good hand with support for opener's suit, informing opener that the hand belongs to his side. Therefore, responder's direct raise can be preemptive.

---

When responder does not have a fit for opener's real suit, you need a way to escape. Most opponents do not have both the agreements and the judgment to penalize Bergen preempts when responder does not have a fit for opener's real suit, nevertheless, you must be prepared when they do. Be philosophical on the rare occasions when your opponents have your area code after a Bergen preempt and collect a telephone number. That is the infrequent price you have to pay for all the good results such methods generate.

Consider a few examples when opener's Two Under preempt gets doubled. The auction proceeds 2♦ (showing spades)-double, and with both sides vulnerable you hold:

(a)      ♠ 2   ♥ KQ1095   ♦ QJ982   ♣ 85
PASS. You have no choice; you have five good diamonds and no fit for spades. If LHO passes 2♦ doubled and opener cannot stand it (knowing you have five or more diamonds), he will most likely redouble and you will then have a chance to introduce your heart suit.

(b)      ♠ K109   ♥ A5   ♦ AQ1076   ♣ 742
REDOUBLE. A maximum vulnerable weak two-bid could easily produce a game opposite this hand. Your redouble is the In-between Inquiry. Opener's descriptive rebid should answer the question of what level you play in spades.

Now suppose partner opens 3♣ (showing hearts) and RHO doubles. With neither side vulnerable, plan your action holding the following hands:

(a)      ♠ J3   ♥ 5   ♦ KQ10965   ♣ J1054
RESPOND 3♦. Remember, the next suit after a Two Under preempt is not the conventional In-between Inquiry after a double (redouble is). The next suit is natural, suggests a place to play, and denies a fit for opener's real suit.

(b) ♠ KQJ98 ♥ — ♦ K1075 ♣ 9854

RESPOND 3♥. You did not want to hear partner open 3♣, especially now that RHO has doubled. Make the best of a bad situation by simply bidding partner's suit. You cannot pass because you do not have five or more clubs. Unfortunately, you probably will have to make an S.O.S. redouble when the opponents hammer your 3♥ bid. Pray that your opponents bid so they will have to play this hand. If they do not, at least partner will be happy for a while — he will not have to play the hand.

(c) ♠ A4 ♥ J106 ♦ AK652 ♣ K103

RESPOND 4♥. Bid what you think you can make. There is no reason to be delicate with this hand. Simply jump to the game you would have bid in a non-competitive auction. This prevents the opponents from exchanging any more information and gets the hand played from the right side.

(d) ♠ A3 ♥ 4 ♦ AKQJ542 ♣ A94

RESPOND 3NT. Again, this is what you think you will make. Partner's 3♣ opening suggests that the opponents will not be able to run the first five hearts tricks. Once you gain the lead you have nine fairly certain winners.

# DEFENSES AGAINST TRANSFER PREEMPTS

To learn reasonable defensive measures against Two Under Bergen preempts, we went to the most experienced partnership in dealing with Bergen preempts — Marty Bergen and Larry Cohen — who have played these methods for many years. Most of the ideas presented here were suggested by them, and your authors are grateful for their assistance.

Against Two Under preempts at the two-level, we advise using methods similar to those we described against ordinary weak two-bids. The following box outlines slight modifications to those methods over the artificial 2♦ opening:

---

### DEFENSES AGAINST A 2♦ OPENING SHOWING SPADES

(1) Double shows 13+ to 15 HCP, or a battleship; your hand tends to be balanced.

(2) 2♠ is a takeout of spades.

(3) 2♥/3♣/3♦ are natural overcalls.

(4) 2NT shows 15+ to 18 HCP with spades stopped. We recommend playing Stayman and transfers after this 2NT overcall.

(5) 3♥ shows a strong jump overcall with an excellent suit and is highly invitational.

(6) 3♠ asks partner to bid 3NT with a spade stopper and usually shows a long solid suit.

(7) 4♣ and 4♦ show a strong two-suiter in hearts and the bid minor, and are game forcing.

---

What action would you take over 2♦ (showing spades) holding:

(a)     ♠ 5   ♥ AQJ109   ♦ 3   ♣ AKJ1065
OVERCALL 4♣. This hand is a perfect example of a strong two-suiter. Make a game forcing call while revealing your distribution.

(b)     ♠ K4   ♥ AQ10   ♦ K1076   ♣ Q1095
DOUBLE. This is a typical example of a card-showing double of 2♦.

(c)      ♠ 3   ♥ —   ♦ AKJ976   ♣ AQ10632
OVERCALL 4♠. Did you remember this
from Chapter 2? A cuebid of opener's suit
at the four-level shows a powerful two-suiter
in the minors.

Defense against Bergen Two Under preempts above the two-level requires some adjustments to the methods discussed in Chapters 3 and 4. Rather than attempting to outline counter-measures to every specific Two Under preempt, we offer the following outline of general understandings that we feel are helpful against all Two Under preempts:

---

## GENERAL DEFENSIVE MEASURES AGAINST TWO UNDER PREEMPTS ABOVE THE TWO-LEVEL

(1)   Doubles of the artificially opened suit are card-showing (typically 13+ to 15 or 16 HCP) and suggest a balanced hand. A double may also be the initial call with a battleship. Double followed by double is penalty-oriented.

(2)   A cuebid of opener's real suit at the three-level is takeout. A bid of opener's real suit when he shows a four-level minor suit preempt promises both majors.

(3)   Simple changes of suit (including a cuebid of the artificially opened suit) are natural over-calls.

(4)   Notrump overcalls show balanced hands with opening strong notrump values.

(5)   Pass followed by double is takeout with a hand not strong enough to make a direct double.

---

If you know that many of your opponents will be playing Bergen preempts — especially in a long match — some special (and specific) agreements will vastly improve your results. For example, suppose LHO opens 2♦ showing a two-level spade preempt. Partner passes and RHO bids 2♥ (In-between Inquiry) or 2♠. You pass, LHO passes and partner bids 2NT. We suggest that the 2NT bid show a minor suit takeout. Partner's hand might be either of these:

(a)     ♠ 3  ♥ 94  ♦ KQ1087  ♣ A10983

(b)     ♠ 42  ♥ A  ♦ QJ984  ♣ QJ1093

We have one final suggestion for defending against Two Under or other wide-range preemptive two-bids. Before play commences against opponents who are using such methods, inquire what their understandings are regarding the minimum and maximum quality and length of suit shown as well as overall strength. This information is often critical in judging the best course of action for your side in the bidding, play and defense. It is information to which you are entitled and it must be given.

This concludes our presentation of Two Under preempts, which we refer to as Bergen preempts out of deference to their leading exponent. They are designed to make life difficult for the opponents playing against them. Played with discipline, they will succeed in accomplishing that objective. For regular partnerships who play in events which permit Two Under Bergen preempts, they are certainly worth knowing.

# CHAPTER 9

# CONVENTIONAL PREEMPTS
## UNSPECIFIED ONE-SUITERS

In addition to the Multi openings discussed in Chapter 7 and the Bergen Two Under preempts described in Chapter 8, other conventional calls have been designed to show one-suited preempts. All have the advantage of getting the hand played from the right side of the table — thus concealing the stronger hand — much more often than standard preemptive openings. Most enable you to distinguish constructive three-level openings from those which are strictly preemptive. In this chapter we present a unique form of conventional preempt — where opener's suit is not immediately known.

## THREE-LEVEL
## MINOR SUIT PREEMPTS

Most artificial 2NT openings (and other conventional bids) which show a three-level preempt are designed to distinguish constructive preempts from those that are strictly preemptive in nature. For example, suppose you pick up either of these hands at favorable vulnerability in first chair:

(a)     ♠ J109   ♥ 7   ♦ AQJ10976   ♣ 85

(b)     ♠ 7   ♥ 43   ♦ QJ10872   ♣ J974

There would be nothing wrong with opening 3♦ with (a) if your partnership plays sound preemptive openings. But if that is the case, do not even consider opening 3♦ with (b). If you open both hands 3♦, you do not need Bob Hamman or Bobby Wolff as a partner; you need a fortune teller across the table from you — maybe his crystal ball can determine the best course of action for your side.

There is a way to show both (a) and (b), using an approach similar to the NAMYATS method of opening four of a major:

(1)     Open 2NT with a weak, preemptive minor suit three-level opening.

(2)     Open three of your suit with a sound, constructive minor suit three-level opening.

The following outlines the requirements and responses for a conventional 2NT opening showing a weak preempt in either clubs or diamonds.

---

## REQUIREMENTS FOR OPENING 2NT SHOWING A WEAK 3♣ OR 3♦ BID

(1)     A weak seven-card suit (sometimes longer); frequently a reasonable six-card suit.

(2)     Little or no outside strength.

(3)     Typically 3-7 HCP.

(4)     No four-card major.

(5)     Preferably, no Ace or King outside your suit.

(6)     Preferably, no void(s).

(7)     Preferably, no "Quacks."

---

What, then are the requirements for opening a constructive 3♣ or 3♦?

## REQUIREMENTS FOR OPENING A CONSTRUCTIVE 3♣ OR 3♦

(1)   A good seven-card suit or an exceptional six-card suit.

(2)   Sufficient values and playing strength to make you hope to hear partner bid 3NT.

(3)   No four-card major.

(4)   Preferably, no void(s).

(5)   Preferably, very little strength outside your suit.

To avoid any possible misunderstanding regarding the differences between a 2NT opening and a 3♣ or 3♦ bid, examine a few hands that you might consider opening with a three-level preempt. Both sides are vulnerable; you are the dealer and hold the following hands:

(a)   ♠ A4  ♥ Q107  ♦ KJ106542  ♣ J
OPEN 1♦ (OR PASS).   This is neither a 2NT nor a 3♦ opening; you have far too much outside strength.  Your authors believe that this hand is worth a 1♦ opening, but conservative partnerships that require more strength for a one-level opening could pass. Maybe they can enter the auction later.

(b)   ♠ K4  ♥ 7  ♦ KQ109652  ♣ 983
OPEN 3♦.   This is a typical constructive three-level minor suit opening that is not close to an opening one-bid in strength. You have a good seven-card suit and a potential outside entry.  If partner bids 3NT, this dummy will delight him.

(c) ♠ 1095 ♥ 43 ♦ 8 ♣ AQ86532

OPEN 2NT. Partnerships that agree to open extremely bad preempts would consider this a good hand and open 3♣ because the Ace of your suit is a potential entry for notrump. Vulnerable, we consider this a maximum 2NT opening. However, if we were not vulnerable, our choice would be 3♣.

(d) ♠ 7 ♥ 109 ♦ K105 ♣ AQ109752

OPEN 3♣. You have an excellent suit and a potential outside entry.

With neither side vulnerable you pick up:

(e) ♠ J107 ♥ 7 ♦ 873 ♣ KQJ1097

OPEN 3♣. As with (c), the correct opening bid may well depend on your partnership style and agreements. We believe this hand qualifies for a 3♣ opening, a good aggressive move non-vulnerable.

(f) ♠ 4 ♥ J1092 ♦ KQ10976 ♣ J6

PASS. There is nothing wrong with your suit for either a 2NT or 3♦ opening. The problem is your four-card major, especially in first or second seat.

(g) ♠ J105 ♥ Q109 ♦ — ♣ AJ108653

PASS. A 3♣ opening could easily prevent your side from getting together in one of the majors. If partner enters the auction, you will be in a great position to compete.

(h) ♠ J10 ♥ 9 ♦ AQJ8732 ♣ 983

OPEN 3♦. A classic constructive 3♦ bid for all partnerships.

When partner is a passed hand, (and especially when you are in third chair), it is permissible to relax the restrictions against opening 3♣ or 3♦ (either direct or via a 2NT opening) with a four-card major.

Your responses to 2NT (showing a minor suit preempt) are:

---

## RESPONSES TO CONVENTIONAL 2NT
## SHOWING A WEAK 3♣ OR 3♦ BID

(1)   3♣ is "**pass** or **correct**"; opener passes with clubs and bids 3♦ with diamonds.

(2)   3♦ is a conventional Rosenkranz inquiry, asking for a three-card major. Opener rebids:

  3♥ = three spades.
  3♠ = three hearts.
  3NT = no three-card major.
  4♣ = three cards in both majors, shortness in clubs.
  4♦ = three cards in both majors, shortness in diamonds.

  3♥ and 3♠ allow the strong hand to declare.

(3)   3♥ and 3♠ are natural and forcing, promising a six-card suit. With a five-card major, use the conventional inquiry.

(4)   3NT is natural, to play.

(5)   4♣ and 5♣ are "**pass** or **correct**."

(6)   4♥ and 4♠ are to play.

---

With neither side vulnerable, partner opens 2NT and you hold:

(a)   ♠ AK1095  ♥ AQ  ♦ K109  ♣ K108
RESPOND 3♦. Four of a major will play better than 3NT if your side has an eight-card spade fit. If partner does not have three spades, you will play 3NT.

(b) ♠ KQ1095 ♥ KQ10 ♦ A109 ♣ AJ
RESPOND 3♦. True, all games may be hopeless if partner holds a poor 2NT pre-empt. Nevertheless, we would refuse to settle for a partscore — the ♥ 10 could easily be the make-or-break card in a no-trump game. Before settling in 3NT, find out if opener holds three spades; since game rates to be better with an eight-card fit.

(c) ♠ QJ109 ♥ KJ7632 ♦ J104 ♣ —
RESPOND 3♣. Hope that partner corrects to 3♦. 3♥ would be 100% forcing, and you do not want to get any higher on what is very likely a misfit. Be grateful you are non-vulnerable since partner is an over-whelming favorite to have clubs.

(d) ♠ AK ♥ KQJ10854 ♦ K5 ♣ Q3
RESPOND 4♥. Even facing a non-vulnera-ble weak minor suit preempt, we would not stop short of game.

(e) ♠ KJ10974 ♥ A5 ♦ AJ10 ♣ K7
RESPOND 3♠. Natural and forcing. Using the conventional Rosenkranz inquiry, three-level major suit responses to 2NT promise six-card suits. Responder can raise with either a doubleton or a singleton honor.

There is no reason to change your responding structure after a direct 3♣ or 3♦ opening. Use the same responses you play if you were not using 2NT to show the weak three-level minor suit preempt. Responder knows that when partner opens 3♣ or 3♦, he holds a sound, constructive three-bid.

The advantage of knowing that opener held a constructive preempt (even at favorable vulnerability) proved most useful to East on the following deal witnessed by one of your authors as Chief Vugraph Commentator for the 1991 European Championships played in Killarney, Ireland. Here is the complete deal, auctions from both rooms, and results:

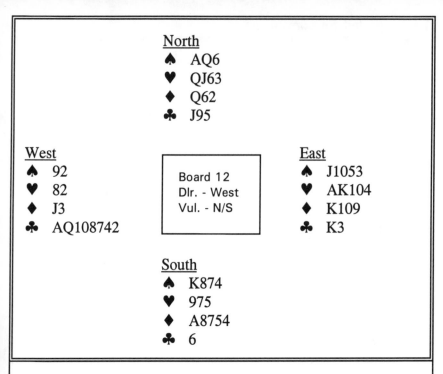

North
- ♠ AQ6
- ♥ QJ63
- ♦ Q62
- ♣ J95

West
- ♠ 92
- ♥ 82
- ♦ J3
- ♣ AQ108742

Board 12
Dlr. - West
Vul. - N/S

East
- ♠ J1053
- ♥ AK104
- ♦ K109
- ♣ K3

South
- ♠ K874
- ♥ 975
- ♦ A8754
- ♣ 6

OPEN ROOM

Opening Lead ♦ 5
N/S -430

| West | North | East | South |
|------|-------|------|-------|
| 3♣ (a) | P | 3NT (b) | P |
| P | P | | |

(a) A sound, constructive preempt; 2NT would have shown a weak preempt in clubs or diamonds.

(b) Armed with the knowledge that partner held a good club preempt, 3NT rated to have some play.

In this room — seen on Vugraph — East did not have to guess. His partner would have opened 2NT with a weak three-level club preempt; 3♣ was constructive. He therefore carried on to game holding the King of clubs and stoppers in the unbid suits.

Hand repeated for convenience:

```
                         North
                      ♠  AQ6
                      ♥  QJ63
                      ♦  Q62
                      ♣  J95

West                                        East
♠  92              ┌─────────────┐         ♠  J1053
♥  82              │ Board 12    │         ♥  AK104
♦  J3              │ Dlr. - West │         ♦  K109
♣  AQ108742        │ Vul. - N/S  │         ♣  K3
                   └─────────────┘
                         South
                      ♠  K874
                      ♥  975
                      ♦  A8754
                      ♣  6
```

| CLOSED ROOM | | Opening Lead ♦ 2 |
| | | N/S -130 |

| West | North | East | South |
|------|-------|------|-------|
| 3♣ (a) | P | P (b) | P |
| P | | | |

(a)  A simple preempt with its strength not clearly defined.
(b)  Reasonable action since the exact nature of the 3♣ opening
     was unknown.  For all East knew, the partnership might
     have been overboard in 3♣!

It is difficult to fault the East-West pair in the closed room for
stopping in 3♣.  East was forced to guess the nature of West's
preempt.  Considering the vulnerability, he decided that the opening
bid probably had been based on a weak hand, or a hand without the
Ace of clubs.

Players using old-fashioned methods would have a far better chance of reaching game on the East-West cards than many of today's aggressive preempters. When you use 2NT to describe a weak minor suit preempt, you should not miss many makeable games when partner opens 3♣ or 3♦.

When RHO doubles partner's 2NT opening, we recommend the following:

---

### RESPONSES AFTER DOUBLES OF 2NT SHOWING A MINOR SUIT PREEMPT

(1)     Redouble informs partner that responder holds a strong hand and may well be interested in penalizing the opponents.

(2)     All bids except 3♥ and 3♠ carry their non-competitive meaning (e.g., 3♣ is "**pass** or **correct**").

(3)     3♥ and 3♠ are natural and non-forcing.

(4)     Pass informs opener that responder has his own minor and wishes to play in that suit. The pass is conventional, asking opener to bid 3♣ which responder will pass (with clubs) or correct to 3♦. A double later is penalty.

---

Using these methods, what action would you take after partner's first-seat 2NT opening gets doubled when you hold:

(a)     ♠ KQ109   ♥ AQ107   ♦ A1095   ♣ J
      REDOUBLE. Inform partner that you hold an excellent hand with considerable interest in doubling your opponents.

(b)     ♠ A1072   ♥ 85   ♦ 4   ♣ KQJ1095
      PASS. This shows a minor suit of your own. Partner is requested to bid 3♣ which you will pass.

Should the opponents make an overcall of partner's 2NT opening, we suggest the following:

---

### RESPONSES AFTER AN OVERCALL OF PARTNER'S OPENING 2NT SHOWING A MINOR SUIT PREEMPT

(1) Double is for penalties.

(2) Bids in new suit (except clubs) are natural actions — invitational, but not forcing.

(3) Any club bid by responder is "**pass** or **correct**".

(4) Cuebids are (game-forcing) slam tries in opener's suit. Opener is asked to show any distributional feature outside his suit.

(5) All game bids are natural, to play.

---

For example, partner opens 2NT, RHO bids 3♥ and you hold:

> ♠ A10932  ♥ 74  ♦ A105  ♣ KJ8
> RESPOND 4♣. "**Pass** or **correct**." This hand is worth competing to the four-level in partner's minor suit.

We do not advise any specific methods to combat enemy intervention over constructive 3♣ and 3♦ openings. Simply add the penalty double and strength-showing redouble to your potential responses and keep in mind that opener has a constructive — not preemptive — three-level opening.

## DEFENSES AGAINST THREE-LEVEL MINOR SUIT PREEMPTS

Successful defense against conventional 2NT openings (which show an unspecified minor suit preempt) requires a few countermeasures. We suggest the following:

## DEFENSES AGAINST 2NT OPENINGS SHOWING A MINOR SUIT PREEMPT

(1)   Double shows at least the values for a strong notrump opening. Partner responds to the double as though the doubler had made a strong notrump opening; i.e., he may bid 3♣ Stayman and use 3♦ and 3♥ as transfer bids.

(2)   Pass followed by double is for takeout.

(3)   3♣ shows a distributional hand, takeout for the majors, with values for a Michaels cuebid.

(4)   3♦, 3♥ and 3♠ are natural overcalls.

(5)   3NT and other game-level calls are to play.

Regular partnerships may want to include transfer overcalls as part of their defense against this convention (e.g., 3♥ shows a 3♠ overcall).

---

Some readers may be unfamiliar with transfer overcalls, which are very simple and can be extremely effective. They can be used in a variety of situations, but are most helpful as a tool to combat enemy preempts — particularly modern types where opener's suit(s) may not be known — and seem to be increasing in popularity and frequency of occurrence.

A transfer overcall is a suit bid that shows the suit directly above it and promises the strength for an overcall at the level bid. Since responder cannot pass a transfer overcall, its strength is unlimited. In response, partner signs off in the transfer overcaller's real suit or makes the bid he would have made over a natural overcall.

The primary purpose of transfer overcalls is to facilitate auctions when the opponents preempt and you have a two-suiter. They can also be used to describe a hand with a long solid suit and a stopper in the enemy suit — similar to a gambling 3NT.

## TRANSFER OVERCALLS AGAINST 2NT SHOWING A MINOR SUIT PREEMPT

(1)    3♣ is artificial and shows both majors.

(2)    3♦ is a 3♥ overcall.

(3)    3♥ is a 3♠ overcall.

(4)    3♠ shows an exceptional minor suit and asks partner to bid 3NT with a stopper in a minor. Lacking a stopper, partner makes an appropriate call. Both 4♣ and 5♣ are "**pass** or **correct**."

Suppose RHO makes a conventional 2NT opening showing a weak three-bid in clubs or diamonds and you hold:

(a)    ♠ AKJ432  ♥ 3  ♦ 7  ♣ AQJ94
OVERCALL 3♥. The danger of making a spade overcall (either 3♠ or 4♠) is that your side may belong in clubs when partner passes your spade overcall. A transfer overcall solves this problem — you will bid 4♣ after partner corrects to 3♠ — insuring that you will find your side's best strain.

(b)    ♠ A7  ♥ AKQ10873  ♦ K4  ♣ K7
OVERCALL 3♦. When you transfer to hearts then bid 3NT you will describe this hand perfectly.

(c)    ♠ KJ107  ♥ AQJ976  ♦ A4  ♣ 3
OVERCALL 3♦. When partner makes the expected 3♥ rebid, you will bid 3♠ showing hearts as your primary suit with a side four-card spade suit. Were you 5/5 or better in the majors, you would have used the conventional, artificial 3♣ bid.

# 2NT SHOWING AN UNSPECIFIED THREE-LEVEL PREEMPT

Some partnerships expand the utility of the conventional 2NT opening we have been discussing to describe a weak three-level preempt in **any** suit. When you have one artificial opening bid (2NT) that describes a weak three-level preempt in any one of the four suits, you have added considerably to the potential difficulty in responding and handling enemy intervention. That is the bad news. The good news is that it makes it far more difficult for your opponents to enter the auction immediately since opener's suit is unknown. Cuebids, for example, are not possible.

The guidelines for opening the more versatile conventional 2NT are almost the same as when the 2NT opening was restricted to the minor suits. The following box repeats those requirements:

---

## REQUIREMENTS FOR OPENING 2NT SHOWING ANY 3-LEVEL PREEMPT

(1) A weak seven-card suit (sometimes longer); frequently a reasonable six-card suit.

(2) A one-suited hand.

(3) Little or no outside strength.

(4) Typically 3-7 HCP.

(5) No outside four-card major.

(6) Preferably, no Ace or King outside your suit.

(7) Preferably, no void(s).

(8) Preferably, no "Quacks."

---

The responses outlined below require a little memorization but are straightforward:

# RESPONSES TO OPENING 2NT
## SHOWING ANY 3-LEVEL OPENING PREEMPT

(1)    3♣ is "**pass** or **correct**."

(2)    3♦ is a strong, game-forcing relay. Opener rebids:

        3♥  =  spade preempt.

        3♠  =  heart preempt.

        3NT =  club or diamond preempt; suit has two of the top four honors (including the Ace or King).

        4♣  =  club preempt; suit that did not qualify for a 3NT response to 3♦.

        4♦  =  diamond preempt; suit that did not qualify for a 3NT response to 3♦.

(3)    3♥ and 3♠ are natural. They usually show a 6-card suit and are game forcing. Opener rebids:

        (i)      game in responder's suit with a doubleton (or better) or singleton honor.

        (ii)     the other major when that is his suit.

        (iii)    3NT with a hand that would qualify for a 3NT response to the 3♦ inquiry.

        (iv)    4♣ or 4♦ natural.

(4)    3NT asks responder to pass with a minor or correct to the major by bidding 4♣ with hearts or 4♦ with spades.

(5)    4♥, 4♠, 5♣ and 5♦ are to play.

Suppose partner opens 2NT showing an unspecified three-level preempt, both sides vulnerable, when you hold:

(a)      ♠ KJ9832   ♥ J   ♦ J75   ♣ A93

RESPOND 3♣. With no interest in game, you want partner to sign off in his suit. Opener will pass if his suit is clubs or bid his suit at the three-level.

(b)      ♠ A5   ♥ AKJ1096   ♦ KQ4   ♣ K10

RESPOND 3♥. Opener's rebid over your forcing response should place you in an excellent position to play your best game contract. With a doubleton heart (or better), partner will raise to 4♥. Lacking heart support opener will bid 3♠ with spades (which you will raise to game), or show a three-level minor suit preempt by bidding 3NT (showing a good suit) which you will pass. If partner rebids 4♣ or 4♦, you will have the option, of raising or correcting to 4♥.

(c)      ♠ AJ10   ♥ KQ10   ♦ A1094   ♣ AJ9

RESPOND 3♦. Partner's response to your forcing relay will identify his suit and should enable you to set the final contract.

(d)      ♠ K109   ♥ AK   ♦ AKQ10763   ♣ 10

RESPOND 3NT. You have a perfect hand for this bid. If partner has a club preempt, he will pass. Should opener bid 4♣ (showing hearts), you will happily bid 4♥. If partner rebids 4♦, showing spades, make a Keycard inquiry (via 4NT) since a spade slam rates to be odds on if you are not missing the two black Aces.

(e)      ♠ AKJ1052   ♥ Q3   ♦ J75   ♣ 109

RESPOND 3♣. You cannot bid 3♠ directly. 3♠ over 2NT would be 100% forcing so you must make the conventional sign-off.

In non-competitive auctions, the expanded scope of the conventional 2NT opening rarely creates serious problems with the proper use of the responses we have suggested. When the enemy intervenes, however, things become more complicated since responder does not initially know opener's suit.

Over enemy doubles, we recommend methods similar to those we suggested over a double of 2NT openings which show a weak three-level preempt in clubs or diamonds. Those methods are:

---

## RESPONSES AFTER DOUBLES OF 2NT SHOWING ANY 3-LEVEL PREEMPT

(1)   Redouble informs opener that responder holds a strong hand and may well be interested in penalizing the opponents.

(2)   All bids carry their non-competitive meaning.

(3)   Pass informs opener that responder has his own suit and wishes to play in that suit. The pass is conventional, asking opener to bid 3♣ which responder will pass (with clubs) or correct to his suit.

---

When the opponents overcall your 2NT opening showing an unspecified three-level preempt, you can respond as follows:

---

## RESPONSES AFTER OVERCALLS OF 2NT SHOWING ANY 3-LEVEL PREEMPT

(1)   Double is for penalties.

(2)   Suit bids below game are natural and forcing.

(3)   Game bids are sign-offs.

(4)   4NT is Blackwood.

---

# DEFENSES AGAINST 2NT SHOWING AN UNSPECIFIED THREE-LEVEL PREEMPT

We recommend essentially the same countermeasures against a 2NT opening showing a weak three-level preempt in an unspecified suit as we did against a 2NT opening showing a weak 3♣ or 3♦ preempt. We still advise playing a 3♣ overcall to show both majors. We also feel that it is more important to play transfer overcalls starting at 3♦.

So much for artificial 2NT openings that show an unspecified three-level preemptive opening.

If you can envision the problems such openings can give your opponents, plus the clarity given to your three-level openings (direct and indirect), then we strongly urge you to adopt the conventional 2♠ opening we are about to present.


# 2♠ SHOWING AN UNSPECIFIED THREE-LEVEL PREEMPT

We favor using 2♠ (rather than 2NT) to show an unspecified three-level preempt for several reasons:

(1)   Playing Multi 2♦ — which we recommend — 2♠ is not needed to show a preemptive 2♠ bid (which can be shown via 2♦).

(2)   A conventional 2♠ opening allows responder to make inquiries via a 2NT response.

(3)   Although the conventional 2NT can be passed by responder, such an action is not really a threat to the other side, nor is it a particularly effective tactic. Passing 2♠, on the other hand, is a distinct possibility if responder has length in spades and no interest in game. It is also a fine tactical psych

when responder knows that the hand belongs to the enemy and is confident that his opponents can record a greater plus by bidding than by defending 2♠ undoubled.

(4)    2♠ can be used without losing the benefit of what often is considered a useful natural opening call: the strong, natural 2NT opening.

For those of you who are bored with the repetitive requirements section of the following box, please skip it and go directly to the section on responses. It includes at least one effective conventional response unavailable over artificial 2NT openings which describe the unspecified three-level preempt.

---

### REQUIREMENTS FOR OPENING 2♠ SHOWING AN UNSPECIFIED THREE-LEVEL PREEMPT

(1)    A weak seven-card suit; more frequently a reasonable six-card suit.

(2)    A one-suited hand.

(3)    Little or no outside strength.

(4)    Typically 3-7 HCP.

(5)    No outside four-card major.

(6)    Preferably, no Ace or King outside your suit.

(7)    Preferably, no void(s).

(8)    Preferably, no "Quacks."

---

Now let us look at the responses to 2♠ openings showing an unspecified one-suited hand:

## RESPONSES TO 2♠ SHOWING AN UNSPECIFIED THREE-LEVEL PREEMPT

(1) 2NT is conventional, asking opener to TRANSFER into his suit (he bids the suit below his real suit).

(2) 3♣ asks opener to pass if his suit is clubs or correct to his suit if it is not.

(3) 3♦, 3♥ and 3♠ are natural and forcing to game; typically 6+ cards in the suit.

(4) All game level calls are natural, to play.

(5) 4NT is old-fashioned Blackwood asking for Aces, then Kings via 5NT. If opener had wanted to use Keycard Blackwood in opener's suit, he would begin with 2NT and then make a Keycard inquiry via 4NT.

Consider some examples of the various responses to the artificial 2♠ opening that describes a three-level preempt in any suit. Suppose partner opens 2♠ (showing an unspecified three-level preempt) with neither side vulnerable and you pick up the following:

(a)     ♠ QJ107  ♥ KJ10  ♦ AK875  ♣ 2
RESPOND 3♣. You undoubtedly have a reasonable play for game if partner has either major, but going plus will be problematic opposite a non-vulnerable 3♣. You cannot afford to use the conventional 2NT response; you do not want to be forced to the four-level in the likely event that opener's suit is clubs. If partner bids 3♥ or 3♠ over 3♣, you intend to bid four.

(b)     ♠ K10  ♥ AK10985  ♦ A102  ♣ KQ
RESPOND 3♥. This is natural and forcing. If partner has a doubleton (or better) in

hearts, he will raise your suit to game. Lacking even modest support for hearts, he will either show his spade suit (which you will raise to game) or introduce his minor directly or via 3NT which shows a reasonably good suit.

(c)     ♠ KQJ10762   ♥ 7   ♦ AQJ9   ♣ 3
RESPOND 4♠. Whatever partner's suit is, you want to play game in spades. Bid what you think you can make.

(d)     ♠ 5   ♥ AKQJ974   ♦ AKQ10   ♣ 7
RESPOND 4NT. Good old-fashioned Blackwood. You want to know whether partner has a black Ace. If he does, you have a great shot at 6♥. If he does not, 5♥ will probably be a make. Note that you do not want to get involved with Keycard. Partner would show the King of his suit, (presumably spades or clubs), which is worthless information opposite this hand.

(e)     ♠ QJ1098   ♥ —   ♦ J1095   ♣ J1076
PASS. We could not resist the temptation to show you what a reasonable gamble might look like. True, partner may not have a spade in his hand, and on a great day he might even hold a suit other than hearts. But you do not care what he holds. If the opponents permit you to play 2♠ undoubled, they are heavy favorites to record a terrible score.

(f)     ♠ AJ7   ♥ AJ7   ♦ K1093   ♣ A65
RESPOND 2NT. If partner's suit is a major, you will play 4♥ or 4♠; if it is a minor, 3NT will be the final contract.

Going back to opener's hand, suppose you open 2♠ and partner responds 3♥. What rebid would you make over this forcing call holding the following?

(a)  ♠ 76  ♥ Q  ♦ A109763  ♣ J1095
REBID 4♥. Yes, we have repeatedly stated that a raise in this position shows at least a doubleton in support. And it does! But the Queen, even singleton, rates to be far more useful to partner than a small doubleton. 4♥ is probably your best game.

(b)  ♠ 1094  ♥ 4  ♦ KQ10965  ♣ J103
REBID 3NT. Without even a doubleton (or stiff honor) in partner's suit, inform him that you do not have spades but do have a reasonably good minor suit for opening 2♠. If your minor suit were weak you would simply bid it.

(c)  ♠ J109  ♥ 3  ♦ 85  ♣ QJ108652
REBID 4♣. You have no support for partner's suit, and with a minimum three-level club preempt, your only choice is to "rebid" your suit.

(d)  ♠ 10  ♥ 85  ♦ KJ10965  ♣ J1094
REBID 4♥. A doubleton is adequate trump support, and this hand could easily be useful for a heart game.

The following deal, which features a conventional 2♠ opening, helped propel one of your authors — playing with British star Tony Forrester — to a second-place finish in the 1992 Reisinger Board-a-Match Teams at the North American Championships in Orlando, Florida. Not only did the 2♠ opening warn responder that opener held a weak preemptive opening; it also got the hand played from the right side of the table. Here was the complete deal, the auctions at both tables and the results:

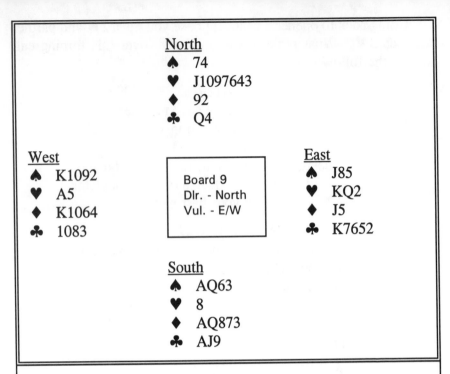

North
- ♠ 74
- ♥ J1097643
- ♦ 92
- ♣ Q4

West
- ♠ K1092
- ♥ A5
- ♦ K1064
- ♣ 1083

Board 9
Dlr. - North
Vul. - E/W

East
- ♠ J85
- ♥ KQ2
- ♦ J5
- ♣ K7652

South
- ♠ AQ63
- ♥ 8
- ♦ AQ873
- ♣ AJ9

| OUR TABLE | | | Opening Lead ♠ 2 |
| | | | N/S +140 |

| West | *Andersen* North | East | *Forrester* South |
|------|-------|------|-------|
| — | 2♠ (a) | P | 2NT (b) |
| P | 3♦ (c) | P | 3♥ (d) |
| P | P | P | |

(a) Not a maximum, even at favorable vulnerability.

(b) Sufficient assets for the conventional inquiry asking opener to bid the suit below his real suit.

(c) Showing hearts.

(d) Too bad! Game rated to be iron-clad if partner's suit were anything other than hearts.

At the other table, North opened 3♥ and South raised to 4♥ which went down two tricks (♠ 5 lead), resulting in -100 for N/S.

Although neither pair of our opponents had a good result on this deal, no one did anything that could be described as terrible. At our table, West's opening lead was unfortunate; only the lead of the Ace of hearts would defeat the contract. At the other table North/South were forced to guess whether or not game was a reasonable undertaking and went wrong. In addition, the defense had the advantage of seeing the strong hand.

When the opponents compete directly over a 2♠ opening, we simply add the penalty double and redouble to our responses. Over a takeout double, pass informs partner that responder has spades and a desire to play 2♠ doubled. Other bids carry the non-competitive meaning they had over the conventional 2NT opening showing an unspecified three-level preempt.

## DEFENSES AGAINST 2♠ SHOWING AN UNSPECIFIED THREE-LEVEL PREEMPT

Our defensive measures when we have the misfortune of having to play against this conventional 2♠ opening are similar to the countermeasures we recommend over conventional 2NT openings. Since 2NT is available as an additional call, we use double to describe a balanced hand with 14-16 HCP (or a battleship too strong for 2NT), and 2NT to show a balanced 17-19 point hand. We play Stayman and transfer responses over that 2NT. A 3♣ bid shows both majors. Other overcalls are natural, and pass followed by double is takeout. Alternatively, you may elect to play transfer overcalls.

This concludes our discussion of artificial openings that describe various one-suited preempts. In addition to placing considerable pressure on your opponents, such openings are used to clarify the nature of your preempt. They also frequently get the hand played from the right side of the table — a considerable advantage.

There is no way we could describe every conventional method devised to show one-suited preempts of various strengths. Even as you read this, someone somewhere is designing another vehicle to impede the exchange of information between opponents while revealing to partner every spot card in a poor hand containing a relatively long suit.

We are now ready to turn our attention to the most sophisticated preemptive weapons devised to date. Some cynics and purists, like the late Victor Mollo, believe they belong in an episode of <u>Star Trek</u>, not in a respectable bridge book. As one of your authors once said to the great British bridge writer, player and philosopher, "I agree with you, Victor, but who are **you** and **I** against so MANY!"

# CHAPTER 10

# CONVENTIONAL BIDS SHOWING
# ONE- AND TWO-SUITERS
## WEAK AND STRONG

Many of the conventional preempts we have discussed (and are about to discuss) are described as **modern** — but they are not. Several were devised and played decades ago. Flint, for example, designed the first Multi well over a quarter of a century ago. Bergen Two Under preempts began to evolve in the 1970s. Many of these conventions have been modified and improved over the years, but many have stood the test of time and remain relatively unchanged.

## 2NT SHOWING
## BOTH MINORS

The artificial 2NT opening showing both minors no doubt is an offshoot of the Unusual Notrump overcall devised by Al Roth in 1948 and developed by him with Tobias Stone. The popularity of this special 2NT opening increased when Howard Schenken made it part of his Schenken Club system in the 1950s.

By today's standards, Schenken's requirements for a conventional 2NT opening showing a two-suiter in the minors were quite
conservative; in fact, they were a bit stodgy.    In addition to
requiring at least five clubs and five diamonds, Schenken called for
13-16 HCP vulnerable and 10-12 HCP non-vulnerable.

We see no reason to waste the potentially valuable 2NT opening
to describe hands that clearly (or nearly) qualify for opening one-
bids (with simple rebids).   Instead, we suggest lowering the strength
requirements considerably from Schenken's standards.   We recommend the approximate high card strength of a weak two-bid — 4-10
or conservatively 5-11 HCP — for an artificial 2NT opening
showing long clubs and long diamonds.   The following box outlines
the understandings and agreements you should have when playing
2NT openings as preemptive showing both clubs and diamonds:

---

## REQUIREMENTS FOR OPENING 2NT SHOWING THE MINORS

(1)   At least 5 clubs and 5 diamonds.   Both suits
      should have reasonable internal strength,
      especially vulnerable.

(2)   Approximately 5-10 HCP concentrated in your
      minor suits.  Strength may vary with vulnera-
      bility, position, texture of suits, form of scor-
      ing, state of game, etc.

(3)   Preferably, no Aces or Kings in the majors.

(4)   Preferably, no voids(s); therefore, no three-
      card major.

(5)   Preferably, no major suit "Quacks."

---

Responses to the conventional 2NT opening showing both
minors are simple yet thorough:

# RESPONSES TO 2NT OPENING
## SHOWING BOTH MINORS

(1)  3♣ and 3♦ are to play.

(2)  3♥ and 3♠ are natural and forcing to game. They promise an exceptional five-card suit or (typically) a good six-card suit. Opener then makes the following rebids:
- Raises responder's suit with two- or three-card support.
- Bids another major or 3NT, whichever is cheaper, with a singleton or void in responder's suit.
- Shows a six-card suit whenever he does not have support for partner's suit.

(3)  3NT is to play.

(4)  4♣ and 4♦ are invitational in the bid minor.

(5)  4♥, 4♠, 5♣ and 5♦ are to play.

(6)  4NT is a Keycard Inquiry for six keycards. The keycards are the four Aces, the club King and the diamond King. Opener responds:

    5♣ = 0; 5♦ = 1; 5♥ = 2; 5♠ = 3
    The next suit bid by responder asks for minor suit Queens (1st step = no Queens; 2nd step = club Queen; 3rd step = diamond Queen; 4th step = both minor suit Queens).

Using these methods, responding to a conventional 2NT opening rarely creates any problems. For example, suppose partner opens 2NT with both sides vulnerable and you hold one of the following hands:

(a)    ♠ KQ983  ♥ KQ964  ♦ J3  ♣ Q
RESPOND 3♦. Do not be tempted to pass 2NT or raise to 3NT with such hands. Show your diamond preference and hope the enemy contests the auction in one of the majors, or 3NT — you will then double.

(b)    ♠ A52  ♥ 7632  ♦ KQ103  ♣ K5
RESPOND 4♦. This is a game invitation. With a conservative partner you might even jump to game although we prefer 4♦. Do not hang partner for an aggressive 2NT opening.

(c)    ♠ AK4  ♥ A52  ♦ KJ104  ♣ AQ9
RESPOND 4NT. If partner holds the Ace-Queen of diamonds and the ♣ K, you should be able to win all the tricks with diamonds trump. Find out if you are missing any key cards in the minors via the 4NT (6 keycards) inquiry.

(d)    ♠ KQ10  ♥ AQ10874  ♦ AJ7  ♣ J
RESPOND 3♥. If partner has two (or three) hearts, you will play your major suit game. Without two or three hearts, partner will either bid 3NT (which you will pass) or show a six-card minor (in which case you will play 5♦).

(e)    ♠ KQ108  ♥ KQ109  ♦ KJ  ♣ A105
RESPOND 3NT. You have both majors triple-stopped and useful cards in both minors. The opponents will be hard-pressed to successfully attack any suit.

Since responder knows both of opener's suits — as well as his approximate strength — enemy intervention over a 2NT opener rarely causes any serious problems for responder. Here are the understandings we advise when the opponents compete:

# THE OPPONENTS COMPETE OVER 2NT SHOWING BOTH MINORS

When the opponents double:

(1) Redouble informs opener that responder holds a good hand. He is frequently interested in penalizing the opponents.

(2) All bids except 3♥ and 3♠ carry their non-competitive meaning. 3♥ and 3♠ are natural and non-forcing.

(3) Pass shows equal length in the minors, and asks partner to choose.

When the opponents overcall 3♥ or 3♠:

(1) Double is for penalty.

(2) 4♣ and 4♦ are natural; opener may raise with a maximum.

(3) 3♠ over 3♥ is natural and invitational.

(4) 3NT and all other game bids are to play.

(5) 4NT asks opener for keycards in both minors.

The opponents overcall 3♣ or 3♦ (cuebid showing majors):

(1) Double is lead-directing.

(2) Pass followed by double is penalty.

(3) 3♥ is a game try in clubs; 3♠ is a game try in diamonds.

(4) 3NT is to play

(5) 4♣ and 4♦ are preemptive and suggest a save.

(6) 4NT asks opener for keycards in both minors.

(7) 5♣ and 5♦ are to play.

If your opponents use 2NT to show both minors, we recommend simple defensive measures. Double shows a strong balanced hand (partner responds to a strong notrump — 3♣ is Stayman and three-level bids can be transfers). Minor suit cuebids describe stronger, more distributional major suit takeouts.

## RUBIN TWO-BIDS

Rubin two-bids were developed by American expert Ira Rubin. They show a weak two-bid in the suit above the one bid, OR a strong one- or two-suiter with the suit opened. The strong hands are balanced (with or without five cards in the suit bid):

---

### RUBIN TWO-BIDS

(1)  2♣ shows one of the following:
   (a)  A weak two-bid in diamonds (most often).
   (b)  A strong one- or two-suiter with clubs.
   (c)  A balanced hand with 22-24 HCP.
   (d)  A strong, artificial 2♣ opening.

(2)  2♦ shows one of the following:
   (a)  A weak two-bid in hearts (most often).
   (b)  A strong one- or two-suiter with diamonds.
   (c)  A balanced hand with 25-27 HCP.

(3)  2♥ shows one of the following:
   (a)  A weak two-bid in spades (most often).
   (b)  A strong one- or two-suiter with hearts.
   (c)  A balanced hand with 20+ to 22 HCP.

(4)  2♠ shows one of the following:
   (a)  A constructive three-level preempt in clubs (most often).
   (b)  A strong one- or two-suiter with spades.
   (c)  A balanced hand, 25-27 HCP, five spades.

---

All responses presume that opener has a weak two-bid in the next suit (or a three-level club preempt when the opening bid is 2♠). Rubin recommends the following relatively simple responses:

---

## RESPONSES TO RUBIN TWO-BIDS

(1) The next suit is a sign-off if opener has the anticipated weak hand.

(2) 2NT over 2♣, 2♦ and 2♥ is conventional. Responder answers via Ogust.

(3) 2NT over 2♠ is a conventional inquiry. Opener responds:
- 3♣ shows a strong hand in spades (responder bids 3♦ to ask if opener holds a one-suiter, two-suiter or balanced hand).
- 3♦/♥/♠ are standard Ogust responses.

Note that opener never opens 2♠ with a weak hand and weak clubs.

(4) New suits (other than the next suit) are natural and forcing. They presume opener has the weak hand.

(5) Jumps are preemptive, presuming the weak hand.

(6) Jumps to game are natural and to play.

---

On the rare occasions when opener has a strong hand, he tells partner immediately. Over responder's sign-off in the next suit (presuming a weak hand), opener:

(1) Rebids the suit he opened with a one-suiter;

(2) Bids a new suit (including raising the next suit) to show a two-suiter; or

(3)     Bids notrump to show a strong balanced
        hand.

Similarly, when responder bids 2NT or a new suit, showing a strong
hand, opener:

(1)     Rebids the suit he opened at the four-level
        with a one-suiter;

(2)     Introduces a second suit at the four-level
        with a two-suiter;

(3)     Bids notrump with a strong balanced hand.

Playing Rubin two-bids, consider a few examples.  What
opening bid would you make with the following hands?

(a)     ♠ KQJ5  ♥ A  ♦ J10  ♣ AKJ1073
        OPEN 2♣.  Suppose partner signs off in
        2♦, presuming you hold a 2♦ preempt.
        You rebid 2♠ to show a good two-suited
        hand with clubs and spades.

(b)     ♠ J104  ♥ KQ10974  ♦ 54  ♣ J9
        OPEN 2♦.  If partner makes a forcing 2♠
        response, rebid 3♠ to show your 2♥ pre-
        empt and your spade support.

(c)     ♠ 7  ♥ AQJ10  ♦ AKQJ52  ♣ K4
        OPEN 2♦.  If partner responds 2♠, jump
        to 4♥ to show your powerful two-suiter
        with diamonds and hearts as a second suit.

(d)     ♠ KQJ107  ♥ 63  ♦ K109  ♣ 985
        OPEN 2♥.  A modern preemptive two-bid
        in spades.

(e)     ♠ 9  ♥ K10  ♦ 984  ♣ KQ109763
        OPEN 2♠.  Typical constructive 3♣ open-
        ing.  Never open 2♠ with a weak three-
        level preempt in clubs when playing Rubin
        two-bids.

When opener shows a strong opening after a constructive new suit or conventional 2NT response, the partnership assets are almost always in the slam zone. Therefore, 4♥ in the following auction is forcing: 2♦-P-2♠-P-4♥.

Conversely, after a simple response in the next suit — indicating no game interest if opener holds the weak hand — opener's rebid shows a strong one- or two-suiter and is not game-forcing. For example, 2♠ in the following auction is forcing only for one round; 2♣-P-2♦-P-2♠. Opener has a strong hand with clubs and spades.

Rubin two-bids are not quite as versatile as several of the Multi openings described in Chapter 7, but have this advantage: responder typically knows opener's suit immediately. Rubin two-bids also simplify the description of strong one- and two-suited hands as well as balanced strong hands that contain five-card majors.

Defending against Rubin two-bids is easier than defending against Multi 2♦ openings because opener's suit usually is known. The defenders should make the same assumption that responder makes, that opener holds a weak hand with the suit above the suit opened. Double can be used to show a balanced 13+ to 15 HCP; 2NT should describe a good strong notrump (with the responses used over the partnership's strong notrump openings), and a bid of the next suit (opener's real suit with a weak two-bid) should be a takeout double of that suit. Other bids, responses and rebids should convey the same meaning they would have had over a weak two-bid.

# TWO-WAY TWO-LEVEL PREEMPTIVE OPENINGS

An increasingly popular artificial two-bid is used to describe a weak two-bid in a major or a major-minor two-suited hand. This type of bid is a favorite with many European players.

## 2♦ SHOWING A WEAK 2♥ BID, OR SPADES AND A MINOR

The following are the requirements for an opening 2♦ bid showing a weak 2♥ bid, or spades and a minor. Opener will have approximately the same high card strength with both types of hands. This simplifies responder's job of judging the partnership assets. He will decide whether the partnership's combined strength is in the partscore, game or slam zone. He also will know when the hand belongs to the enemy.

---

### REQUIREMENTS FOR OPENING 2♦ SHOWING A WEAK 2♥ BID, OR SPADES AND A MINOR

Opener will have one of the following:

(1)   A hand containing your usual partnership agreements regarding suit length and quality, outside strength and distribution for a weak two-bid in hearts.

(2)   A two-suiter (at least 5-5 in spades and a minor) with 5-10 HCP. The quality of the suits and playing strength will vary in accordance with vulnerability and position.

---

Following these guidelines, we would open 2♦ with any of the following hands:

(a)   ♠ QJ1095   ♥ 7   ♦ KQ1094   ♣ 98

(b)   ♠ AJ1093   ♥ 84   ♦ 5   ♣ QJ983

(c)   ♠ 7   ♥ KQJ107   ♦ QJ107   ♣ 984

(d)   ♠ J109762   ♥ 5   ♦ 8   ♣ KQJ65

(e)   ♠ KJ1073   ♥ 4   ♦ KJ9854   ♣ 9

(f)   ♠ 98   ♥ AQJ1094   ♦ J109   ♣ 43

Hands (a) and (b) are typical 2♦ openings containing a spade-minor two-suiter. Example (c) is an acceptable five-card weak two-bid at any vulnerability. It is fine to be 6-5 in your two suits, as illustrated in (d) and (e); (f) is a classic 2♥ preempt. Note that neither vulnerability nor position should affect your decision to open 2♦ on any of these hands.

Here are the responses to the opening 2♦ bid:

# RESPONSES TO 2♦ SHOWING
# A WEAK 2♥ BID, OR SPADES AND A MINOR

(1)    2♥ and 2♠ are "**pass** or **correct**." If opener does not have hearts, he promises only five spades, plus a minor.

      If responder bids 2♥ and opener corrects to 2♠, responder's 2NT asks opener to bid his minor suit.

(2)    2NT is a forcing inquiry. Opener rebids:
     3♣ = spades and clubs.
     3♦ = spades and diamonds.
     3♥ = minimum weak two in hearts.
     3♠ = medium weak two in hearts.
     3NT = maximum weak two in hearts.

(3)    3♣ is artificial and forcing with hearts. Opener rebids:
- 3♦ with no heart support.
- With heart support, opener cuebids 1st- or 2nd-round controls in side suits. Without controls he bids 3NT.

(4)    3♦ is artificial and forcing with spades. Opener rebids:
- 3♥ with no support for spades.
- With spade support, opener cuebids 1st- or 2nd-round controls in side suits. Without controls he bids 3NT.

(5)    3♥ and 3♠ are "**pass** or **correct**."

(6)    3NT is to play.

(7)    4♣ says that responder has a self-sufficient major. Opener is asked to bid 4♦, after which responder signs off in his major.

(8)    4♥ and 4♠ are "**pass** or **correct**."

Surprisingly, responding to these 2♦ openings rarely creates much of a problem. Consider a few examples. Suppose partner opens 2♦ and you hold:

(a) ♠ J1095  ♥ QJ104  ♦ A85  ♣ 94
RESPOND 3♥. Your side has either a nine-card spade fit or a nine- or ten-card heart fit. The LAW demands you elevate the bidding immediately to the three-level at any vulnerability and any form of scoring with a fit and some outside values. Jump to 3♥, which is "**pass** or **correct**."

(b) ♠ 52  ♥ 3  ♦ QJ10962  ♣ K1093
PASS. Perhaps 3♣ would be better if opener holds a black two-suiter, but there is no reason to inquire. 2♦ is playable and the hand belongs to the opponents. Perhaps they will be confused by your pass. Maybe RHO was trapping with a good hand and both majors, leaving LHO badly placed to contest the auction.

(c) ♠ AKJ10985  ♥ 85  ♦ AJ10  ♣ 4
RESPOND 4♣. Force partner to bid 4♦, over which you will sign off in spades.

(d) ♠ KQ10  ♥ 7  ♦ AK1065  ♣ J1042
RESPOND 2♥. "**Pass** or **correct**." You do not want to be higher than 2♥ if opener holds the likely weak 2♥ bid. If partner corrects to 2♠, we would recommend a raise to game.

(e) ♠ A1095  ♥ KQ4  ♦ AJ1095  ♣ 7
RESPOND 4♥. "**Pass** or **correct**." You want to play game in opener's major.

In addition to the responses we have already discussed, there are a few useful tools that should be added to your responding arsenal when responder has slam interest:

## SLAM TOOLS OVER 2♦ SHOWING A WEAK 2♥ BID, OR SPADES AND A MINOR

(1) When opener has shown the two-suiter:
   (a) After opener has identified his minor, a bid of four of that minor is Keycard in that minor.
   (b) 4♥ is a Keycard inquiry in spades.

(2) When opener has shown a weak two-bid in hearts:
   (a) 4♠ is a Keycard inquiry in hearts.
   (b) 4NT is a spade cuebid promising heart support.
   (c) 4♣ and 4♦ are cuebids in support of hearts.

Since the methods we recommend for handling competition over 2♦ are practically the same as our agreements over competition of a 2♥ opening, we will first review the 2♥ opening and then consider enemy intervention over both.

## 2♥ SHOWING A WEAK 2♠ BID, OR HEARTS AND A MINOR

The following are the requirements for a two-way 2♥ opening bid:

## REQUIREMENTS FOR OPENING 2♥ SHOWING A WEAK 2♠ BID OR HEARTS AND A MINOR

Opener will have one of the following:
(1) A hand with your usual partnership agreements for a weak two-bid in spades.

(2) A two-suiter (at least 5-5 in hearts and a minor) with 5-10 HCP.

Using these guidelines, choose your opening bid with each of these hands:

(a) ♠ KJ1076 ♥ 5 ♦ KQ1094 ♣ 94
OPEN 2♦. Do not open 2♥ with this hand; 2♥ shows a two-suiter with the suit opened and a minor, not spades and a minor.

(b) ♠ K4 ♥ Q9652 ♦ Q8542 ♣ 7
PASS. Even at favorable vulnerability your suits are far too weak for a 2♥ opening based on a two-suiter. Only when desperate for a good result with favorable vulnerability would we ever consider opening 2♥. Even under those circumstances, we would prefer that our HCP be concentrated in our suits.

(c) ♠ J97432 ♥ K ♦ K73 ♣ Q95
PASS. If you are considering opening this hand with 2♥ to describe a 2♠ preempt in first or second seat, you need to reread Chapter 2. Even in third chair, it is probably wrong to make a preemptive two-bid with so much strength outside your suit.

(d) ♠ 5 ♥ QJ1087 ♦ 4 ♣ KJ10752
OPEN 2♥. This hand is perfect for a 2♥ opening showing hearts and a minor.

(e) ♠ KJ1098 ♥ 4 ♦ J1093 ♣ J104
OPEN 2♥. This is not a classic two-bid, but the excellent spade spots tip the scales in favor of a five-card two-bid. Meck-Well would say, "What's the problem?....We've done it on far weaker suits!"

(f) ♠ AQJ987 ♥ 72 ♦ J108 ♣ 976
OPEN 2♥. It is legal to have a traditional weak two-bid in spades. This hand meets all the requirements for a classic 2♠ opening.

Here are your guidelines for responding to opener's 2♥ preempt:

# RESPONSES TO 2♥ SHOWING
## A WEAK 2♠ BID, OR HEARTS AND A MINOR

(1) 2♠ is "**pass** or **correct**". With a two-suiter, opener bids his minor.

(2) 2NT is a forcing inquiry. Opener rebids:
   3♣ = with hearts and clubs.
   3♦ = with hearts and diamonds.
   3♥ = minimum weak two in spades.
   3♠ = medium weak two in spades.
   3NT = maximum weak two in spades.

(3) 3♣ is artificial and forcing with hearts. Opener rebids:
   • 3♦ with no heart support.
   • With heart support, opener cuebids 1st- or 2nd-round controls in side suits. With no controls, he bids 3NT.

(4) 3♦ is artificial and forcing with spades. Opener rebids:
   • 3♥ with no spade support.
   • With spade support, opener cuebids 1st- or 2nd-round controls in side suits. With no controls, he bids 3NT.

(5) 3♥ and 3♠ are "**pass** or **correct**."

(6) 4♣ shows a hand with a self-sufficient major. Opener must bid 4♦, over which responder will sign off in his major.

(7) 4♥ and 4♠ are "**pass** or **correct**." Over 4♠, opener corrects to his minor.

(8) Pass is very rare. However, pass may be appropriate when responder has a long heart suit and does not care which type of hand partner has.

Let us examine some responding hands after partner has opened 2♥.

(a)    ♠ — ♥ AJ983 ♦ K1065 ♣ Q1063
RESPOND 2♠. This is not an easy hand, but do not blame the 2♥ opening. Would you have been better off if partner had opened a direct 2♠ preempt (which is most likely what he holds)? As our friend Tony Forrester would say, "It is surprising how often such artificial openings avoid the blade; and, you do have a classic S.O.S redouble if 2♠ doubled is passed back to you."

(b)    ♠ K103 ♥ AJ4 ♦ KQ762 ♣ A5
RESPOND 2NT. Use the conventional 2NT inquiry to learn the nature of partner's 2♥ opening. This information will place you in an excellent position to determine the best final contract for your side.

(c)    ♠ 7 ♥ AKQ1074 ♦ A109 ♣ K98
RESPOND 3♣. This is artificial and forcing in hearts. If opener rebids 3♦, he denies heart support; you will settle in 3NT.

You might add the type of slam tools to your responding methods that we suggested over 2♦ openings when responder's interest goes beyond the level of game. They help you avoid poor slams and reach good ones. To determine whether a slam is a good or bad proposition, we favor the objective standard recommended by Bob Hamman. The Hamman Rule states: "A good slam is one that MAKES; a poor slam is one that DOESN'T!!" It is difficult to fault this logic.

What should your countermeasures be when your opponents compete over your 2♦ and 2♥ openings? We advise making as few changes as possible in your responses and rebids. It is best to maintain our general approach over any enemy interference.

Here are suggested methods to combat an enemy double:

## WHEN THE OPPONENTS DOUBLE 2♦ OR 2♥ SHOWING A MAJOR SUIT WEAK TWO-BID OR A TWO-SUITED HAND

(1) Pass shows a willingness to play the suit doubled, if that is one of opener's suits when he holds a two-suiter. (Some partnerships play that a pass shows a desire to play the suit doubled even if opener does not have that suit as one of his two suits).

(2) Redouble informs opener that responder holds a strong hand and often is interested in penalizing the opponents.

(3) 2NT is still the conventional forcing inquiry.

(4) 3♣ and 3♦ are natural and non-forcing.

(5) All other bids carry their non-competitive meanings.

Using these countermeasures to enemy intervention, what call would you make if partner's 2♥ opening is doubled when you hold:

(a) ♠ J10  ♥ 32  ♦ A9854  ♣ QJ72
RESPOND 2♠. "**Pass** or **correct**." You want to play 2♠, and will be happy to be at the three-level in opener's minor.

(b) ♠ 9  ♥ 85  ♦ Q1065  ♣ KQJ973
RESPOND 3♣. The enemy double enables you to sign-off in 3♣ (natural and non-forcing) and get your lead-director in.

(c) ♠ 7  ♥ KQJ10  ♦ AJ104  ♣ AJ95
REDOUBLE. If partner has the likely 2♠ preempt, you are about to collect a telephone number for defending clubs, diamonds, hearts or notrump doubled.

Responder's bids will have slightly different meanings depending on whether the opponents make a simple or jump overcall:

---

## WHEN THE OPPONENTS COMPETE OVER YOUR TWO-WAY 2♦ AND 2♥

After a simple overcall:

(1)  Double is negative.  Opener will pass if the suit bid by the enemy is one of his suits.  Otherwise he will describe his hand.

(2)  Any major suit bid is "**pass** or **correct**."

(3)  Any minor suit bid is natural and forcing.

(4)  2NT is the conventional forcing inquiry.

(5)  3NT is to play.

(6)  4♣ forces opener to rebid 4♦.  Responder then signs off in his major.

After a jump overcall:

(1)  Double is penalty.

(2)  3♠ is to play (almost impossible).

(3)  3NT is to play.

(4)  4♣ and 4♦ are natural and forcing.

(5)  4♥ is "**pass** or **correct**."

(6)  4♠ is to play.

(7)  A cuebid shows slam interest.

---

RHO overcalls partner's 2♦ opening with 2♠ and you hold:

(a)      ♠ Q5  ♥ A32  ♦ K1065  ♣ K1072
         DOUBLE.  If opener passes with five spades and a minor, you are delighted because your side has more trumps than declarer's.  If opener rebids 3♥ the LAW is on your side.

(b)     ♠ KQ10952   ♥ 3   ♦ 984   ♣ Q103

PASS. Even if a double were for penalty, which it is not, you should pass 2♠. You do not need to double spades to record a sensational result on this deal. Your opponents obviously have at least one better place to play.

(c)     ♠ A754   ♥ K104   ♦ AQ105   ♣ 72

RESPOND 2NT. Use the conventional 2NT inquiry, asking partner to describe his hand. If opener has more than a minimum, game should be a reasonable undertaking.

The enemy will usually have far more difficulty handling 2♦ and 2♥ openings than responder. Using the methods we have suggested, you should have no trouble when the enemy competes over your opening two-level preempts.

## 2♠ SHOWING THE MAJOR OR THE MINORS

Since 2♦ and 2♥ describe major-minor two-suiters (in addition to major suit weak two-bids), 2♠ is used to describe the remaining two-suiters — hands with both majors or both minors. The requirements for a 2♠ opening are identical to those for 2♦ and 2♥ openings describing two-suiters.

---

### REQUIREMENTS FOR OPENING 2♠ SHOWING MAJORS OR MINORS

(1)    5-5 or better in the majors or minors.

(2)    5-10 HCP.

(3)    Strength concentrated in the two long suits which should have reasonable internal strength.

---

We would open 2♠ with either (a) or (b):

(a)      ♠ KJ985   ♥ J109652   ♦ K2   ♣ —

(b)      ♠ K2   ♥ 5   ♦ QJ1087   ♣ QJ985

Avoid opening 2♠ with:

(c)      ♠ Q9843   ♥ K7532   ♦ A4   ♣ 7

The long suits in (c) are simply too weak. When you open 2♠ you are practically forcing the bidding to the three-level with limited high card strength. To compensate for your lack of high cards, you must have two reasonably good suits especially since partner may not have a fit for you.

    The responses to 2♠ are similar to those over 2♦ and 2♥.

---

## RESPONSES TO 2♠
## SHOWING MAJORS OR MINORS

(1)   2NT is a forcing inquiry. Opener rebids:
       3♣  =   minors (minimum).
       3♦  =   minors (maximum)
       3♥  =   majors (minimum).
       3♠  =   majors (maximum).

(2)   3♣, 3♦, 3♥ and 3♠ are "**pass** or **correct**."
     Opener rebids:
       3♦ over 3♣  =   majors (maximum).
       3♥ over 3♣  =   majors (minimum).
       3♥ over 3♦  =   majors.
       3♠ over 3♥  =   minors (maximum).
       3NT over 3♥  =   minors (better diamonds).
       4♣ over 3♥  =   minors (better clubs).
       3NT over 3♠  =   minors (maximum).
       4♣ over 3♠  =   minors (minimum).

(3)   4♣ and 4♦ are "**pass** or **correct**."

(4)   4♥ and 4♠ are to play.

---

Using these responses, suppose partner opens 2♠ and you hold:

(a) &spades; 75 &hearts; 4 &diams; J10762 &clubs; QJ1065

PASS. You do not need a long spade suit to take this action. If you suspect that opener holds the majors or if you are weak enough that you do not care, then it is perfectly acceptable to pass 2&spades;. With this hand, responder knows the opponents have at least 26 HCP. If partner has the minors — fine — the opponents have at least a game in the majors. Vulnerability may be a factor if responder does not know which suits opener holds and is considering a pass.

(b) &spades; A104 &hearts; 3 &diams; J10952 &clubs; Q943

RAISE TO 3&spades;. Take up some of your opponents' valuable bidding space. If partner has the minors, your 3&spades; bid may cause some confusion for your opponents. Besides, you want to play at least four of a minor and will not mind going to the five-level at anything other than unfavorable vulnerability. In the likely event that opener has the majors, you have strong preference for spades.

(c) &spades; K9832 &hearts; A1097 &diams; J7 &clubs; Q9

RESPOND 3&clubs;. Be grateful you have honor-doubleton in both of opener's likely suits. This is an excellent responding hand for a 2&spades; opening; if the opponents compete they are likely to be in serious trouble. If you play in 3&clubs; you may go plus.

(d) &spades; AKQJ972 &hearts; A5 &diams; Q7 &clubs; J3

RESPOND 4&spades;. Bid what you think you can make. Remember, 4&spades; (and 4&hearts;) over 2&spades; is a natural sign-off; it is NOT "pass or correct." 4&spades; will play well from opener's side of the table.

Consider a few hands from the other side of the table: opener's hand after responder's initial response. Suppose partner responds 3♥ ("**pass** or **correct**") to your 2♠ opening when you hold:

(a)      ♠ KQ1093   ♥ QJ9542   ♦ 3   ♣ 7
         PASS. Do not be tempted to carry on to game with this hand. If partner had any game interest he would have used the conventional 2NT inquiry to find out whether you had a minimum or maximum 2♠ opening. Except for your sixth heart, you have no extras.

(b)      ♠ 972   ♥ —   ♦ KQ1095   ♣ AJ1076
         REBID 3♠. This shows a maximum 2♠ opener with the minors.

(c)      ♠ 5   ♥ 9   ♦ KQ10872   ♣ KJ1074
         REBID 3NT. This shows the minors with better diamonds than clubs.

If partner responds 2NT (the conventional inquiry) after you open 2♠, what do you rebid with:

(d)      ♠ AQ1096   ♥ QJ9854   ♦ 3   ♣ 6
         REBID 3♠. You have a maximum 2♠ opening with the majors.

(e)      ♠ 9   ♥ 5   ♦ QJ8732   ♣ QJ1094
         REBID 3♣. This is a minimum 2♠ opening with the minors.

(f)      ♠ KJ1096   ♥ KQJ109   ♦ 54   ♣ 6
         REBID 3♠. This shows a maximum 2♠ opening with the majors.

(g)      ♠ 86   ♥ —   ♦ KJ1096   ♣ KQ10987
         REBID 3♦. Show your absolute maximum 2♠ opening with the minors.

When responder's aspirations go beyond the level of game after partner has opened 2♠, we recommend a few simple understandings for slam exploration. These understandings are:

## SLAM TOOLS OVER 2♠
## SHOWING MAJORS OR MINORS

(1) When opener has shown the minors:
  (a) 4♣ and 4♦ are Keycard inquiries in the suit bid.

(2) When opener has shown the majors:
  (a) 4♣ is a Keycard inquiry in hearts.
  (b) 4♦ is a Keycard inquiry in spades.

Keycard inquiries are made by responder only. Partnerships that play six-card Keycard should use that convention here.

---

We do not fear competition over our 2♠ openings; we welcome it. Our simple countermeasures to enemy intervention are:

## WHEN THE OPPONENTS DOUBLE 2♠
## SHOWING MAJORS OR MINORS

(1) Pass is to play if opener has the majors.

(2) Redouble shows a strong hand with interest in either penalizing the opponents or reaching game.

(3) 2NT asks opener to bid 3♣, allowing responder to sign off in his own long suit. Note that 2NT is not a forcing inquiry.

(4) All suit bids (3♣ through 4♦) are "**pass** or **correct**."

(5) 4♥ and 4♠ are to play.

Note: 3NT is always TO PLAY over all intervention.

---

If 2♠ is doubled, plan your response following our guidelines:

(a) ♠ J109 ♥ J10 ♦ K1074 ♣ J872

PASS. If opener holds the majors, responder will be happy to play 2♠ doubled. With the minors, opener will correct.

(b) ♠ AJ1098 ♥ KQ109 ♦ A10 ♣ 98

REDOUBLE. If opener holds the minors, responder is interested in penalizing the enemy. In the unlikely event that opener has the majors, game will be a reasonable shot.

When the enemy bids over your 2♠ opening, your responses are:

---

## WHEN THE OPPONENTS BID OVER 2♠ SHOWING MAJORS OR MINORS

When the opponents make a simple overcall:

(1) Double is negative. Opener may convert for penalty or rebid at the cheapest level; clubs shows the minors; hearts the majors.

(2) Suit bids through 4♦ are "**pass** or **correct**."

(3) 4♥ and 4♠ are to play.

When the opponents make a jump overcall:

(4) Double is penalty.

(5) Suit bids through 4♦ are "**pass** or **correct**."

(6) 4♥ and 4♠ are to play.

When the opponents bid notrump (natural):

(7) Double is penalty.

(8) Suit bids through 4♦ are "**pass** or **correct**."

(9) 4♥ and 4♠ are to play.

Note: 3NT is always TO PLAY over all intervention.

---

If RHO overcalls 3 ♦ over partner's 2 ♠ opening, what do you bid with the following hands?

(a)    ♠ A1072  ♥ KJ7  ♦ 9  ♣ K10642
DOUBLE.  We expect partner to convert our negative double to a penalty double holding the minors.  With the majors, opener will bid 3 ♥ and we will jump to a game in spades.

(b)    ♠ A5  ♥ KQJ109654  ♥ —  ♦ J108
RESPOND 4 ♥.  Even if partner holds the practically certain club-diamond two-suiter, we want to play game in hearts.

The advantages of playing the 2 ♦, 2 ♥ and 2 ♠ openings we have just described are too numerous to list.  Some of the outstanding features of these bids are:

(1)    They enable you to open the bidding on all two-suiters containing sub-opening (one-bid) strength and to handle major suit preempts.

(2)    They facilitate bidding good distributional games and slams as well as taking profitable sacrifices because they allow you to show your two-suiter with your first bid.  This would be difficult, if not impossible, if you pass initially.

(3)    They make it very difficult for opponents to compete when there is no known suit.  Neither takeout doubles nor cuebids are available to the defenders.

Look at the problems one of our 2 ♥ openings — and an effective "**pass** or **correct**" response — caused the opponents.  Here is the complete deal, auction and result from Board 13 of a round-robin match between Germany and Japan in the Venice Cup competition.

## North
♠ KJ7654
♥ 974
♦ Q95
♣ 2

## West
♠ A2
♥ Q8
♦ J764
♣ QJ984

Board 13
Dlr. - North
Vul. - Both

## East
♠ 93
♥ AKJ3
♦ K32
♣ K1075

## South
♠ Q108
♥ 10652
♦ A108
♣ A63

---

OUR TABLE

Opening Lead ♠ 5
N/S +500

| *Banno* | *Zenkel* | *Miyaishi* | *von Arnim* |
| West | North | East | South |
| --- | --- | --- | --- |
| — | 2♥ (a) | P (b) | 3♥ (c) |
| P | 3♠ (d) | Dbl. (e) | P |
| 5♣ (f) | P | P | Dbl. |
| P | P | P | |

(a) A weak two-bid in spades, or a two-suiter with hearts and a minor.

(b) Judging that no direct action was appropriate.

(c) Typical "**pass** or **correct**" response.

(d) "I have a weak two-bid in spades."

(e) A takeout double of spades, by partnership agreement.

(f) Aggressive, but not unreasonable.

With the benefit of hindsight it is easy to find fault with West's aggressive 5♣ call. Many experts would bid either 3NT or 4NT (showing the minors) with the West cards. Neither would be a winner, and the latter would result in the same final contract. In short, this is not an easy hand to bid. The winning action (passing 3♠ doubled) is impossible to find and rates to be a loser in the long run. Credit von Arnim for making a well-judged penalty double.

What defense do we recommend against the two-way two-level openings we play and endorse? We were afraid you would ask. Frankly, we have not had very good luck against such openings. Consequently we contacted Eric Rodwell for the Meck-Well defense against such openings. Eric's initial remark is worth repeating and is an endorsement of the openings: "They are the pits to defend against!" We agree.

Nevertheless, here is what Meck-Well recommends. It is the best defense your authors have heard of; it is the one we now play.

---

## MECK-WELL DEFENSE AGAINST TWO-WAY TWO-LEVEL OPENINGS

Against "either/or" 2♦ and 2♥ openings and 2♠ showing the majors or minors:

(1) Double shows 13-15 HCP, balanced or semi-balanced, or stronger than a 2NT overcall.

(2) 2NT shows 16-18 HCP, balanced or semi-balanced. Partner bids 3♣ Stayman and uses transfers.

(3) Overcalls are natural.

(4) 3NT is to play with a long suit as a source of tricks.

Against the "either/or" 2♦ and 2♥ openings you defend similarly to the way you do against Multi. You may prefer to use transfer overcalls over two-way two-level openings.

---

The key to defending against two-way two-level openings is often to contest the auction immediately with reasonable values. Waiting often proves fatal, particularly when responder has been able to make a preemptive response knowing his side has a fit somewhere.

## FORRESTER-ROBSON 2♦ OPENING

In the same family of either/or two-level openings is a 2♦ opening — played by the leading British pair Tony Forrester and Andy Robson — which shows a major-minor two-suiter with limited high card strength. Neither of opener's suits are immediately known with this opening bid. The requirements for this 2♦ opening are:

---

### REQUIREMENTS FOR FORRESTER-ROBSON 2♦ OPENING

(1) A five-card major; at least four cards in a minor.

(2) Approximately 5-9 HCP non-vulnerable; approximately 6-10 vulnerable.

(3) High card strength should be concentrated in the two long suits.

(4) Always have a two-suited hand; avoid 5-4-4-0 three-suiters.

---

Consider a few hands that may qualify for the Forrester-Robson 2♦ opening:

(a)     ♠ KJ1093   ♥ 76   ♦ QJ108   ♣ 52
OPEN 2♦. This hand meets all the requirements. Your high card strength is in your two suits.

(b)    ♠ 7   ♥ A10974   ♦ 85   ♣ K10983
OPEN 2♦. Another good example of a 2♦ opening. Note the good internal strength of your two suits. This is often critical when you open the bidding with limited strength — partner may have no fit for either of your suits.

(c)    ♠ 7   ♥ AQ1097   ♦ A10976   ♣ 109
OPEN 1♥ OR PASS. Your authors believe this is clearly an opening one-bid. However, a pass is possible if your partnership requires ultra-sound openings. What is NOT acceptable on this type of hand is a 2♦ opening — even though it technically meets both the distributional and high-card requirements. It is far too strong.

(d)    ♠ J8732   ♥ AQ   ♦ 107632   ♣ K
PASS. Your high-card strength is acceptable, but it is in all the wrong places. Only 10% of your HCP are in your long suits. Partner is very likely to misjudge both your offensive and defensive prospects if you open 2♦ on hands like this.

(e)    ♠ AJ1094   ♥ 1095   ♦ AJ986   ♣ —
OPEN 1♠. Yes, this is a major-minor two-suiter with 10 HCP, but NO, it is not a Forrester-Robson 2♦ bid. It is a 1♠ bid. Remember, 2♦ openings are preemptive in nature (and you have a void).

(f)    ♠ QJ954   ♥ 7   ♦ 4   ♣ J109543
OPEN 2♦. This is a rare example of a 6-5 2♦ opener. Despite your excellent distribution, this is a weak, preemptive hand — as it should be.

As you might expect, the responses to this 2♦ opening are a bit complex. The following outlines our recommended structure:

# RESPONSES TO FORRESTER-ROBSON 2♦ OPENINGS

(1) Pass is rare, but possible.

(2) 2♥ is "**pass** or **correct**." Over 2♠, responder can bid 2NT, asking for opener's minor.

(3) 2♠ is to play if opener holds spades. With hearts, opener rebids:
- 3♣ or 3♦ to show hearts and the bid minor; medium strength.
- 3♥ to show hearts; minimum strength.
- 4♥ to show hearts; maximum strength.

(4) 2NT is a game-forcing inquiry, or it may be used to play in opener's minor. Opener rebids 3♣ with clubs and 3♦ with diamonds.
Responder's next-step bid asks opener to bid a major.
> Opener's rebids over 3♦: 3♥ shows **spades** and 3♠ shows **hearts**. Over 3♥: 3♠ shows **hearts** and 3NT shows **spades**.

Once the major is known, four of the **other minor** by responder asks for keycards in opener's major. Four of **opener's minor** asks for keycards in opener's minor.

(5) 3♣ is invitational in both majors with either better hearts or equal holdings in the two majors. Opener bids 3♦ to find out the nature of responders hand. Responder bids:
> 3♥ with equal major suit holdings.
> 3♠ with better hearts.

(continued)

## RESPONSES TO FORRESTER-ROBSON 2♦ OPENINGS (continued)

(6)   3♦ is invitational in both majors with better spades.

Over 3♣ and 3♦ opener signs off in three of a major with a minimum or bids game with a maximum.

(7)   3♥ and 3♠ are "**pass** or **correct**."

(8)   3NT is to play.

(9)   Four-level responses are preemptive and opener will "**pass** or **correct**" to his major or his minor, whichever is cheaper.

What call would you make if partner opens 2♦ and you hold:

(a)   ♠ AQ105  ♥ 7  ♦ AKQ10985  ♣ 3
RESPOND 2NT.   Do not presume that partner has hearts and clubs (which is most likely).   Find out via the game-forcing 2NT inquiry.

(b)   ♠ J10  ♥ 73  ♦ KJ98  ♣ A10643
RESPOND 2NT.  Use the conventional 2NT inquiry to locate your side's minor suit fit. You have no interest in game.

(c)   ♠ KJ105  ♥ AJ4  ♦ A1087  ♣ J10
RESPOND 3♦.  This conventional response shows invitational values, both majors, with better spades than hearts.

(d)   ♠ 9865  ♥ J1093  ♦ A98  ♣ 74
RESPOND 3♥.  This is preemptive, "**pass** or **correct**."  The hand belongs to the enemy and the LAW says you will be safe at the three-level.

Should the enemy compete over 2♦, Forrester recommends these guidelines:

---

## HANDLING ENEMY INTERVENTION
## OVER FORRESTER-ROBSON 2♦ OPENING

When the enemy doubles:

(1)  Pass is to play if opener's minor is diamonds.

(2)  Redouble commands that partner bid 2♥, enabling responder to place the contract.

(3)  2♥ and 2♠ are "**pass** or **correct**."

(4)  2NT asks for opener's minor, OR it is a conventional game force. Responder clarifies with his rebid.

(5)  3♥ is "**pass** or **correct**."

(6)  3NT is to play.

After an enemy overcall:

(1)  Doubles are negative through 4♦. Opener will convert this for penalties with an appropriate holding in the enemy suit.

(2)  A cuebid asks for a minor if a major has been bid; it asks for a major if a minor has been bid.

(3)  2NT asks for opener's minor OR is a conventional game force. Responder clarifies with his rebid.

(4)  3♥ is "**pass** or **correct**."

Other suit bids are natural, non-forcing and show a decent hand.

---

As you may have noticed, the suggested responses after the enemy competes over a Forrester-Robson 2♦ opening are quite similar to the guidelines we outlined after competition of an either/or 2♦ or 2♥ opening. Responder must have simple vehicles to use to find out which suits opener has.

If your opponents play the Forrester-Robson 2♦ opening, or a similar structure, we recommend the Meck-Well defense against either/or 2♦ and 2♥ openings previously outlined.

## OTHER TWO-WAY
## TWO-BIDS

The predecessor to the 2♦ opening we have just described was a 2♣ opening with the same basic requirements. It is most effective when playing a forcing club system since 2♣ no longer has to be reserved for battleships. The designers of this 2♣ opening used the bid to show a balanced 22-24 HCP in addition to the major-minor two-suiters with 5-10 HCP. By adding the balanced battleship to the 2♣ opening, 2NT openings became available for lesser duty — much less, since they frequently were used to describe other preempts instead of showing smaller battleships.

One advantage of using 2♣ rather than 2♦ to describe major-minor two-suiters is the availability of 2♦ as a response. The best way to utilize 2♦ is to make it a weaker relay than 2NT. Other responses can carry the same meaning they would have over a 2♦ opening that describes a major-minor two-suiter with less than opening one-bid strength. Enemy intervention can be handled in the same fashion.

If you play a forcing club system and can work out a way to describe a limited opening containing a long club suit without using 2♣ for that purpose, perhaps you should consider using 2♣ to describe preemptive major-minor two-suiters. If nothing else, it will make life more difficult for your opponents.

In addition to 2♣ and 2♦, it is possible to use other triggers for the preemptive weapon describing a major-minor two-suiter. For example, one of your authors, when playing with Tony Forrester, uses a 2♥ opening to show a weak hand containing a five-card major and a minor suit. Our responses to 2♥ are extremely simple. The following are your guidelines for a conventional 2♥ opening.

---

### REQUIREMENTS FOR OPENING 2♥ SHOWING A WEAK HAND WITH A MAJOR-MINOR TWO-SUITER

(1) At least 5-5 in the two suits in first and second seats. May be 5-4 (with a five-card major) in third and fourth chair.

(2) 5-10 HCP concentrated in the two long suits.

### RESPONSES

(1) 2♠ is "**pass** or **correct**."

(2) 2NT is a forcing relay. Opener rebids:
- 3♣ or 3♦ with a minimum in the suit bid. The next step by responder asks for the major.
  Opener rebids 3♥ with **spades** and 3♠ with **hearts**.
- 3♥ and 3♠ show a maximum in the suit bid. The next step by responder asks for the minor.
  Opener rebids 4♣ with diamonds and 4♦ with clubs.

(3) Three-level bids are natural and forcing.

(4) 4♣ is "**pass** or **correct**" (to diamonds).

(5) 4♦ is preemptive in diamonds.

(6) 4♥ is "**pass** or **correct**" (to spades).

(7) 4♠ is to play.

---

We use essentially the same methods for handling competition that we recommended after the enemy intervenes over a 2♦ opening showing a preemptive major-minor two-suiter. For example, passing 2♥ doubled means the same as passing the conventional 2♦ opening — it instructs opener to pass if the suit doubled is one of his two suits.

Opening 2♥ bids can also be used to describe two-suiters with either the majors or the minors (like the 2♠ openings we discussed earlier). Chicago expert Gerald Caravelli — playing with one of your authors — used 2♥ to describe such hands. In addition we played Multi 2♦ openings and 2♠ showing an unspecified weak three-level preempt. We found playing those three conventional openings together most useful and effective.

When you play 2♥ openings to show either the majors or the minors, 2♠ becomes the usual "**pass** or **correct**." Add the other responses previously outlined for the responses over two-way two-level 2♠ openings and you are all set.

It is also possible to play two-way either/or bids at the three-level. In fact, one of your authors once played that an opening 3♥ bid showed either a preempt in hearts or solid clubs; and 3♠ showed either a preempt in spades or solid diamonds. This unique treatment enables 3NT to be played from the right side of the table when opener holds a solid suit with little or no outside strength. It also makes it a bit more difficult to defend against 3♥ and 3♠ openings.

The popularity of this relatively obscure conventional 3♥ opening was not enhanced by perhaps the most famous deal in the history of Venice Cup competition. This deal still gives one of your authors nightmares. We include it since your authors feel that tragedy is more instructive than triumph — there are more lessons to be learned from it.

The scene of the following horror story was the 1989 World Championships in Perth, Australia. It was board 114 (of a 128-board match) between Germany and the Netherlands. The winner — assured of a silver medal — would play the U.S.A. for the Venice Cup Gold. With 15 deals to go, Germany led by 29 IMPs. The score was 279 to 250. Here is the complete deal:

## Board 114
Dlr. - East
Vul. - N/S

**North**
- ♠ J643
- ♥ AK93
- ♦ Q542
- ♣ J

**West**
- ♠ AQ107
- ♥ J
- ♦ KJ
- ♣ KQ9754

**East**
- ♠ K9852
- ♥ 6
- ♦ 983
- ♣ A862

**South**
- ♠ —
- ♥ Q1087542
- ♦ A1076
- ♣ 103

---

**CLOSED ROOM**

Opening Lead ♥ A

N/S -450

| Schroeder West | Arnolds North | Vogt East | Vriend South |
|---|---|---|---|
| — | — | P | P |
| 1♣ | P | 1♠ | 2♥ |
| 4♠ | P | P | P |

Although purists might object to Schroeder's jump to game, we approve of her practical bid opposite a passed hand. North's pass of 4♠ is the call that surprises us. True, partner is a passed hand, but a vulnerable overcall missing the high heart honors — with known extreme shortness in spades — should have propelled North to bid 5♥. We will never know what would have happened in the closed room had Arnolds bid 5♥; what we do know is that Vogt won 11 tricks in 4♠ for an excellent result for Germany.

Plus 450 was not nearly enough for Germany to even maintain their useful 29 IMP lead after the following result in the open room.

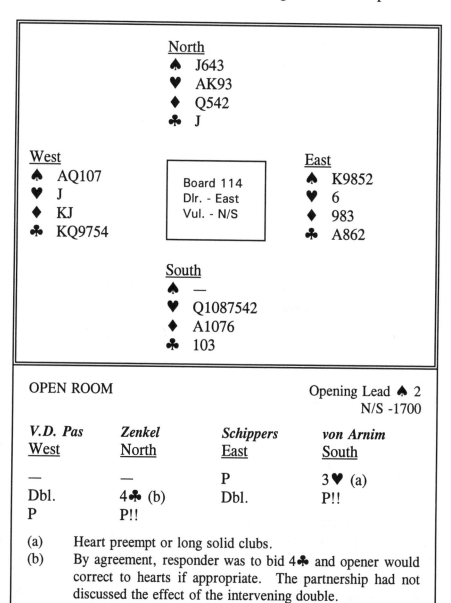

North
♠ J643
♥ AK93
♦ Q542
♣ J

West
♠ AQ107
♥ J
♦ KJ
♣ KQ9754

Board 114
Dlr. - East
Vul. - N/S

East
♠ K9852
♥ 6
♦ 983
♣ A862

South
♠ —
♥ Q1087542
♦ A1076
♣ 103

OPEN ROOM

Opening Lead ♠ 2
N/S -1700

| *V.D. Pas* | *Zenkel* | *Schippers* | *von Arnim* |
| West | North | East | South |
| — | — | P | 3♥ (a) |
| Dbl. | 4♣ (b) | Dbl. | P!! |
| P | P!! | | |

(a)    Heart preempt or long solid clubs.
(b)    By agreement, responder was to bid 4♣ and opener would correct to hearts if appropriate. The partnership had not discussed the effect of the intervening double.

It was certainly reasonable for North to bid 4♣; indeed, it certainly looked as if South had solid clubs looking at the North hand. South, in turn, reasonably presumed that North would simply pass the double of 3♥ and await clarification unless she really had a long club suit that rated to play better than opener's hearts. The only unreasonable thing about this was the result: -1700. A trump lead would have netted the defenders 2600, but that was of little consolation to declarer who managed two spade ruffs in the dummy in addition to her two red Aces.

Aided and abetted by this spectacular result (and the 15 IMPs gained), the Netherlands gained a berth in the Venice Cup final. One of your authors could only lament, "For of all sad words of tongue or pen, the saddest are these: 'It might have been.'"

Nevertheless, Board 114 provides a valuable object lesson. The Star Wars two-way either/or bids of the modern era require exhaustive partnership understandings and agreements so that they do not inflict the devastation on the side that uses them that is intended and designed for the enemy. They are like hand grenades in that regard.

Having issued this warning, it is time to bring down the curtain on our review of conventional two-way preemptive openings. Time and space do not permit us to describe every preemptive weapon that has been devised. Even some of those we felt worthy of inclusion will no doubt soon be revised, modified or discarded in favor of more devastating weapons to make life difficult for the opponents. Such is the nature and evolution of war and our favorite game.